The Heart Has Its Own Reasons

Mothering Wisdom for the 1980s

The Heart Has Its Own Reasons

Mothering Wisdom for the 1980s

Mary Ann Cahill

La Leche League International
Franklin Park, Illinois

July 1983
Copyright ©1983 La Leche League International, Inc.
All Rights Reserved
Printed in the United States of America
83 84 85 86 9 8 7 6 5 4 3 2 1
Book and cover design by Lucy Lesiak
Library of Congress Catalog Card Number 83-81672
ISBN 0-912500-13-1

The heart has its own reasons, which reason does not know.

Blaise Pascal

Contents

Preface

The question is begging to be asked: Why is La Leche League, the authority on breastfeeding, putting out a book on money matters?

Actually, *THE HEART HAS ITS OWN REASONS,* filled as it is with tips on how to save and ideas for earning money, fits comfortably on the League's bookshelf. It has become obvious in recent years that the nursing mother and baby may need to be involved in saving ways. In our modern world, the union of the two often becomes necessary if the nursing couple is going to remain intact; only by astute money management can many mothers remain at home with their babies. Practical information about living on one income is a fitting companion to the League's philosophy that babies need their mother's milk and equally as much, they need their mother's comforting presence.

Although the connection is clear, the idea for the book evolved slowly. On an informal basis at League gatherings, mothers would regularly discuss problems and share ideas on creative homemaking. The sensible thing to do, we decided, would be to gather helpful information and make it available to all interested families. Mother-to-mother help, we know, is a powerful form of support.

A notice was placed in *LEAVEN,* our quarterly publication for LLL Leaders, inviting the readers to share their saving ways. How do they manage to make ends meet on one paycheck? And how do they feel about being a mother-at-home?

Close to 300 replies were received, some quite lengthy, others including only a few comments, all warm and enthusiastic. Sincerity was uppermost; style was secondary to content. "It's difficult to type with a two-year-old on one's lap," wrote one mother. Another mentioned that her handwritten letter was penned in her son's room "by the glow from a Mickey Mouse night-light."

I feel privileged to have been able to get to know the writers as I have through their letters. If anyone were to ask me what I think of the present generation of young parents, my answer would be unqualified admiration. I feel as though I personally know many dedicated, even heroic, mothers and fathers. They are the inspiration and in good measure the authors of this book. Their words give form and substance to THE HEART HAS ITS OWN REASONS.

A book is always a joint effort, with many people working to bring it about, transforming an idea into words on typewritten sheets of paper and eventually to the printed pages between the covers of a book. I am especially indebted to Kevin Thornton, LLLI Publications Director, and to Judy Torgus, LLLI Executive Editor, for their understanding, patience, and talented touch. My family has earned my gratitude by their unfailing support and for never once complaining about the sound of a typewriter at odd hours of the day or night. Finally, I dedicate this book with love to the memory of my late husband, Chuck, who for so many years was my partner in creating a family and in making dreams come true.

*I*ntroduction

As a mother, you may find the ideas proposed in this book very old-fashioned or quite avant-garde. Actually, they are a mixture of both, which makes them somewhat exciting and somewhat comforting. If you give them more than a passing glance, you will be faced with some hard questions that may be challenging or disconcerting or both. This book may tear at straw idols and make outrageous demands on you—but it also holds exquisite promise.

What is the book about? Simple ideas, really, but ones that have long been a cornerstone of society:

Your baby needs you. Consider setting aside, for the time being, your outside job and rethink your career plans.

Give yourself time to discover the tremendous satisfactions that can come with being a mother-at-home.

And at the same time, make a good life for yourself and your family by outwitting the money monster that gobbles a family's resources and drives mothers out to work.

This is no small order. Mention these ideas at a social gathering, and questions and comments are likely to explode around you like a fireworks display. Most of a mother's concerns are of two types: 1) What will this decision mean to me in a personal way, as an individual? 2) How will this decision affect my family?

The decision to stay at home with your baby must be reconciled with the image you carry of yourself, with those deep feelings that define you as a woman, and with your plans for all the things you hope to accomplish in life. These feelings are colored by social pressures and the thinking of the time. Women today are on the move. They are doing things in and outside the home that more than ten years ago, they didn't dream were in their realm. Of course you don't want to be out of the mainstream! You want to be in on making things happen! We are proposing that a mother-at-home does not have to be stifled, bored, or unfulfilled. People can be stifled, bored, and unfulfilled in places and positions far from home.

This book will explain why it is important for a mother to be at home with her young children even though many people are saying that women owe it to themselves and their families to pursue jobs outside the home.

The period when children are small and need a full-time mother is a comparatively short time in a woman's life. Sandra O'Connor will probably be remembered as the first woman to serve on the U.S. Supreme Court. What is equally worthy to note is the fact that when her children were young, she stepped back from her work in the practice of law to concentrate on being a mother. Obviously, her time away from law did not limit her ultimate job opportunities. The woman who is interested in knowing how to stay involved in her career and still minimize separation from her baby can find the help she needs in La Leche League's publication on this subject, planned for fall of 1983.

But what about the economics of your present situation? Your need for feelings of self-worth and fulfillment are important, but they may be secondary to your need for money. Many women work to help support their families. Where will the money come from to allow you to be a mother-at-home? Parents nowadays want to share equally in maintaining the family; if you stay at home, what is your contribution to the nitty-gritty of making ends meet?

This book will help you by offering a wide range of possibilities for saving and earning money which can make your time at home with your children an economic possibility. In great part, it is a book about income substitution, though you'll also find numerous ways to augment your income. The suggestions we present here are family-tested and the people who shared them with us have done so eagerly and enthusiastically. These families do not consider that having a mother-at-home is a luxury, certainly not in the sense that it is something over and above what is important and necessary.

Although the accumulation and allocation of money is given considerable attention here, it is not the real reason for this book. Other books can undoubtedly serve that end much better. This book is about how money can *serve* a family and about how you, as a mother, can serve the best interests of your baby and, in the long run, yourself and your family. Listen to your heart—to the quiet yet insistent voice coming from deep within you and urging you to be with your baby.

No one can replace you as mother. From all the evidence, from all that is known about how babies grow and learn to live and to be competent adults, it can be said that a mother is the one most perfectly suited to be nurturer in the early years.

Someone else may care for your child very much as you do, change diapers regularly, be attentive to feedings, even hold and rock your baby, but what comes of this care will not be the same as when you, as mother, are the nurturer. Something very important will be lacking. And doubts are raised. How much of a mother's absence can this child tolerate? How much mothering can be missed? No one can say; no one knows the answers to these questions. What you can be sure of is that you are important to your baby. Too important, many would add, for you not to be there in the beginning when your baby forms and develops so much of his character. Your baby needs your responses appropriate to his already unique self and to his accumulating range of experience. Only the sensitivity born of a mother's love is likely to achieve optimum fulfillment for this unique individual.

It is an awesome responsibility to be a mother—grand and wonderful but awesome—and at times, rather overwhelming. You are not the first to wonder if you're equal to the task. Take heart. Mothering is the original one-day-at-a-time job. Mothers, as well as their children, need time in which to grow. The same holds true, of course, for fathers. Parents are still the ones best qualified to raise a child. When other systems of caring for children have been tried, the results have all fallen short.

There are no perfect parents; there is always room to grow. There is no better guide in the important undertaking of bringing up your children than the experience of other parents. We can be one another's greatest support. Sharing the experiences of other parents is the basis for this book. Mothers and fathers will tell you of their commitment to parenting and, in this context, explain how they have managed to live satisfying lives on a limited budget. At the end of their rainbow they have found a variety of answers. We hope that sharing their experiences will help you keep bread on the table, a roof over your head, a spring in your step, and peace in your heart that no money can buy.

Part One

New Frontiers—
New Pioneers

CHAPTER 1

The Heart of the Matter

Sometimes you can have the best of reasons for doing something, yet you cannot explain it with any degree of logic. In fact, there seem to be logical reasons for selecting a totally different course of action. Deep down, in your heart, you feel that your choice is right, but at the same time it seems you're going in one direction while the rest of the world is going in another. You may have made a brave move, but it can be a lonely one. It's easy to feel unsure when you're following your heart.

If you are a mother who has chosen to stay at home with your children, your reasons for this choice may not be easy to explain, even to yourself.

If you are considering this choice, you may be hesitant to give up a good job and stay at home with your baby because everyone expects you to continue working. And if your financial situation is tight, it may seem totally logical to continue working—or to look for a job.

What are the reasons, then, why more and more mothers are following their hearts to stay at home with their young children?

During pregnancy, planning to stay at home with your baby may not be an easy choice.

It's a difficult question to answer with logic because, as a mother in Ohio, Diane Grubb, writes, "the reasons are mostly feelings and they are harder to describe than any specific reason. I wanted children so I could be with them, not so I could leave them in someone else's care. If I left them, I would feel very cheated and deprived of something that is so important and wonderful."

Other mothers who have pondered this question share their feelings and explain how logic gives way to deeper needs. As Linda Lawrence from Ontario, Canada, explains: "My children range in age from five months to eight and a half years. Since eight months before my youngest child's birth, I have been virtually functioning as a single parent. It has taken 100 percent giving on my part this past year, and I am convinced that no one else would have had quite the patience, tolerance, and love for my children that I have had. I would do anything in order to remain with my children in the crucial early years."

Linda Coates, from Oregon, adds: "My husband and I are living below the taxable income level and yet we seldom feel deprived or overly anxious. Many items I used to consider necessities are not really necessary after all. When they're slowly eliminated so it's not too traumatic, I find I'm quite happy without them—ice cream, a daily newspaper, regular haircuts at a beauty salon, new books and records, frequent long-distance phone calls. Being able to really put family first makes us feel very good about our choice of lifestyle."

In simple terms, Marsha Stoeberl from Wisconsin expresses her reason for staying at home, "It would break my heart not to be home with my children!"

For hundreds of mother like these, the explanation for why they stay with their babies may not seem logical in today's world, but it is simple. The practical arguments for getting a job are overruled by the wisdom of the heart.

New Frontiers

Yet for all its simplicity, the concept of mothers and babies being together is in jeopardy. There is a need to rediscover the beauty of the mothering career. In a world that is preoccupied with outer space, the home is a new frontier, one that is attracting new pioneers. We believe that the pioneering spirit is in evidence among the families whose stories you will find in these pages. They share a firm conviction that mothers and babies need to be together in order to build a foundation for the family and for a healthy society. And like pioneers of old, they are eager to show others the way. While they admit that the road they are taking is not the smoothest (it seldom is when one leaves the beaten path), they vouch for the rewards to be gained and they willingly explain how it can be managed.

Many of the newcomers to the art of pioneering look to those earlier pathfinders for survival techniques. With a reduction of family funds as the mother quits her job, there is a resurgence of interest in saving. They become very self-reliant, looking to yesteryear for ways to grow or make many of the things they need.

Even though they have adopted a frontier style of living, they are realistic enough not to view the past in a rosy wash of nostalgia. Pioneering is a feet-firmly-on-the-ground, one-foot-ahead-of-the-other kind of work. There is nothing haphazard about it. Careful planning is necessary. The first step lies in taking a stand against the all-too-prevalent thinking that added income will solve all of a family's problems. If this added income means separation of mother and baby, then it may not be the solution; it may be a new source of stress. The long-range effects of separation are seldom as easy to correct as a temporary shortage of funds.

Modern pioneer families bear little outward resemblance to the early settlers who have been commemorated in bronze. But certainly, like their predecessors, they view life in its basic components. It's an approach that simplifies choices. These new pioneers are blazing new trails in finding ways to preserve the values that are known to keep families strong. As with many undertakings, the heroic proportions of the accomplishment are best appreciated with the passage of time.

It isn't all that far-fetched an idea to think of yourself as a pioneer. Home is your base of operation, and some of your best work will be conducted in your rocking chair. From this vantage point, you can strike out in a new way, take a chance, and take up with the new pioneers.

Who Are the New Pioneers?

Who are these home-based pioneers, these courageous mothers and fathers, the subjects of this book? Where do they come from. How do they live?

If you were to see them strolling along an avenue, in a park, or perhaps at a fair, you probably wouldn't look twice at them. They appear as a typical family group—father, mother,

Modern pioneer families face hardships to avoid the separation of mother and baby.

© Richard Ebbitt

and children, probably with a baby in arms or in a stroller. Often, too, the older children will be skipping alongside or holding a parental hand. Occasionally, a single-parent family will consist of just a mother and her children.

If you observe them for a while, you'll notice that the parents and children enjoy being together. They're relaxed and at ease with each other. There is considerable interaction between mother, father, and children.

These parents unanimously see the child-rearing years as a good period in their lives, though not necessarily an easy one. Providing for their families is a continuing concern. There is no question that they are resourceful. With hammer and nails, with thimbles and nimble fingers and flour to the elbows, by barter and with a bit of banter, they are creating a foundation of security for themselves and their children.

Most of the pioneer couples are young, and they see their earning capabilities increasing over the years. Time is on their side. They are confident that ability and a firm belief in what they are doing will see them through. For now, they are high on hope. They aren't afraid to dream or to wait on their dreams. In the long run, they have no doubt they will come out ahead for having chosen to keep mother at home with the young children rather than have her work elsewhere, for someone else.

It is hard to imagine a more important work to which a mother could devote herself. Judy Dorris, Kentucky, reflects:

> Five years ago I stopped teaching math to seventh and eighth graders to become a mother. I took advantage of a year's maternity leave thinking I'd return to teaching at that point. After all, how could a baby compete with all the excitement in a classroom of thirty boys and girls? However, Melinda's early responses to my voice in a crowd of people showed me I had a special place in her heart. Week by week, month by month, our relationship grew, and I knew she depended on me to be there when she needed me. In the summer, I told the school superintendent what I'd known months earlier—I would not be returning to the classroom. I had a full-time teaching position at home.
>
> Recently, our second daughter, Marci, was born at home because I still did not want to leave Melinda and I didn't want to be separated from my new baby, either. Each fall, new students will fill the classrooms, but "my season of children" is the present. I have to take advantage of it while I can.

There is overwhelming evidence that these pioneer men and women are thinkers, innovators, and problem solvers. The vast majority of the women have had job experience, and many have college credits or degrees. In many cases, both husband and wife have advanced degrees. "About four weeks after our first son was born, we both graduated with PhDs," Jean Giesel of Florida writes, "and we moved to a new town. I thought I would try to get a part-time teaching job when the baby was old enough. It soon became apparent that this little fellow needed me full time, as did his brother and sister who followed."

Where do these new pioneers live? They come from small towns, the heart of cities, and rural areas. Such heroic parents come from all over the world, but the English language is a common denominator, and not surprisingly, the United States and Canada have the highest representation in this book, although letters were received from a number of other countries.

It is highly unlikely that very many of these pioneer families would be characterized as wealthy. From what their letters reveal, these families represent a fairly wide range of incomes, but by far, most would probably count themselves among the struggling middle class. Many are paying on a house rather than renting, but it is usually a modest house. When the wife quits her job, the drop in income, sometimes by as much as half, hits like a falling weight and has a profound effect on their lifestyle.

They aren't afraid to dream or to wait on their dreams. . .

A number of these families have gone through very difficult periods when the family income was drastically cut either because of illness or more often because of a job layoff. At such times, they switched gears and adopted survival tactics. One woman commented that it's like driving through a rough stretch

of mountainous road. You're glad when it's over, but on looking back, you're amazed at the challenge you've surmounted.

Many of the families would say that living on one income
is a matter of holding one's own and not backsliding. Even
when the husband has steady employment, inflation can out-
pace income. These families manage by being cautious con-
sumers. They're careful that no excess creeps into their spending.
Their buying habits are comparable to a dieter's eating habits.
They know that it's the little extras and treats day after day
that blow a good diet or a good budget. These couples save
in a 1,001 ways, from doing many household and auto repairs
themselves, to prolonging the life of a scouring pad. Many of
the things they do to economize are far from spectacular, but
put them all together and the savings are substantial.

Another much smaller group of respondents come from
the upper middle class. "We increase our savings each year,
and a large portion of the interest earned is reinvested," one
woman explained in stating that, at the present time, they do
not have immediate money worries. For a time in the past,
they had had very little money. While they are now enjoying
a time of plenty, neither she nor her husband has forgotten
the saving ways that saw them through the lean years.

A sizable portion of those who wrote in would be considered poor. Their yearly income is below the poverty level. They
are the long-term survivors, the ones who are on the most
intimate terms with living lightly. These people consider themselves impoverished only in monetary terms. There is a richness about their lives that does not depend on purchasing
power. Their housing and clothing are usually adequate, though
perhaps not in the latest fashion. Many of these survivors eat
more nutritiously than the majority of the population. More
than most, they are adept at living by the maxim "Use it up,
wear it out, make it do, or do without."

Living in a money-scarce world promotes a lifestyle that is
not dependent on spending money. Or perhaps it's the other
way around; when there isn't the money to shell out, one

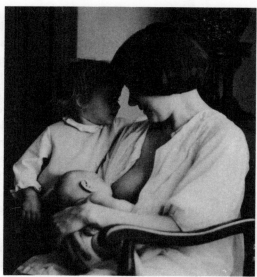

*Those special moments
with young children cannot
be scheduled.*

© Richard Ebbitt

adopts a lean lifestyle. "We are looking forward to releasing ourselves from the slavery of auto ownership," Barbara Dick writes from Washington. "For two years we did not own a car and for another year and a half we rarely used one. What heaven! We just bused or walked. I shop by busing—yes, with both kids." Barbara further explains their philosophy of living, "There's no need for bigger, better, brighter, whiter, faster, and shinier. But there is a need for simpler, smaller, slower, and saner. People need to rediscover the joys of being together, working together, and sharing together, instead of isolating one another and competing against one another."

The Four-Part Plan

When money is limited and you're living on basically one income, you can't afford many wrong moves. Travelers have road maps, builders look to their blueprints and pioneer families usually follow The Plan. They probably don't think of it as such and may not even be conscious of it, but nonetheless it is in operation. The Plan combines a strong sense of realism and a large measure of resourcefulness. This plan bears no resemblance to a corporate multiyear plan, the kind that projects goals and outlines the steps for achieving them. The Plan functions more as a strong undercurrent that provides direction and momentum. Each family develops its own strategy and style, yet when you look closely at the survivors, you find that certain attitudes or characteristics are evident again and again. There is a discernible pattern, a winning formula for surviving, that consists of four basic elements: *a people priority*, a *saving sense*, an *enterprising spirit*, and a *reliance on support*.

People Priority   Underlying the entire Plan is an attitude that people come before things. This belief is the foundation for a basic value system and makes all the effort worthwhile. "People before things" is a neat, simple little philosophy. Few people would argue with it; most would swear they live by it. In practice, it is far from simple. If not watched carefully, "people" and "things" can change places. The move is imperceptible, with few warnings alerting you to the shift in the critical balance, until one day you look back and wonder when and how things went awry. It happens, of course, because of the unquestionable need that people have for things. There is no living without them: everybody needs some things. The critical issue is the distinction between *needs* and *wants*. Wants aren't bad themselves; problems only arise when the line separating the two becomes blurred.

One of the best ways to keep the distinction clear and sharp, possibly the only way, is to stand back a bit from the vast and wonderful array of things that constantly beckon. To do so is somewhat like leaving the fast lane of the expressway and taking a less traveled country road. There's a letdown at first and the feeling of diminishing progress. But after a bit, you adjust to the slower speed and begin to notice the trees and little half-hidden flowers growing next to the road.

When you have less money, the pace for getting ahead will be slower. You will often find yourself standing back and thinking twice about whether you need something. In fact, you'll become a very selective shopper. The realization grows that you can manage without a good many things. But what is even more apparent is that life would be infinitely poorer without the people who are dear to you. Living on less, pioneer families have found, can be an intensive course in people appreciation.

A Saving Sense With the matter of putting people first at the top of the list, you can turn your attention to the second element of The Plan—making the most of the things in your life. Living on a limited budget need not be a steady diet of sacrifice. Doing without is a small part of surviving. Much more important is doing, making, and creating.

An attitude that people come before things. . .

The foundation for the good life lies in being selective, in being a "choosy shopper." For one thing, being selective is a good way to avoid the clutter of too many possessions doing too little for you. What you acquire should be worth at least what you must put out to get it, which may be a considerable amount of time and effort, if not money. You must look for value. Sharpening your sense of value is part of The Plan. The pursuit of value calls for the development of a rating system. You won't always be successful at obtaining top value every time around. Expect to make mistakes along the way. Even so, by being a questioning and observant shopper and by investigating how well things perform, you'll come out ahead in the long run.

To be a smart shopper, you need to develop good money sense. You'll need to keep a finger on your financial pulse, know how much money you have to spend as well as where the best buys are to be found. The Plan calls for a consistent but not elaborate effort at money monitoring. A complicated system is always short-lived. Furthermore, you don't want to draw the budget string too tightly. If a little slack isn't built into a budget, it's sure to collapse. Another vital part of The Plan is sharing and knowing when to splurge.

An Enterprising Spirit An eye for value and a sure money sense will get you going, but nothing keeps things perking like an enterprising spirit—the third element of The Plan. A dash of daring, the willingness to seek out-of-the-ordinary methods (legal and proper, of course) will often make up for a shortage of money in getting the things that you need or want. An enterprising spirit is the innovative side of surviving and is comparable to engaging in a challenging game. To get from "start" to "goal" you look at all possible options and seek the greatest maneuverability. The more options you have open to you, the better your chances of getting where or what you want. If an obstacle cannot be removed, you put your efforts into getting around it. In The Plan as in a game, trading is encouraged. Your real-life trading will most likely involve an exchange of talents or possessions with some other enterprising pioneer. Sometimes you'll make a series of trade-offs, giving one thing up in order to gain another. You're willing to try new things and take some chances.

For example, think of that continuous source of financial concern: the high cost of keeping the family well-nourished. Suppose that your family enjoys eating steak, but you find you can no longer afford it. Perhaps you pass the steak at the meat counter and instead choose the chicken, which is on sale. It isn't a bad choice, considering that it is more healthful in ways, with less fat and fewer calories, than beef. To further increase your options, you could introduce some high-protein foods like

Young children need great quantities of quality time.

© Richard Ebbitt

tofu to your family, having first learned all you can on how to prepare it. What you save on high-priced meat protein can help pay some of the bills you're getting tired of looking at, or you may find that you're able to afford steak now and again.

There are all kinds of variations on the theme of trading. One mother relates that she enjoyed music but had never had the opportunity to learn to play an instrument. With the arrival of the children, there wasn't money for such an extra, yet she did not give up her dream. She contacted a piano teacher and arranged to clean house in exchange for piano lessons. Being able to play has brought her immense pleasure, and she has also been able to give beginning lessons in piano to each of her children.

A trade-off is giving up one thing in order to get something else. If the budget is strained because of one or two large-expense items, there may be a sacred cow in the value lineup, a costly house or second car. A number of families came to the realization that the nice house they had in the good neighborhood, while certainly an asset, was also taking a disproportionate share of the money coming in. Overall, they decided, the family would be better served by a smaller house in a different area. Sometimes a change of location brought benefits beyond a lower house payment. A number of families moved to a rural area in order to raise more of their own food. Others relocated closer to the city to lessen their dependence on a car and to take advantage of low-cost cultural events.

A Reliance on Support You would not have to observe new-pioneer families long to notice another common characteristic: loners they are not. Like pioneer families of old, they know the value of support. They band together in a figurative wagon train, getting together in work projects and to have fun. They are drawn to kindred souls who understand the special demands that come with living on one income. As some very astute person once said, pleasure is doubled and trouble halved when shared with friends.

Look down the road, take the broad view, and chart your course. . .

One example of such a support group is a food co-op, the formation of which allows the members to buy better food at more economical prices. Enterprising savers also form exchanges, which are an avenue for trading time and services. La Leche League includes many mothers-at-home, who find it a prime support group which provides social ties as well as information and support in breastfeeding and mothering. As the spirit moves them and time allows, mothers also form play groups, exercise classes, and craft or cooking clubs, and they pitch in with church or other community work. They get together to make big jobs easier, from cleaning house to canning or freezing the harvest. It's more fun working together, and there is always someone available to keep things moving when a mother has to take time out to care for a child.

New pioneers must be able to look down the road a way, to take the broad view, and chart their course accordingly. If you are hard pressed for cash now, there are steps you can take to pull clear of a crisis situation. Once past the financial shoals, you can reset your sights and ready the family for the long haul. Once you are open to change and are ready to do some reshuffling in your life, you're well on the way to coping. Perhaps only a slight shift in habits will be needed to keep a lid on expenses, or you may decide to adopt a whole new lifestyle. It's important to check options—and it helps to be in close touch with others who are going your way.

The Pioneer Plan

So these are the basics of the pioneer plan, the philosophy for living on less.

1. People First
2. A Saving Sense
3. Create and Innovate
4. Seek Support.

In later chapters, these main points will be further developed, and you'll find the practical tips on saving and earning that can make the theory a reality.

What is important now is to set your goal and go for it. Make your decision and *do it!* Julina Hokanson lives in Wyoming, a part of original pioneer territory. She writes,

> We do mostly what everyone around here does, *we just do it!* When presented with a new challenge, a new baby, another hardship, an extra child or two (we are now supporting a foreign student for a few years), we never consider the cons, *we just do it!*

If you're presently employed, the prospect of doing without your salary can seem frightening. Leaving a safe job to pioneer on the homefront may look like a step into the unknown. Suddenly, financial obligations appear insurmountable. Interestingly, this hesitancy to let go of the second income may be as strong in a couple who are well-fixed as it is in a financially struggling family. Even when a husband is doing quite well in his job, there can still be a long list of reasons why the wife should not quit hers. A second income can become a security blanket.

As parents (or prospective parents) of a little one, you have the best incentive in the world for making the break from being a two-income family. One new mother refers to her difficult decision to stay home with her baby, as "taking the plunge." Once she made the decision, she said she experienced "a tremendous sense of relief." In a sense, taking the step is like going off the high dive in swimming for the first time. The only way to do it is simply to let go. Take a deep breath and jump.

At first, your efforts at saving money may seem of little consequence. You gain confidence as you go along. Susan Soderberg, an experienced saver from Pennsylvania, tells young mothers who are interested in learning more about managing on one salary, "Getting organized, gathering information, and setting priorities may take some time in the beginning. Once you make a plan and adapt your life to that plan, you find that with each new experience, you become more self-reliant, more creative, and enjoy yourself and your family more."

Once you're started in your new resolve, what carries you through to your goals? Not theory, of course. Not pages or

Quiet moments spent rocking together lay the foundation for a future that's emotionally secure.

© Richard Ebbitt

volumes of how-to suggestions, though all of these help. The crucial elements are determination and effort—or, as a pioneer would say, guts and hard work.

Pioneers in Rocking Chairs

Mothers and babies need time together, time that is not fragmented by the pressure to punch a timeclock or complete an assignment for a waiting boss. In itself, the rocker holds no magic. It is simply a warm invitation to a mother and child to rest and snuggle for a spell. What a baby needs most is mother. When you are there with your little one, there is a fundamental rightness to the order of your world. Being there is the most precious gift, after life, that you can give your child.

To get you started with The Plan, the simple non-technical rocker may be exactly what you need. The gentle motion of rocking back and forth soothes the restless spirits within. Mind and body relax. Some excellent thinking can take place in a rocker, especially when rocking a baby to sleep. Rockers and babies go together.

When you and your baby settle into your favorite rocker for a song and a bit of nursing, baby's round little head nestled against your breast, big eyes intently watching the expressions on your face, words are not needed. The message is unmistakable. Sight, sound, smell, taste, touch all convey that which is more important than food to your child: love. To love and be loved in return is so vital to survival, we humans never cease to yearn for it. The baby or young child focuses on the mother; when mother is within sight or better yet, within touch, the reassuring signal is clear. When the mother goes away, the line of communication is broken. Not until some time in the future, years ahead, will the baby have developed the ability to think in abstract terms and to associate feelings and ideas with words. Not until this and much more has taken place will the young child know that although mother leaves she will return and that in the meantime, all is well. Let's consider then, the underlying theme of this book, the motivation of our pioneering spirit—namely, the child's need for mother.

CHAPTER 2

*I*mportance of *M*othering

Parental lifestyles may change, and undoubtedly have over the course of the centuries and the millenniums, but babies do not. The baby born in the twentieth century has the same needs and will respond in the same way as the infant who arrived before time was tallied. The human baby has an inner drive to be fully human and in that context, a baby's wants are a baby's needs.

Baby the Baby

Why do we say to baby the baby? The baby still has an immature sense of himself. He does not perceive himself as being totally separated from his mother. To the infant, mother is an extension of self. He feels complete only when close to her. As Louise Kaplan, PhD, writes in *Oneness and Separateness: From Infant to Individual:* "From the infant's point of view there are no boundaries between himself and mother. They are one."

From living in the womb with the umbilical cord supplying all his needs, he has progressed to a position outside of, but near, mother's body. He is meant to be within close proximity of her warm breast and the sound of her voice. It is nature's careful way of providing a transition from the infant's old world to his new one. The little newcomer has the freedom needed to grow, yet is assured of continuous, loving support. The all-important mother-child bond replaces the umbilical cord.

The ideal environment for nurturing a new life includes mother. Mother is buffer zone and reassurer all in one. Her young child is blissfully secure when he is with her. Such security is as much a prerequisite for optimal development as is being well nourished and adequately stimulated mentally. Slowly but steadily, the child expands his horizons and discovers greater self-awareness. Psychologically speaking, he cannot be expected to stand on his own two feet until about the age of three. Louise Kaplan goes on to explain: "By three years a child will have achieved his initial sense of separateness and identity. However, the reconciliations of oneness and separateness have only begun. The three-year-old has but a small degree of constancy—just enough to allow him to feel safe in the world even though he now recognizes that his self is separate from the self of his mother."

Unlike growing bigger or learning a new skill such as walking, being emotionally secure is not readily visible or measurable—it would be so much easier to repair insecurity if it were. All future accomplishments rest on the foundation laid in the early years. Little should be left to chance in the process of a young child becoming a caring, loving adult, able to function productively in society and to form lasting relationships with others.

A Personal Tutor

Nature has gone to elaborate lengths to assure success in this critical phase of growing up. A personal tutor in the art of living has been designated—mother, of course. Since she is the one

Importance of Mothering

The daily interaction between mother and infant provides a learning experience that's not easy to replace.

© Richard Ebbitt

who can provide the most complete nourishment to her infant, both in body and spirit, there is a superb allocation of responsibilities. As mother's milk flows to her child, so does her love. The one intensifies the other. The baby knows this and so does mother.

Around the clock, the interaction between mother and child constitutes a message, a lesson in life. As a way of passing on the complexities of social living, none of the experiments tried over the years comes close to being as effective as mother at home.

There is something wonderful and exciting about the unfolding of a new personality. The young child's growth in self-esteem is a joy to see, but it is based on a fact of life with which we are all very familiar. People do their best when they know they count, when they are confident that they are important to those who mean the most to them.

In *Your Child's Self-Esteem*, psychologist Dorothy Corkille Briggs explains:

Your child's judgment of himself influences the kinds of friends he chooses, how he gets along with others, the kind of person he marries, and how productive he will be. It affects his creativity, integrity, stability, and even whether he will be a leader or a follower. His feelings of self worth form the core of his personality and determine the use he makes of his aptitude and abilities. His attitude toward himself has a direct bearing on how he lives all parts of his life. In fact, self-esteem is the mainspring that slates every child for success or failure as a human being.

The baby grows in response to mother and her gift of herself to her child. The giving is reciprocal. The baby is a most generous little soul, ready to give his heart. In fact, he falls unconditionally, madly in love with his first teacher, mother. A loving child is an apt pupil. His unreserved bonding is also a clue to his behavior. What lover, especially in the first throes of love, can bear to be apart from his beloved for any length of time? The young child has not yet acquired the maturity to know that even though mother is gone for only an hour—or even twenty minutes—she will be coming back to him. For all he knows, she is gone forever. A child becomes upset when his mother goes away because he is heartbroken. He mourns her leaving. He cries from grief. There is a void, an aching emptiness in his world that no substitute can fill. This is explained by Selma Fraiberg in *Every Child's Birthright: In Defense of Mothering:*

> The baby has discovered that his mother is, for the time being, the most important person in his world. And he behaves the way all of us behave when a loved person is leaving for a journey, or is absent for a while. ("I can't bear to be without you. I am lost. . . . I am not myself without you. . . . You are my world and without you the world is empty.")

Such exclusiveness does not lessen baby's fondness for father, sisters and brothers, grandparents, and other dear ones.

These other caring people add another important dimension to the young child's world, but not one of them can substitute for what is, at this time of the child's life, the central relationship. Selma Fraiberg continues:

> The baby who has formed a deep attachment to his mother is also moving toward some degree of independence and autonomy. His own mobility brings him to explorations of the world around him. He tends to go off on brief excursions around the house or the yard, then return to "touch base" with his mother. She is the safe and comforting center and must continue to be so for some years to come.

When Mother Isn't There

As is often the case, the value of what is essential in life is realized most in its absence. Babies need their mothers because babies seldom survived, at least not until recently, without breast milk. Then came the history-changing merger of technology and advertising; the former made cow's milk somewhat more suitable for the human baby, and the latter sold the idea to the adult world. It was quickly assumed that with regularly scheduled feedings of the new formula and proper hygiene, even a motherless infant would thrive. (Rigid hygiene and schedules achieved the status of gospel for a time. They have yet to be completely exorcised from the thinking on child care.)

Unfortunately, science's best effort was not the whole answer to the question of the foundling. Babies in institutions were fed carefully and changed regularly, but they consistently lagged behind other children in their development. Even those who were dedicated to solving the problem came to realize that more than good physical care and good intentions are needed. One authority on child development, John Bowlby, tells of the experience of D. Burlingham and Anna Freud in running a residential nursery in England. "As time went on

© Richard Ebbitt

Parents who want to instill their values on their children know the importance of the early years.

they became increasingly aware of the evil effects of maternal deprivation and of the difficulties of providing substitute care, in an institutional setting. In the end, they concluded that so many helpers were necessary if their infants and young children were to receive the continuous care of one mother-substitute, which their observations showed to be essential, it would be better for each helper to take a couple of children home with her and close the nursery."

Children who are deprived of mother feel the loss in varying degrees. There is no predicting whether a particular child will weather the separation with only temporary discomfort or whether the repercussions will be more severe and long lasting. Children who have less of mother than they need often display antisocial behavior. Their relationships with others are shallow. They may have difficulty understanding the difference between fact and fiction. Commonly, there is an unrealistic and debilitating need for attention that may persist throughout life. All else being equal, having numerous caretakers is not broadening for the young child but is, to a greater or lesser degree, crippling. The evidence is sobering and it continues to accumulate. Selma Fraiberg reports:

> It has been determined that children who do not have the benefit of a single, sustained contact with a loving mother-figure for at least the first three years of their lives, will—depending upon the degree of deprivation—manifest a diminished capacity to love others, impaired intellectual powers, and an inability to control their impulses, particularly in the area of aggression.

Mother's Viewpoint

Mothers who have chosen to be at home with their children have often made this choice because of personal experiences. Some gained insights into the needs of the young child before they had their own children, often through their work. For others, the consequences of mother-baby separation were observed in caring for young children whose own mothers were working. These women have learned from their own experiences what is normal behavior for children, and more importantly, what is not normal.

Betty Aviles from Maryland is convinced that "Babies really need their mothers. From all my observations, I'm convinced that *no one can take the place of mother.* I have been 'babysitting' for the past three-and-a-half years. Mostly, I care for bottle-fed babies. These children are different from breastfed babies. Breastfed babies cry more for their mothers. A breastfed baby knows his mother's arms and won't stay happily with others. The day-care babies are used to being away from their parents. They will go to anyone. They also have a great need to put things in their mouths. Some eat a lot and talk incessantly." Betty concludes, "A babysitter and/or bottle cannot replace the love and caring the mother brings to her baby."

"I took care of three children for a week while their parents went on vacation," Jane Hunt Morford of Idaho relates. "This taught me *not* to leave my children with others, especially a child under the age of two. The little guy was so sad! He would not let me hold him while he was being fed, preferring to hold his own bottle. The bottle was 'mother.'"

Flor Constantino of Oregon was not yet a mother herself when she began thinking about what it can mean to a child to have a mother at home.

I am home because of the things I saw in children before I had my own. While doing student teaching, I saw a variety of children with working parents. I saw the ways they tried to cope and compensate for not having the most important person in their lives there.

In Las Vegas, there were children who would go days without seeing their parents because mother and dad were working some crazy shift in that twenty-four-hour city. There would be little kindergartners who would get themselves up, pour out their cereal, and get dressed for school all timed to certain television programs.

You could almost always pick out the child whose mother was home. Please understand, I am talking about little ones, first graders. Oh, it wasn't just how they were dressed or how their hair looked. I am talking about the way they interacted with other children and the teacher. They were more confident of themselves, almost always the initiators, the "leaders." They could deal with correction without sulking or crying and having it become a big issue. They also displayed a gentle considerateness, a kind of mothering toward others—if another child was crying they'd walk over and whisper something kind and put their arm around the upset child. I wanted my children to be like that.

Marjorie Corrington from Texas was herself a working mother at one time.

I enjoyed my job as a mechanical engineer. During an almost five-month maternity leave following the birth of our son, I had some problems adjusting to being a full-time housewife.

When my husband and I discussed our financial situation we just didn't see how we would make the house payment, pay utilities, and still eat. I looked for "at home" work or part-time work but found nothing suitable, so I went back to my full-time job.

Several weeks before I had to return to work, I learned to express my milk so Nathan could continue to get the best milk possible. I also put an ad in the local paper for a sitter. Like all working mothers, I felt I had found the best sitter, a young grandmother with several school-aged children who wanted to care for only one baby.

I had no problems expressing milk, and Nathan seemed to be just fine with the sitter. However, during the second month after I returned to work (he was then six months old), the sitter just could not keep him happy. She had to hold him continually.

The "unhappy baby" problem was soon followed by a very bad diaper rash. We thought it was something that he was eating, but even when we went back to total breastfeeding, it never completely healed. Sometimes it seemed to be getting better on weekends but then would get worse again during the week.

The sitter just could not keep him happy...

After a week of hearing, "We didn't have a very good day today; Nathan wasn't very happy. I think something is wrong," the babysitter took the time to visit our home to tell us that she didn't want to babysit for Nathan any longer. We discussed all the problems she was having. What worried me the most was that Nathan was not sleeping well. She would rock him to sleep, but he would never be in a deep or peaceful sleep.

The babysitter thought that perhaps Nathan would be happier if someone would watch him in our home. At the time, my parents were visiting us and they took care of Nathan for a couple of hours during my workday. They informed me that Nathan was a different baby after I walked out of the door. He seemed to be such a happy baby when I was around, but he had to have constant attention when I was gone. I told myself that if a seven-month-old baby cannot take a nap during the day, he must really be upset. I quit work. I'm glad I did.

The diaper rash went away. It was then that I realized it had been an emotional problem that caused the rash, not his diet. My staying home has helped him to be a more emotionally sound little individual. Now he is a nursing two-year-old and can accept some separation from me. I hope that if my story reaches other working mothers, they will be more aware of the problems involved in working and will realize the unhappy signals babies may send.

Young babies are not the only ones to be affected by mother's work schedule. Another mother writes briefly of the conflict she faced when her child was three years old.

It was unpleasant to have to tell my young daughter that she *had* to go to the day-care center despite her fears of the bully-in-residence. It was hard juggling work responsibilities when she was ill, and I have no doubt that she went to school sometimes not feeling too well because I couldn't afford another day off from work.

A Matter of Values

Christy Stamps of Illinois says: "By experiencing all the good times and the bad times, I've grown very close to my little ones. I've learned to see my children as little people rather than small bodies to be cared for. I've learned to be considerate of their needs and feelings and to put my needs aside temporarily. If my children were to stay with a sitter or at a day-care center, or even with a friend while I would work, the other adults would become the parent and I would be the evening-and-weekend sitter.

Christy Stamps knows the time she spends with David and Timothy will affect their future well-being.

"My husband and I want to put our personal mark on our children, and unless I'm there all the time for them, our mark is weakened. The time when we have the greatest influence on each child is so short, just about five years, and then peers and other adults start to become a larger part of children's lives."

A mother of three, Christine Hilston of Ohio, makes a similar point. "As parents, we want to instill our values in our children. We want to decide how they will be raised, to guide them toward becoming loving persons, respectful of the feelings of others. This doesn't mean that we want to totally control our children's lives or stifle all natural inclinations. We want them to be free to discover their own interests, strengths, and weaknesses. We want them to know that we will be here as a refuge, a sounding board, a place where they are always free to share their feelings."

Joyce Bartels of New York tells this story: "My sister-in-law returned to work last year, and I babysat for her four- and two-year-old sons for four months. I saw what she missed by working. I got the hugs when Tommy learned how to snap for the first time. I was the one Dougie said 'Mommy' to. I was there for the daily trials and errors, and I received great enjoyment watching the smiles of triumph. I could only tell Kathy how it was. I couldn't give her the feelings I felt."

Joyce feels there are even more important reasons for a mother to be with her very impressionable young children. "My kids are learning their values from me," she says. "They learned of death, sex, and divorce from me. How would a babysitter have answered questions like 'Why did your mommy die?' 'What made her body stop working?' 'Where did Michael and I stay when Valerie was in your belly if we weren't born yet?' 'Doesn't Uncle Bruce love Aunt Kathy any more?' 'Does he still love Tommy and Dougie?' 'Will you stop loving Daddy?'

"How could a babysitter answer any of these questions? Would the kids even have the inclination to ask them if I had not been with them from birth, always willing to talk to them and enjoying their inquisitiveness?"

"How can children really relax and let their feelings show if they are not home?" Linda Couvillion of Georgia observes. "My four small boys are struggling to grow up, and their daily little disappointments are important to us as a family." In New Mexico, Donna MacFarlane concurs. "Emotions and feelings can be expressed freely at home with familiar people. There is no need to bottle up feelings that beg for release because the child does not feel comfortable enough to release them in the company of strangers. With older children, arguments can be worked out immediately. And hugs and kisses can be freely dispensed whenever the mood strikes." Sue Publicover of Nova Scotia relates, "My children get to know me as they will perhaps never know anyone quite so well, at least not until they find partners of their own. They see me cry, laugh, hate, fear— all the emotions—and they see me at work—cooking, cleaning, teaching, typing, knitting. They see also the sharing, loving, praying—all that I do as a person—as wife, mother, and member of a community. I believe that young children need to see an adult in all types of interaction and work in order to learn. This role generally falls to the mother, as the father is usually out of the home."

How children learn from their mothers comes through in letter upon letter. From Wisconsin, Jj Fallick writes, "My kids are learning about work from working with me, not from a storybook or television. Of course, it is much more than that. As we are approaching the time for our eldest to go off to school, we know that she has learned some important values. Just today she figured out all by herself something that had apparently been on her mind for a while. She told me, 'I know how I can be both a ballet dancer and a mommy! I can dance before I have babies, and then, when I have my babies, I will stay home with them.' I told her that sounded just fine to me and that I was sure her babies would enjoy learning to dance from their expert mama.'"

*E*motions can be expressed freely at home. . .

Sue Sperry of Missouri reflects, "As each of my babies became older, I thought I might eventually go back to work for 'fulfillment.' They seem more independent every day, but their need for me doesn't diminish; it just manifests itself in a different manner. The benefits from guiding a newborn baby into a healthy happy person cannot be seen as quickly as the return from a healthy paycheck, but it is so much more fulfilling to meet the needs of one's own child than to satisfy the boss or a company. While I cannot give my children 100 percent quality time 100 percent of the time, I care very deeply for them. And always, I keep trying to do my best for them."

John Bowlby, MD, explains this in *Maternal Care and Mental Health*:

> The mothering of a child is not something which can be arranged by roster; it is a live human relationship which alters the character of both partners. . . . The provision of mothering cannot be considered in terms of hours per day but only in terms of the enjoyment of each other's company which mother and child obtain. Such enjoyment and close identification of feeling is only possible for either party if the relationship is continuous.

Janis McCauley's words are echoed by many other mothers. This Virginia mother writes, "I stayed home with my first child simply because my husband wanted me to. I accepted the idea intellectually, but I had no experiential proof to back it up. Sometimes, I did it grudgingly.

"My oldest daughter will be six tomorrow, and I have seen her grow from an infant who nursed almost nonstop into a confident, intelligent, independent little girl. Her need for intense mothering was met and was outgrown and left behind. This second time around, I am doing things the same way but enjoying it more. I know the results are worth it."

The child's need for mother is so important, La Leche League has recognized it as one of its basic concepts.

> In the early years the baby has an intense need to be with his mother that is as basic as his need for food.

The baby's need for mother, like the hungry person's yearning for food, is not easily ignored. For a time, something else may

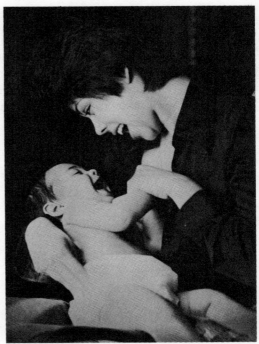

Mother and baby spend time enjoying each other's company as the child's personality begins to unfold.

© Richard Ebbitt

serve as a diversion, but it will never fully satisfy the hunger. Only mother, or in the case of a motherless child, a *single* mother figure, can fill the void and provide the needed nourishment. Food and mother are both vital, and in the case of the baby or young child, much more is at stake than a full tummy.

As Herbert Ratner, MD, philosopher and long-time friend and advisor to La Leche League states, "It is a wise and providential nature that gives each newborn his or her private caretaker and tutor—the mother. The more we study nature—the bonding and attachment phenomena; the special love relationship of mother and infant engendered by pregnancy, child-birth, and the postpartum period; the unique developmental needs of the infant—the more we learn that the dynamics of the mother-infant dyad (optimally the nursing couplet) encompass much more than the nutritional. The mother is truly a nurturer of the person—of the psyche and soma as they intimately interrelate."

CHAPTER 3

*E*xploring the *Q*uestion

"Is being a mother-at-home enough? Should I be doing more with my life? If ever I have to support myself, then what? Employers look for work experience, not years of mothering, on a job resumé. . . ."

The above questions probably have a familiar ring to them. Mothers say that these questions and others like them are a source of concern. You can hardly avoid them in this day and age. If you push them to the back of your mind, they're sure to resurface, like the theme melody of a movie or play. A relative will mention that a mutual acquaintance is "really making something of her education," having recently received yet another job promotion. It makes you wonder anew if you should be doing more to ease the financial strain on your husband.

At the end of a busy day when you're tired and the baby is fussy, the thought of getting away can even seem downright appealing. But it's during the quiet moments, perhaps when you're in your trusty rocking chair, that you find yourself mulling over much of what you've heard and read since first you thought about what it means to be a woman.

A Time of Change

In the last twenty years or so, views of women's roles have changed dramatically. As a prelude to these changes, the roles of women in the past, (predominantly involved with motherhood) have been held up to view, stripped of all sentiment, and scrutinized in a strong harsh light.

Without a doubt, past societal influences imbued motherhood with heavy doses of sentimentality and placed the role of mother-at-home on a pedestal. In reality, there were few other opportunities open to women. That too has changed.

In retrospect, women can take pride in many of the new opportunities that have been opened to them as a result of their concerted efforts. It is important, however, to recognize that some women have paid a high price for their gains. While advances were being made by women in business and government, the traditional work of women as mothers and homemakers was being devalued. We can all be pleased to see more choices available to women, but those who choose motherhood as a full-time career deserve society's respect. Our society encourages mothers to look outside the home for fulfillment and, in the process, to give their babies over to someone else's care. A one-time advocate of child day-care, British authority on social psychology Penelope Leach, writes, "I am sorry for mothers who cannot look after their babies themselves, but I do not believe that it is helpful to conceal the fact that group care is a bad alternative to individual care." How foolish to dispel one set of myths regarding a woman's role only to replace them with new myths which are equally damaging!

For the most part, women in the past knew that society as a whole supported them in what they were doing day after day. Many of them were not at all stifled by being at home. They regarded the home as their special domain, one that offered them considerable freedom. Many truly functioned as equal partners along with their husbands in maintaining the home and raising the family. Grandmother and great-grandmother served as household managers, character builders to their children, and they were truly the heart of the home.

Today's women, of course, live in a different kind of world, one that offers a tempting array of things to do outside the home. I do not know of anyone who would turn back the clock to what was a simpler though much more limited era. Along with a variety of choices, of course, comes the agony and ecstasy of having to make a decision.

A New Beginning

For the first-time mother in particular, the birth of a baby means a major reorganization of her life. The thought of returning to the comfortable, familiar routine of a well-liked job can seem very reassuring.

Initially, many of the mothers we heard from were reluctant to sever the ties they had formed to their places of employment. They enjoyed their work and liked the people they worked with. Many feared that, once home, with only a baby for company, they would be lacking for mental stimulation and would end up "crawling the walls."

In reality, many a well-intentioned young mother has stepped into the brave new world of combining a career and motherhood only to realize some time later that mothering a young child is in itself a full-time career. The concept of combining motherhood with an outside career promises the best of both worlds. However, many women do not find that to be the case: "Handling a part-time job while trying to be a mother doesn't sound difficult, but it is," one mother writes. Another acknowledges, "I never felt I could give as much to the job or to mothering as I wanted to give."

The Need to Nurture

It can all sound very simple and sensible: Have the baby, get back on one's feet, and get back to work. The reality of what takes place is another matter. Becoming a mother is unlike almost any other experience, and it is impossible for a woman to know beforehand how deeply the experience will affect her. Until your baby is born and in your arms, nursing at your breast, you cannot know what it means to have a child, and then to leave your child. "I cried a lot" is a very common reaction among mothers who leave their babies to go back to their jobs. The female has been primed for her nurturing role over millions of years. Upon the birth of the baby, the full impact of nature's intent is felt. A mother may attempt to ignore the message or even fight it, but the odds are stacked against her. She stands to lose something that is basic to her nature as a woman.

As if coping with her own feelings were not enough, the baby's reaction to the separation adds to a mother's dilemma. If the baby is visibly upset, all the guilt feelings the mother is already feeling are further intensified. On the other hand, if the sitter reports that "everything is just fine," the young mother doubts her own importance in her child's life. In either case, some distance is created between mother and baby. This distance almost becomes necessary, because it serves as a safety zone, preventing either from being hurt too much by the experience. In the long run, it can affect the long-term relationship between mother and child.

Feeling Inadequate

Many first-time mothers are faced with a feeling of inadequacy which can motivate them to leave the baby with "a perfectly super sitter" and return to their former pursuits. For all her joy at having this most wonderful little being in her care, the new mother may also feel an unsettling sense of unsureness about her own capabilities as a mother. In contrast to other areas of her life—her job, for instance—in which she feels confident and successful, the caring for a baby may be something of a puzzle that in ways intimidates a still inexperienced mother.

Perhaps breastfeeding gets off to a slow start, and mother and baby have a hard time adjusting to this new phase of life together. Even before that, at the time of the birth, perhaps the momentous moment of greeting her newborn arrived and mother's response was emotionally flat. While other mothers might gush rapturously about the wonder and excitement of having given birth, perhaps her most vivid recollections are those of relief at having labor and delivery end. These reactions may in turn provoke feelings of guilt or the fear that she is not sufficiently maternal.

In many ways, mothering is a learned art. . .

A new mother needs support and some pampering. Her appetite should be tempted with a variety of good, nourishing things to eat to replenish her strength. Others should take over household duties for a time, but it is anything but helpful for someone else to take over the care of the baby, even with the well-meaning intention of letting mother get some rest. Mother and baby rest best when resting together. Mothers and babies need each other. The time a mother spends with her little one is the rich soil that nourishes motherliness. In many ways, mothering is a learned art. The good news is: your baby does not expect perfection. The power of the mother/baby connection is illustrated in the story of a mother who considered herself anything but the motherly type. Nancy Clay Edmond of Oklahoma tells the story:

I had never understood why people enjoyed holding babies and playing with small children. I didn't want to be anywhere near a crying baby or even too close to a happy one. Even so, when Joe and I had been married for seven years and I was thirty, we started our family. I loved being pregnant. Watching my stomach grow and feeling the little one move inside held an endless fascination.

When Jennifer was born, she was a beautiful baby. I was amazed at her beauty. My husband was overwhelmed with joy. But when they brought Jennifer to me, she took one look at me and screamed. I thought, "She already knows what a lousy mother I am." The nurse brought her to me later and she furiously refused to nurse. Much to my relief, the nurse took her back to the nursery and I lay there knowing that she must be disappointed in getting me for a mother and wishing I could put her back inside and be pregnant again.

Every four hours they brought her to me with strict instructions to nurse only five minutes on a side. Each time they brought her she was more eager to nurse, and I wasn't able to limit her to five minutes, no matter what anybody said. It was a nice feeling when they brought her in crying and I could comfort her so quickly. I began to feel a little better.

But then I had to take her home. I was responsible for her twenty-four hours a day. Meanwhile, I was hearing many doubts about my milk—there wasn't enough, it was too thin, it was too rich. I was encouraged to give her sugar water, cereal, a little formula, anything to help her sleep. I was told she had diarrhea; on the same day, I was told she was constipated. When she broke out in the typical baby acne that the doctor told me might occur, I could not convince people that it was not an allergy to my milk.

I probably drove my La Leche League Leaders, Beckie Greenshaw and Becky Hencke to distraction. Still I clung to the nursing relationship for dear life, because something inside me was telling me it was vitally important. I refused to supplement because breastfeeding was the *only* thing that made me special to my baby.

You see, she preferred being rocked by her soft-shouldered grandmas. My shoulders were bony. Her grandmothers could change diapers neatly and in a snap. They would bathe her without sending her into hysterics. My sister-in-law knew exactly how to talk to her and was an expert burp-popper. I realized that almost anyone who walked in my front door would have been more skilled at giving the baby a bottle than me, and I could not allow that to come between us.

With nursing, we had a special relationship between just the two of us. We had to be together during those times. We had to be close. However incompetent I might have been at anything else, it was *me* she needed at those times. It was a comfort knowing I could provide what Jennifer needed most.

Then one night in the wee hours, something very special happened. I began talking to her and she smiled at me. It was impossible to hold back my affection and all the silly things I wanted to say to her. It was as if I had motherly love collecting in a secret place in my soul for all my life and Jennifer unlocked the door. It was like a miracle. I had finally become a mother.

That was about eighteen months ago. I love holding my baby. I love being responsible for her. I enjoy all the little things I do in taking care of her. Our nursing relationship has made both of us grow. She has opened the door to the happiest time of my life. If anyone asks what my ambitions are, I cannot say. I am too content and too thankful for this glorious day. The best of my dreams have come true. Thank God for Jennifer, for the miracle of breastfeeding, for Beckie Greenshaw and Becky Hencke, and for La Leche League!

The Outside World

The need to have mother at home with baby does not mean that a mother must remain cut off from the world. You owe it to yourself and to your family to develop a daytime social life. While you may not want to give up old friends from your former job, you need to find support in your new work of mothering. Every new mother should have access to a La Leche League Group or its equivalent. Mothers need other mothers.

The change of status from working woman to mother will take some time. Many a former working woman recalls a transition period when, as a new mother, she was finding a new social base to replace the one she lost when changing from an outside job to her in-the-house job. Initially, she had to take steps to contact other women in new settings. Breaking away from the old haunts of a job and familiar patterns of living requires openness and a willingness to make necessary adjustments.

Mother versus Housekeeper

Many women return to work after having a baby because of their distaste for or disinterest in housework. One mother explains, "My husband knows he has to help around the house when I'm working. He may not feel that way if I stay at home."

The fact is, many mothers who stay at home place housework very far down on their priority list. They see themselves as most effective when interacting with people, mainly their family, rather than with dirt and scrub mops. The all-too-common thinking that equates a mother's role at home with that of housekeeper is sure to bring sparks to their eyes—and speech. Hilary Rocca of France relates: "Many people here are shocked to see Patrick, my husband, helping me with the housework. They are shocked to see him doing the weekend shopping and getting breakfast on weekdays, not because a man shouldn't do such things but because I should be earning my keep by doing all the household chores. It's acceptable for the husband to share household chores if the husband and wife both 'work.' But they don't see raising children as a job! Nor do they understand why my house doesn't look like something out of

Ideal Homes. They don't realize that because we're living in it all day long, it has that lived-in look."

Hilary adds that two of her neighbors are upset "because their children spend their free time in our home—our topsy-turvy, minimum-of-furniture home. They're both working to have a beautiful home *now* and don't understand why their children prefer our lunar-landscape garden to sitting in their beautiful lounge watching television."

Husband and wife working together in the home is not a new idea. It has been going on since people discovered that cooperation is the quickest and easiest way to get a job done. Husbands and wives work best together when each is able to respect the other's contribution to the family.

"It's a tradition in my family that weekends are for wives, too," Hilary explains. "I remember my grandfather and father with a tea towel on their shoulders washing dishes on Sunday while granny and mama were getting ready for the family's Sunday outing. Even in those days, it was recognized that mothers were doing a very important, time and energy-consuming job."

Cooperation is the quickest and easiest way to get a job done.

On the other hand, having mother at home can mean a more relaxed time together as a family in the evening. Many mothers say they don't mind doing as much of the housework as they can during the day—consistent with caring for the children first of all—and dismiss the idea that doing so makes them the maid. "I enjoy making our home a pleasant place to be," one mother says. "I'm happy when my husband can come home at the end of a workday and relax or do things with the children, rather than doing chores.''

A Family Team   Mothers stressed again and again how important it is to do things with their children, household chores as well as other family projects. At such times, mother functions as teacher; she works alongside the children, imparting lessons in how to organize one's work and carry it through completion. The younger the child and the less his ability, the greater is his enthusiasm. Take advantage of it! Toddlers, who are great mess makers, also love to run and get things for mother. A smart mother will keep her toddler busy putting things away as well. Example certainly plays a big part in teaching children, but so does repetition—mother being there, reminding, encouraging, and if need be, insisting on the job being done. A lively tune and the promise of a treat when the chores are completed help motivate big and little members of the family team.

Earning Respect

The reason why many women work is to bring home a paycheck. Many women equate earning a paycheck with feelings of independence—or even a sense of power. This feeling may be more difficult to replace than the actual income. A frequent comment from working women is ''I'm accustomed to having my own money to spend. I don't want to have to ask my husband for every penny.''

Before marriage, of course, most of us had only ourselves to provide for. If there was extra money in our pocket, it was ours to spend as we pleased. All that changes with marriage and a family. Occasionally, there may be a twinge of regret for the carefree days, but that lifestyle was set aside for the closeness of family life. Husband and wife are co-workers in a common enterprise, and money that comes in—from whatever source—is to be used jointly.

The wife who has to ask her husband for every penny while he is accountable to only himself had better sit down with her husband for a serious talk. Much more is at stake than money. To sidestep the issue by getting a job and money of her own is a poor substitute for cooperation and communication. In the long run, money becomes a wedge between the couple rather than a means to an end.

The wife's value to the family by staying at home and caring for the children deserves to be respected on an equal basis with the husband's contribution to the family. If you add to that the economizing ways we will be discussing later in this book, there is all the more reason for recognition that her role is as important to the family's financial situation as her husband's is.

Career Considerations

Complicating the matter further when a woman gives up her job is the loss of seniority or rank that she may have attained, often through considerable hard work. In practical terms, women fear that they will go rusty in their line of work or have to start again at the bottom when applying for a new position in later years. They see themselves one day being passed over for younger workers with current work records or with recent degrees who are familiar with the latest techniques.

There is no reason for the mother-at-home to be out of touch with her chosen field. She can continue her subscriptions to trade journals, check the local library for recent books or other publications, even take a part-time course at a local college when the children are in school all day.

Gwen Rosentrater says that she told the fifth-grade class at a Career Fair in their Colorado school that homemaking is a unique career because "you can have other careers before and after a career in homemaking."

But still, mothers wonder how successful they will be in

finding a job once the children are grown or if they are faced with the need to support the family on their own.

For the mother spending years at home, there are really no answers to that question, but there are also few guarantees for the woman who remains in the work force. Job security is a tenuous thing at best. People who have given years to a job may one day walk into their office or plant and learn that a shutdown is imminent, that another corporation has bought them out, that the department has been eliminated, that the company is moving, or that there is any one of a number of other reasons why they will be out scouting for a new job. Today, more and more people change jobs or make career changes in the course of their working life. Gone are the days when one would pick a line of work and a safe company and stick with them through thick and thin.

The woman who is re-entering the job market after a hiatus spent at home raising her family will have plenty of company. She should recognize that she has a great deal to offer a prospective employer. Don't ever sell yourself short. Technical experience on a job can carry one only so far, and many needed skills can be updated fairly easily. The difference between a competent and an outstanding worker almost alway lies in personal qualities—the ability to work well with others, the ability to bring out the best in others, and often, the ability to look at old ways of doing things with fresh eyes. A conscientious mother at home has been fine-tuning such skills over the years. Far from being wasted years in a personal sense, the time you spend at home with your children can be a time of fruitful development.

As always, mothers are solving the problem of re-employment in unique ways. Marsha Hardin from Illinois is a case in point. She recounts:

> I was at home full time for eleven years during which time our three children were born. When my youngest child was six, economic need prompted me to look for a way to earn money.

Marsha Hardin (shown here with Alena) treasures the years she spent at home with her children.

© Richard Ebbitt

I decided to do housecleaning. The work was no more difficult than I was used to doing, and I didn't have to travel far or spend money on a wardrobe. I could work during the hours the children were in school, and I had a certain amount of freedom regarding the days I would have to work. Many people thought I was crazy to clean other people's houses when I had a degree in chemistry. But I thought it was smart since I could be home when I was needed.

In time, we again felt the need for additional income, but still I did not want to work full time. A neighbor who was employed part time herself encouraged me to look for part-time work in my field. I told her I thought that was a daydream—I had not heard of part-time jobs in chemistry, even as a technician—but she challenged me to give it a try.

When I went out and applied, I got raised eyebrows and negative remarks, but I kept trying. Finally, I decided to take a rather unorthodox approach. I visited the Village Hall and took down the names and phone numbers of all local businesses that looked promising. I then proceeded to call only company presidents or lab directors, totally bypassing the personnel department, which, I had come to realize, could not evaluate my technical skills anyway.

This resulted in two job offers, and I opted for the one that was part-time and offered the most flexibility. I had to really shine to make it clear that I *could* do the work well. That way, when I couldn't come in, or had to leave early, or answer a distress phone call in the middle of a business meeting, management would feel the inconvenience to them was worth it.

Things worked out well until the job grew to the point that it required someone full time. I knew that would not work for me. The company did hire a technician to help, but I knew the job would soon need two full-time people, possibly more. I was not willing to compromise the good job I had already done or my family's needs, and so, after a year and a half, I resigned.

In the meantime, one of the consultants associated with the company had been impressed with my work, not only in chemistry but also in plant and employee safety, business negotiating, and other areas. He suggested that I go into consulting as he felt I would be good at it. He pointed out that consulting could give me the flexibility I was looking for, adding that he admired my commitment to my family.

I am now a self-employed consultant, and I feel I am successful at it. I have also co-founded a corporation, still working part time, primarily from home.

A most vital, important part of my story, I feel, is the fact that I had a span of years at home during which I had the opportunity to grow, stretch, discover new talents, develop them, and *then* go out and try to set the world on its ear. At home, I learned how to deal with different personalities (mine, my children's, my husband's), and how to deal with institutions and negotiate with them (board of education, special-education boards, church committees, parent groups, political groups, to name some).

There is no way on earth that I could have come close to being who I am now had I done the traditional thing of working in a lab and taken the normal route to career building. I have so much more expertise now. I am better able to analyze situations and make decisions and cope with problems. Through my work in La Leche League, I have gained greater skill in writing and speaking before others. I believe that everybody has some special talents, but I would not have recognized and developed mine to the extent that I have had I not had the time at home. It will practically shove you into growth, if you will let it happen.

Not Always a Stay-at-Home

Most mothers-at-home do not limit their efforts exclusively to their families. There are times when staying close to home is in everyone's best interest—when there is a new baby in the family, for instance. But as the home operation smoothes out and mother's time frees up, she frequently lends a hand and a part of her heart to helping elsewhere doing volunteer work. As Marsha Hardin points out, these experiences in community and service organizations are an asset when the mother-at-home again chooses to seek employment.

A community is served and strengthened through the combined efforts of its volunteer force. Women do not volunteer their time just to keep busy. Many women are well organized and bring a high degree of talent and dedication to what they do. The needs they meet would rarely be met by the paid sector because the price would be too high. If a dollar value were placed on volunteer labor, the figure would be astounding. In La Leche League alone, the contribution of its Leaders has been estimated at being worth millions of dollars a year. Add to this the church work and other volunteer efforts of the many mothers at home with small children and you find that volunteering is big business. It's a two-way street, of course. The community benefits, but so does the volunteer.

Recently, a La Leche League Leader wrote on the subject of retiring from the League.

During my years in LLL I grew as a mother, as a person, and interestingly I grew *professionally*. I had taught for many years before having children and was a very successful teacher. As a mother, I learned to set aside some of the efficiency for warmth and adapted to new priorities—those of the children. Today I feel I am an even better teacher. Although I teach in the classroom only two hours a week, the teacher under whom I work felt I was valuable enough to seek special funding. Ironically, I have been offered teaching jobs I would never have been considered for before my training in LLL.

I grew as a person by learning new skills. As Coordinator of Leader Applicants, I had tremendous experience in writing and loved the opportunity to develop this interest in working with words. I learned to keep records, organize files, and deal tactfully no matter what the situation. But through LLL I also grew as a mother, and that's the best of all. I learned to accept and enjoy my children instead of having unrealistic expectations for them. Loving my children was never a problem. I just had to learn how to show it and to give the really important things in my life first priority.

The Costs of a Second Income

The reasons why mothers back off from full-time mothering are undoubtedly as complex as women are themselves. If you were to ask an individual mother to rate her reasons for working, she would probably be hard pressed to do so. The desire to help out, to clean up a few bills, and to get ahead a little would probably head the list. Even mothers who admittedly would rather be home with their babies will put themselves out in order to bring in some extra money. The sad fact is that many times there is little to show for the many sacrifices they and their families make in order for mother to work. The hourly rate that mother earns, or her basic salary, may look substantial enough, but deduct the many obvious expenses connected with working and the not-so-obvious costs, and the remainder is a mere shadow of what started out looking like a windfall.

The price of working can be considerable, especially for the mother of young children.

Below are some of the more common expenses incurred by the mother who heads out the door to a job. Circumstances will differ for each family, of course, so possibly some of these items would not apply in your case. But it pays, literally, to know realistically what you would earn if you did take an outside job. Compare this amount to what you can save and possibly earn as a mother-at-home. With few exceptions, the difference in dollars is not that great. This knowledge can allow you to smile and feel not even a twinge of regret when you hear of another contemporary joining the ranks of the employed. One study of working mothers earning a yearly income of $10,000 (hourly wage of $4.80) revealed that once work-related expenses were deducted, a slim $1,159 was left.

Taxes You'll pay more taxes, federal and possibly state (depending on your area). Frequently, a wife's earnings put the couple's joint income into a considerably higher bracket than would be the case with the husband's earnings alone. A higher tax bracket means not only a higher amount of tax, but a higher *percentage* of total income paid as tax. In the U.S., along with income taxes, social security (FICA) will also be withheld from paychecks.

Child Care Child care can be a major expense if you must pay for it. Hourly child-care rates may be low, but the total cost can take a sizable chunk out of a mother's earnings. Often a husband and wife try to avoid this expense by staggering work shifts—one working days, perhaps, and the other at night. Although such an arrangement doesn't take dollars, it is costly in a variety of other ways.

Transportation A working mother needs a reliable means of getting to her job. If you use the family car, there will be the cost of extra gas and wear and tear, and your husband will not have use of the car while you're gone. Having a second car eliminates this last problem, but a portion of what you earn will be offset by the cost of owning and running the second car. The last thing you want to do is work to support a *car*.

Clothing There's quite a range of choices for what the well-dressed employed woman wears, from casual outfits to a highly fashion-conscious look. While always eye catching, the latter can also be highly expensive. A newly employed mother may tell herself that she'll settle for wearing the things she already has, the smart dresses and suits from her former working-woman days with the addition of only a few new blouses. Inevitably, however, the old things succumb to age and wear. In the meantime, co-workers show up regularly with attractive outfits. The contrast becomes increasingly evident, and soon mom finds herself replenishing her wardrobe—another job-related expense. Some jobs require the purchase of a special uniform, including perhaps, special shoes. If the job doesn't work out, she is out the cost of the then useless items.

*F*atigue is often the employed mother's constant companion. . .

The clothing budget for the rest of the family may also increase. More money is likely to be spent on family clothing because no one has the time to mend a tear, to take down a hem or move buttons as a child grows, or to otherwise brighten or rejuvenate a garment. "I would buy new tights for my little girl," one mother reports, "because I couldn't get around to sewing up the rips in the ones she had. The mending sat around so long, the kids outgrew the clothes and I gave them to charity. In a way, I felt we would have qualified for charity." Another mother recalls going out and buying new shoes for a youngster "simply because a shoe was lost somewhere in the house, and it was simpler and less time-consuming to buy a new pair than search for the missing shoe." The woman who previously enjoyed sewing pretty new things will find herself hurrying past the fabric displays.

Maintaining Health and Sanity

Working at an outside job takes time and energy, and employed mothers look for ways to compensate, most of which take money. Convenience foods are usually the first lifesaver for which an employed mother reaches. Convenience costs. The food bill increases, but the family is seldom as well fed as would be possible if mother could devote more time to preparing nourishing and tasty meals. Also, there isn't time to take advantage of sales such as an unadvertised special or surplus produce that requires quick handling. Working mothers also tend to forgo serious coupon savings. Organizing these money savers, which can take several hours a week but add up over a period of time to hundreds of dollars, is just another task for which the mother with an outside job often finds she has no time.

Fatigue is often the employed mother's constant companion, especially if she is working full time and has a young child. Housework drops lower and lower on the list of priorities—which is only proper when there are people needs to consider—but an everlastingly dirty house gets to be depressing. A working mother may pay for cleaning help as a way to give her flagging spirits a lift.

A Michigan mother, Joey Latterman, tells a fairly typical tale of the cost of working:

I never thought I particularly saved money at home until I worked away from home. I accepted a substitute teaching-aide position the last couple of months of school this past year. The pay was low—$4.25 an hour—but I love working with kids, I have a teacher's degee, and I had not taught for sixteen years. So it was a temptation I couldn't resist. I'd been wondering if I was ready to work at a full-time job. My sixth child was five years old, and the others were all in school. This was a chance at a temporary opportunity to find out.

My take-home pay after subtracting expenses such as income tax—almost half of my salary—and day-care for my five-year-old—$50 a week—brought my income down to "not too much," but it was the hidden little expenses I hadn't thought of that made me realize you'd have to make a considerable amount of money per hour to make it worth your while in dollars and cents to work.

With errands to run and children to chauffeur here and there, quite often it would suddenly be dinnertime, and I found myself buying many more convenience foods or eating out more often. Whenever cookies or treats were needed at school or for the church or a community affair, I had to buy them instead of baking. There just wasn't enough time at home anymore.

In the spring, I like to wash the windows, but this year, with less time, I hired someone to do them. The children were supposed to pitch in and do the heavier housework in addition to their regular chores. It worked for awhile, but that's all. I've read of households that maintain such a schedule, but we lacked something to make it click, so I was cleaning toilets in the evening instead of reading stories to the little ones or going to bed. Hired cleaning help on a regular basis would be another twenty or so dollars a week.

I didn't put up asparagus because it was not possible to get to the market. Also, by working all day I quickly discoverd the fallacy of the "quality time" argument. I had practically *no* time at all with the children. Either they weren't there or I wasn't, or they were too busy and not available or I was too busy. I was always shorting out something, or worse yet, somebody.

As meaningful and pleasurable as the job was, I decided against working for next year. I'll go back to volunteering in the schools. Plenty of adults want the teaching jobs and can do a good job, but no one can replace me in my job as a mother and wife. They come first for now!

Non-monetary Costs

Another word for these job-related expenses without price tags is stress. After quitting her job in order to stay home, a mother of a preschooler comments "The extra money was not worth the strain."

The employed mother is affected in varying degrees, most directly from the day-to-day strain of keeping up with the work load and, on a secondary level, from the tension of knowing that waiting on the sidelines, credentials in hand, is a growing number of job seekers eager to replace her. The continuing need to prove oneself is built into every job. It can be argued that the accompanying challenge lends excitement to life— which it does—but it also takes its toll.

Work-related stress, it is becoming increasingly evident, can affect a woman's hormonal balance. Women in demanding jobs may be troubled by infertility, depression, insomnia, and irritability all directly related to stress.

There is no sure or easy way to figure a profit/loss statement on what it means for mother to work. If she is exceptionally successful, the job is almost certain to become ever more important in her life— to the exclusion, at times, of the very things she set out to preserve when first taking the job. If the father is given the opportunity to advance in his job by transferring to another area, the mother may be reluctant to leave her position. In such a situation, someone or something has to give—not infrequently, it is the marriage.

Non-overlapping work shifts that make it possible for one parent to be with the children while the other is at work may seem attractive for a number of reasons. The little ones benefit from having a familiar, loving parent caring for them, and there's a financial savings from not having to pay babysitter fees. But it is not a cost-free arrangement. The marriage, rather than the budget, suffers.

A woman who is now a grandmother says she made up her mind as a young girl that a smart wife would not leave her husband alone evening after evening. An experience she had as a high school freshman confirmed this opinion. When she was eager to earn a little extra money for new records or a sweater, but too young to work in the business world, she got a job as a sitter after school for a ten-month-old girl whose mother left for work before her husband arrived home in the evening. This woman recalls, "The husband began coming home later some evenings, but I didn't mind too much because once the baby was asleep, I could do my homework or read."

The job ended abruptly, however, one evening, "when the husband, who had adopted the habit of sharing a bottle of cola with me as he asked about the baby and about my day, sat down, put his arm around my shoulder and said something about my soft hair and pretty rosy cheeks." She remembers that "I was horrified at the time. He was married, and besides, he was old." In retrospect, she realizes he wasn't old but was lonely. "How much better if his wife had been there instead of a teenage babysitter."

In a sense, the question of whether or not to take an outside job (*all* mothers work) *can* be settled in mathematical terms. Time—not money—is the most important consideration. Each of us has only twenty-four hours in a day, and no matter how energetic and organized a woman may be, she can only be in one place at a time. When she is at her job, her employer has first call on her time, energy, and attention.

A mother must make a decision about who deserves the "first call" on her time. If she decides her baby—her family— deserve not just a small portion of her time, but a large quantity of quality time, then she knows what she must choose. In the upcoming chapters we'll offer you a way to make being at home an economic possibility in addition to being the choice of your heart.

Part Two

Staying on Course

CHAPTER 4

*S*etting the *P*lan in *M*otion

Whether you're expecting your first baby or have several children already, you realize that you might want to be a mother-at-home. Now you want to know where to begin. How can you set The Plan in motion and apply it to your family situation?

Or perhaps you're already a mother-at-home, enjoying the good life with your children, but you're feeling the pinch of living on one income and you want more information on making ends meet.

This chapter will present step one in managing your money and embarking on The Plan.

Where Are You Now?

It's important that you know where you are in the financial sea. Perhaps you have already been getting behind on some bills, so you wonder how you'll survive (or continue to survive) on just one income.

With a few sheets of paper (ruled notebook paper will do) and about an hour's time, you can find out where your money is going, and where there's room to economize.

Divide a sheet of paper into two columns, heading one "In" and the other "Out." Under "In" write your husband's earnings, as closely as you can estimate them, for the coming month. Remember to use the take-home pay figure—income after taxes. If you have any other regular source of income, list that, too. (Don't include your salary if you are still employed outside the home.)

Next, get out your checkbook register or your paid bill file. Pull out or check off those items that must be paid each month, such as the rent or mortgage payment, the car payment, other loan payments, utility bills, the telephone bill. *Skip anything that you paid for in full at the time of purchase,* such as food and entertainment and a host of miscellaneous items. You want to get an idea of what you would owe in the coming month even if you didn't buy another thing.

List these monthly regulars under "Out" on your sheet. Where there is no set amount, as with the utilities, figure a rough average of the bills from the last six months. To make things easier for yourself, round off all figures to the nearest dollar.

You may also have bills that are paid quarterly, such as the water bill, or every six months, such as insurance premiums. For any bill that must be paid within the next six months, estimate what you think the coming bill will be, based on the old one. Record this amount and the date due on a *second* sheet of paper. Total these amounts and divide by six. Include this figure in your monthly "Out" column on the first sheet.

Look over the two columns on the In/Out page one last time to make sure you haven't forgotten any item. Then add together the items in each column. A calculator will help you at this point.

The totals tell the tale. On the one side is income; on the other is the amount already owed, or claimed, against that income. True, it's only an approximation, but it will give you a good idea of where you stand. Any other purchases you make during the coming month will also have to come out of your income. Since these discretionary purchases include your family's food, clothing, medical expenses, and entertainment, they're a pretty important item! Knowing the actual amount you will have available for these expenses will help you adjust your spending accordingly. If your In and Out totals are close, some adjustment will need to be made to bring income more in line with expenses so you can continue as a mother-at-home. The options include:

1. An increase in income
2. A decrease in fixed expenses—housing, car payments, energy costs.
3. Finding a way to economize in food, clothing, and other discretionary expenses.

All of these options will be explored in this and other chapters of this book.

Managing Your Money

The In/Out sheet and the sheet with the long-term bills are master lists of the expenses you know will be coming up. The next step is to think seriously about setting up a more complete system of money disbursement. How you spend your money—however much or little you have— can help you make ends meet or at least keep them within sight of each other. I hesitate to use the term *budget* because there are those of us who panic at the mention of the word.

For years, I smugly said that I married an accountant because I had no knack for keeping records. For a good many years I had a free ride in this regard, which was very nice! Now that I am on my own and must manage the family finances, I've discovered that, given the need, one can learn quickly. A budget doesn't have to be a complex system.

All you need is a simple form for keeping track of your

	ESTIMATED BUDGET	ACTUAL EXPENSES	OVER [UNDER]
John's Salary	$1190.00	$1190.00	$ _____
Expenses:			
Mortgage (Rent)	350.00	350.00	_____
Food	280.00	295.00	15.00
Gas for Car	60.00	80.00	20.00
Utilities	110.00	85.00	[25.00]
Telephone	40.00	42.00	2.00
Work Expenses	65.00	70.00	5.00
Clothing	50.00	18.00	[32.00]
Medical Expenses	20.00	20.00	_____
Car Payments	175.00	175.00	_____
Total Expenses	$1150.00	$1135.00	$ 15.00
Difference-Income Over [Under] Expenses	$ 40.00	$ 55.00	$ 15.00
Payment to Savings Account or Credit Union for Large Expenses (e.g. Car Insurance, Large Medical Bills, etc.)	30.00	30.00	_____
Cash Balance at end of month	$ 10.00	$ 25.00	$ 15.00
Cash in Checking Account at beginning of month	200.00	200.00	_____
Cash in Checking Account at end of month	$ 210.00	$ 225.00	$ 15.00
Savings Account (or Credit Union) beginning of month	$ 400.00	$ 400.00	_____
Addition [subtraction] from above	30.00	30.00	_____
Savings Account end of month	$ 430.00	$ 430.00	$ _____

This is for illustrative purposes only; your budget will vary according to income, fixed expenses, and family size.

money. The sample budget outline shown here was prepared by La Leche League's knowledgeable controller, Bob Kirk. If you don't already have a system, check this one out. A Maryland mother, Angie Martin, emphasizes, "Since becoming a mother-at-home, I have found it essential to keep a written budget, something that I never did when we were both working." The Martins regularly set money aside each payday for upcoming bills. This money is deposited in a separate checking account. "We acquired a second account at our credit union," Angie says. "It pays interest but requires no minimum balance or service charge." She finds this second account "the most helpful aspect of my budgeting."

The Martins began using their second account for long-term bills, such as insurance premiums, which they converted from monthly payments to annual and semiannual payments. (On the subject of insurance, periodically reevaluate your policies. Ellen Martyn of Canada advises calling in a broker if necessary, to help you replan. "We were able to save several hundred dollars," she says.) Once the Martins had set up their budget checking account they expanded it to cover some regular monthly bills in addition to the long-term bills. There were fewer unpleasant surprises this way. "The important thing is to put in enough to pay the bills," Angie points out, "and to only use the account for the purpose it was intended. Otherwise, you may get hopelessly overdrawn."

Budgets Can Work Jean McNertney of Texas finds that "making a master list of all expected expenses is really necessary." She, too, suggests allotting a certain amount for each bill early in the month as a way to "enable budgets to stretch further towards the end of the month when there tends to be some lapse of funds—and unexpected expenses." At the present time the Fowlers in Washington can happily say that they have "no money worries," yet Helene reports, "We still maintain a budget, with a certain amount allocated for the various categories of home management. Staying within a self-imposed budget controls impulse buying and allows more for extras, such as vacations and remodeling."

"We Need Help!"

If you made an income/expenditure comparison as suggested earlier in this chapter, and your "In" column total is *less* than the "Out" total, you have a case of what one father calls "financial indisposition." More than likely, you feel like yelling "Help!" and looking seriously for a job, or keeping the one you have now. Calling for help is a step in the right direction, but the outside job that would take you away from your baby is not your only recourse. There are a number of measures you can take immediately to see you past this crisis, keep you securely at home, and keep the bill collectors from your door. If you rally your forces, you'll find they are far greater than you think.

A two-way approach—shoring up inflow and reducing out-flow—is most effective. Let's start by considering ways to fatten the "In" side of the ledger.

Check into Hidden Assets Tap all available sources of money. Do either you or your husband have a retirement fund, perhaps from a previous job, that you can cash in? There will be many years ahead of you to think about retirement. More important now is getting through this week and the months to come—securing the present.

Is there an insurance policy that you can borrow against? Check your policy or call your insurance agent for information.

While you're digging, look carefully through your jewelry. The gold in an old class ring can be converted to money for buying groceries or paying a heating bill.

Is there a musical instrument on a shelf gathering dust along with the pleasant memories? Think of it as a means to bring enjoyment to some other player and needed cash to you. In fact, this could be the time to move out other items around the house—such as a seldom-used bike or a second television set. Take advantage of free community advertising such as supermarket bulletin boards. Run a small ad in a local paper offering your surplus treasures for sale, or clean out the closets and the basement and hold a garage sale. (For more on garage sales, see Chapter 14.)

Kitty Desmarteau of Oregon explains that because her husband is establishing a new career, her family has had to change their lifestyle. "We've gotten to the point of selling the sailboat, the motor boat, and the scooter and having garage sales," she writes. "Occasionally a fleeting thought crosses my mind: Should I work? I completed four years of college (I'm a teacher) and we're still paying on college loans—Good grief!" When Kitty's oldest, Heather, was seven months old, Kitty signed up to substitute teach. Kitty recalls, "I taught one day and left Heather with another mother who was thrilled to have her for the day. When I got back to the house, I sat and nursed and cried for half an hour. It was awful. I decided that wasn't for me." The Desmarteaus now have two children, and like many mothers of young children, Kitty says that shes feels "very overwhelmed, off and on" but "every moment is filled from early morning until night."

Another source of potential cash can be municipal or federal savings bonds. If there are any either in your name or the children's names, they can be turned in for cash even before they mature.

Rob the Piggybank?   If you like many other parents have opened savings accounts for your children, look upon this money and also the return from any bonds as a way to help them *now*. Sue Dion of Massachusetts recounts, "Our children often received money for birthdays and special occasions, which we deposited in their own savings accounts. When things got tight for us financially, we found ourselves 'borrowing' from these accounts. When it became evident that we could not repay, we felt guilty. But then it occurred to me that this money of the children's was paying bills so their mother didn't have to leave them and go to work. The guilty feelings are gone. There is no gift that I could 'buy' my loved ones that is better than myself."

If you're still awaiting the arrival of your baby, let it be known that a gift of money will look much better to you than even the most darling new baby outfit. As Cynthia Cuevas of Illinois points out, "Baby clothes are so cheap at garage and church sales. I hate to have anyone buy them for me as a gift." Actually, a new baby requires very little in the way of furnishings and other paraphernalia. A supply of diapers, some wrapping blankets, enough outfits to keep baby warm and dry, and your good milk and loving arms will be all that is needed for many a month.

Beg or Borrow   What about a loan? A loan may help you pay off some of the bills and take the immediate pressure off you. Do you have relatives who can help you? The grandparents, perhaps? Don't be shy! After you, nobody is more interested in your children than their grandparents.

Help may come in a way other than a conventional loan of money. One couple found that a single expense—the rent— overwhelmed all their efforts to economize and make ends meet. (For more on this big-expense item, see Chapter 7, "Housing.") In this case, the young parents talked to the husband's father, a widower living alone in a large house. He invited the young family to move in with him. They now have enlarged living quarters for a fraction of what they had been paying, and baby and grandpa have become great buddies. A bonus for grandpa is that he can take an extended vacation whenever he likes without the worry of leaving an empty house.

Moonlighting   As a way of bringing in extra income, dad could consider taking an extra job—but you and your husband should first discuss this possibility carefully. Especially if your husband is already working full time, another job isn't an ideal solution. Many couples have found, however, that it's the lesser of two evils. "I took on two part-time jobs to make ends meet," Dennis Campanell of New Jersey writes. "As far as I'm concerned, we did the right thing." Both Dennis and his wife, Sandi, were convinced that baby Alexis and later her brother should have mother at home. Dennis concludes, "Those jobs got us through so our children got the most important part, someone always there, always guiding, always loving." Eventually Dennis found a new job that enabled him "to say goodbye to the part-time humdrums and spend more time with the family," an important consideration for these family-oriented parents.

Depending on the age of your baby and your circumstances, you may be able to earn money at home without leaving your baby. This option has proven worthwhile for many

Sandi Campanell refinishes a table with baby Alexis peeking over her shoulder.

families, but it, too, calls for careful thought. We discuss at-home earnings in more depth in Chapter 14.

Bills to be Paid It may be that despite your best efforts, there is still a considerable gap between income and expenses. There's the temptation, of course, to shut outstanding bills out of your mind by shutting them in a drawer, but, unfortunately, ignoring them will not make them go away. Brew a pot of tea or your favorite soothing drink and look the dragon in the eye. Remember, there are no debtor prisons, and this is only a temporary state of affairs.

Probably the most common way of dealing with the problem of having more bills than money is to pay the most pressing bills and postpone payment on the rest—making sure that the next time around the leftovers are given first priority.

Keep in mind—especially if you are staring at a number of critical bills—that it will pay you to do some telephoning. You have everything to gain and nothing to lose by notifying the proper parties of your financial situation. Creditors are people, too, and they appreciate being kept informed. This is particularly important in regard to certain obligations. The mortgage payment, for example, does not age well. If you begin missing payments, you are placed on the delinquent list. If you continue to miss payments, your house can be subject to foreclosure. As grim as this consequence sounds, there is room for hope. "No lender in the world," emphasizes the president of one savings and loan association, "wants to take a house back. We're in the business of finance, not real estate." He stresses that what a lender does want is proof of good faith. If your house payment—or perhaps the car payment—is in trouble, make an appointment to sit down with the lender and discuss a reduced payment schedule. The importance of honest communication also applies to other creditors.

Once an understanding is reached, follow up by sending a payment *every* month. Even if you can't send the full amount, send something. A partial payment is an indication that you're aware of the situation and making an effort to pay. "Keeping our bills paid is sometimes a problem," Cindy George from Michigan admits. She and her husband Brian live in an economically depressed area, and Brian was laid off from his job as a design draftsman some time ago. Cindy says that they manage to make the house payment, which is small because they did much of the work to upgrade the house themselves, but the heating bill is another story. "We have found, though, that by working with the electric company and by letting them know we are trying to keep up, they will accept partial payments and late payments."

During the month you may receive calls from the credit people asking you for more money, even though you had previously notified them of your situation. These calls are often a routine procedure. If you receive such a call, do a lot of listening and simply reassure them again and again that you're doing the very best you can.

Finding the Help You Need

In a tight financial situation—such as the layoff of your husband—you must seek out all possible sources of help. There are numerous special programs for the family in need, from food supplements to tax breaks and low-cost health programs. Taking advantage of such programs is *not* something to be ashamed of. Social programs provide a shelter that can help you keep your family intact—and the family is one of society's most important resources. You paid for these programs with your taxes, and in the future, you'll be paying into these programs again, but in the meantime the program funds are being put to good use in helping you safeguard your children's future.

Seek all possible sources of help. . .

Some support programs are national in scope, while others originate in the community. Check with your local officials about what is available. If there is a township supervisor in your area, talk to him or her. The social-service arm of your church or temple or your pastor or rabbi should be able to direct you to the proper agencies.

The families who wrote to us are mainly from the U.S.A. So the government and social service programs discussed here are those available in most parts of the U.S.A. Other countries have similar types of programs to aid families in need. If you live outside the U.S.A. contact the appropriate government agencies in your country for further information.

Supplemental food programs—such as the government food-stamp program in the U.S.A.—can be a valuable source of aid. The amount of aid available will vary from case to case, but we heard from one family of five who received $89 a month in food stamps in addition to benefits from other programs.

The Bartels had two children when Jerry lost his job due to a company relocation. "We decided to live off the government," Joyce states. "Through those next ten months we lived on unemployment checks, food stamps, and a lot of love from friends. We got excited over bags of hand-me-down clothes from League friends, invitations for dinner at the end of the food-stamp month, and prayers from all."

"Once the baby arrived I could not leave her. . ."

Possibly less well known but directed specifically toward pregnant or nursing mothers, infants, and children under the age of five is the WIC (Women, Infants, and Children) program. This special supplemental food program provides nutritious foods, such as milk, eggs, cereals, fruit juices, and cheese, to those who qualify. Susie Wing of Texas says, "I save between $40 to $50 monthly through WIC. This program along with the tutoring and babysitting that I do out of my home has helped make it possible for me to stay home and do the most important job in the world—mother my children." Susie says that before her youngest child was born, she had "heard of mothers who were so determined to stay home they would go on welfare, but I never thought I would be one of them. My husband went into business for himself several months before I learned I was pregnant with our third child, Emily. I had planned to return to teaching since our boys were school age, but I knew once the baby arrived that I could not leave her. A friend told me about the free checkups and immunizations available through the well-baby clinic of the Health Department. We took Emily there, and that's when we learned about the WIC program."

Other Government Programs   Be aware, too, that there may be a tax-relief program in your area. Doris Franz Poling tells us that property taxes where she lives in Maryland are among the highest in the nation. The Polings discovered a program called "a tax circuit breaker." Doris says, "If you qualify, your taxes will be reduced or you may be given a refund. This has kept our house payments low."

Home Energy programs are available to persons or families with certain income levels for help in meeting fuel bills. A few phone calls to local social agencies should put you on the right track for getting help with these seasonally high bills.

Creative Health-Care Services   Health-care programs that prorate the cost of the service to the income of the recipient can be helpful to young families. Dental and eye clinics are often associated with a teaching medical facility. "For regular dental cleaning and checkups, we go to the local university, which has a dental-hygiene program," Donna MacFarlane writes from New Mexico. "It takes longer because the people who clean and check the teeth are students and sometimes are being tested on what they do. But the cost is low, only $8 for adults and $6 for children." Donna and her husband make an effort to learn about good health practices and feel that, as a result, they have saved considerably in medical expenses. "We have only used our family-practice physician twice for children's illnesses, and each time the illness was not severe enough to warrant medication." She says that she always questions if a medication is really necessary to cure the illness or if it would "just cover up the symptoms for a while."

Major medical expenses can be a worry, but there are ways to handle these, too. One mother experienced a prolapsed cord when expecting her last child and had to have a cesarean delivery. Her husband had been unemployed for some time, and it was an unexpected expense. The good news is that mother and baby did fine, and financial aid obtained through the hospital is helping them meet the bills.

Investing in Your Children

Cindy George says that she knows there are those who "can't understand why I'm not hitting the employment agencies with my secretarial skills. I tell them, 'If you could buy something for your children that would make their early years the happiest and give them a super head start, wouldn't you go into debt for it?' " In answer to her own question, she acknowledges, "I guess that is what we are doing. But we truly believe that by my being home we are making a substantial investment in our children's future happiness as well."

Our children and their children and many future generations are affected by our choices. I remember vividly a family years ago that struggled through very hard times. In later years "Mrs. B" said that during the hard times she and her husband would look at each other and say that they really couldn't afford to get up the next morning. But they did, and they made it through the rough periods with careful economizing and copious amounts of prayer. Now they look with pride on their children and grandchildren and great-grandchildren. When family members come together for family celebrations, they reminisce about the times when they were children around the big table eating mother's fresh baked bread and homemade soup—and no one gives a second thought to the fact that there were a great many lentils and vegetables and very little meat in the big soup pot.

Sound Waves You can set the direction and keep The Plan true to course by sending and receiving sound waves. At times the sound will be strong; at others, it will be soft. Most important there must be a regular, continuous signal. Sound waves we are referring to are transmitted when you and your spouse communicate with each other.

There is no way that a husband and wife can make it through a tight financial situation without good communication. When money is plentiful, two people can go somewhat separate ways, and the relationship can still work out. When funds are limited, however, sensitive communication acts as a form of sonar, keeping you on course. Talk to each other; pay attention to each other. The greater part of communication is verbal, yet the most telling part for a couple is nonverbal. Start by letting each other know how you feel about your situation.

Coping with Financial Crisis

Pam and Terry Ahearn explain the importance of good communication. Pam had left a well-paying job to stay at home when her first child, Tim, was born. She intended to breastfeed him because "it was the natural thing to do," she says. But nursing lasted only four months, due mainly to "a lack of confidence and knowledge, a fussy baby, and the chorus 'there is something wrong with your milk.' " Soon after she stopped breastfeeding, she recalls, they experienced a financial crisis. "The only way out seemed to be for me to return to my former job. Tim was receiving formula, and my mother-in-law lived only a few blocks away. She was most anxious to care for him while I'd be at work."

Pam says she felt trapped and torn. She remembers thinking, "How could this have happened to us?" She says, "Everywhere I turned people just assumed I would return to work. They thought I was very lucky to have someone so close who was willing to take care of the baby and to have a good job waiting for me. Ever since I had left my 'lucrative job' I had been thought of as a fool for not returning to it." Worse yet, Pam says, "The situation had left Terry and me feeling there was little to say to each other. So I set the wheels in motion to return to work."

It wasn't that simple, of course. Pam says, "I will never forget the night I became quite angry with Terry and said I really did not want to return to my job, but I would do it just to get the money we needed. He very quietly said he did not want me to go back either. He did not feel right about my leaving Tim. He just did not like the whole idea. When I asked him what we should do he said he needed time to think it over.

"Several days later, Terry announced he would get a second job and I would stay at home. When we told my mother-in-law our plans, she was most upset. She felt it was too much for Terry and that I was being selfish."

Determined, they forged ahead. "It was not easy, believe me," Pam recounts. "There were times of self-pity (that's my specialty), loneliness, and resentment at our lot in life for we certainly didn't have much, or at least as much as I saw others having. Terry would come home very tired and I would rub his aching muscles."

In time, this Indiana couple found a positive side to the experience. "What we received from this, other than the needed money, is priceless. I learned a new respect for my husband, a new depth to my love for him. We were pulling together and this was a foundation for some even harder times that we were to face, not only as husband and wife, but as a family."

Dealing with a Layoff   The high unemployment figures that are a part of newspaper headlines are also reflected in the letters we received. No one is happy about the layoffs, yet here are some unexpected compensations. Anne Harvey describes their experience in Kansas.

In December of last year, my husband was laid off from his job. It is now mid-July, and we are still on unemployment benefits. We make ends meet from the extra money he makes doing auto mechanic and body work out of our garage here at home.

This has been the best year we have ever spent as a family. We have three children, and after a few weeks at home, my

Fathers often miss a lot of their children's growing up.

© Richard Ebbitt

husband said, "I never realized how much of their growing up I was missing." He has come to see what I had been saying about a relationship between the children's diet and their behavior, and now I have his support in this area. Many dilemmas that I faced alone during the day while he was at work are now shared, and this makes for more and better communication between us. While we haven't had a lot of money, this year of unemployment and hard times has brought us closer together and has taught our children much about what is really important in life. It has made a tremendous impact on the direction of our lives. It has truly been a blessing in disguise.

From Ontario, Canada, Ellen Martyn writes, "Ron lost his management position eleven months ago and has been job searching ever since. For nearly a year now, he has received polite refusals. He was one of the top two applicants but still didn't get one job, he joined and quit a company that is now nearly bankrupt, and now he has established a consulting business out of the house that so far is mainly potential. In spite of it all, our marriage is better than ever and our two boys, aged four-and-a-half and two-and-a-half, are happy."

Ellen explains how they faced up to the situation. "When Ron lost his job, we sat down and talked and decided that we have been through harder times—our firstborn had died at three months—and we could certainly face unemployment." But she admits that "It has not been without rough times and many, many sleepless nights for Ron."

Ellen had been a special-education teacher before the children were born. "The thought certainly occurred to us that I could go back to work," she says, but "upon closer examination, we felt that my role at home could not be compromised. I was a steadying force, and I envisioned the household going to pieces if I wasn't here. I'm sure it would not have, but I don't think it would have held together as well as it has if I had not been here. We were going through enough adjustments without adding one more huge one—Mum going back to work—to the list. To get by on very little money, we feel that both parents must be at the same level of wanting to economize without the martyrdom syndrome setting in."

When the husband is not working, Ellen emphasizes that "the spouse *has* to be supportive." In their own case, she says, "We are pulling through and our lives have been enriched." The Martyns find that having little money automatically simplifies one's life. When her husband was wondering one day if they could continue their current simplified lifestyle once they have more money, she says, "We both agreed that we hoped we would. But we also look forward to the day we will have some financial security."

Holding a Family Together

Certain words and phrases come through repeatedly in letter after letter even though the writers are miles apart. In Maryland, Doris Franz Poling expresses her fear that, had she gone out to work when her husband was unemployed, their family life would have crumbled. She says that for those nine months when her husband was not working, "I perceived myself as a glue that helped hold us together." She says that she sometimes felt very guilty about not doing something at home to make money but that she now considers herself an expert on saving. The youngest of the Polings' three children was born six months ago, and Doris's husband has since found a job with a future although to start he has had to take a substantial cut in pay. "As we are emerging from this difficult period, we realize we are closer, more patient, more appreciative of each other," Doris writes. "There is a bond between us now that comes from remaining together and helping each other."

To respond to the question, "How do you keep your marriage together during a financial crisis?" Doris says she thought long and hard. She agrees with one of her friends that regardless of how much money is coming in, there will always be financial differences in a marriage. "It is one thing," she admits, "to disagree on whether to buy a pop-up camper and quite another to wonder if there is money enough to buy food till the end of the month."

"I envisioned the household going to pieces. . ."

Both she and her husband feel it is important for other family members to try to understand what it is like for the man in this situation. He sees himself as the breadwinner in the family and knows that the others depend on him. When he cannot find work, his self-esteem is at an all time low. Doris feels it has taken her husband two years to fully rebuild his self-esteem. Doris passes on several other observations.

1. Each man is different and will react differently under stress. When unemployment is prolonged, depression is common. Other reactions include bouts of insomnia, yelling at family members, a short temper, weight loss, or a greater amount of drinking. The wife should recognize that these behavior changes are temporary and should stress that this time of being unemployed—as endless as it may seem—is also temporary.

2. If the husband is home during the day, the wise wife tries to make as much space as possible for everyone.

3. If he has spent fruitless days looking for a job and going on interviews, try to imagine how he feels being rejected again and again. A nonjudgmental, supportive attitude on the wife's part is essential. During this time, the wife is the main source of encouragement, supplying courage for the husband to continue the search. "Try very hard not to shoot arrows in what self-esteem he has," Doris advises.

4. Some commiserating together will be comforting for both of you, but be careful of complaining. He may perceive a complaint as an attack, and you could get it right back in your face when he says, "If you don't like it, get out or get a job."

5. Fantasize together—or alone—about how it will be when he is again working. Dreaming about the future is a positive act, not just wishful thinking. It can help define goals for both of you.

6. The stress may affect the man sexually; it is possible that he may occasionally be impotent. Be patient. Just being together can be very satisfying. Another couple may have a greater than usual need for each other. Making love relieves tension and is reassuring as nothing else is. Make time in the evening to be together, to talk, to be lovingly attentive toward each other. Tomorrow could be the day you reach that light at the end of the tunnel.

CHAPTER *5*

*S*pending *P*ower

Anyone who is serious about saving money has to give some thought to the matter of spending it. A philosophy of spending is part and parcel of The Plan. Such a philosophy is a means to an end, a tool—like a fine, sharp knife—that cuts through the outer layers and reveals the core of money management. Once you've incorporated a philosophy of spending into your life, you're in a much more secure position, whether you're rich or poor.

The first rule of spending goes back to the premise of The Plan: look for value. If something is inferior in quality, it's not worth a cent of your money—limited or not. Second, if buying something takes funds that are needed elsewhere, that item is not a good buy. Only someone with money to burn can afford thoughtless shopping.

A Quest for Quality

The quality item will not necessarily be the one with a famous label but will have the nuts-and-bolts durability that is more than surface deep.

It takes time and practice to recognize quality, and even the most experienced shopper will on occasion be fooled. One way of tipping the odds in your favor—especially when making a substantial purchase or buying a mechanical item—is to consult a testing authority, such as *Consumer Reports*. Copies are available at the public library. Another way of finding out what brands or models hold up is to check a good secondhand shop. The quality items still look good the second time around while lesser merchandise has been junked.

Once you are sure you have found a quality item, you must decide on quantity. How much of this quality item do you need—and can you afford? (Was a more difficult question ever asked?)

Coleen and Ken Mast, a couple from Illinois, break their decision down into several parts when contemplating a purchase. "Do I need it?" is the logical first question. There may be any number of good reasons for buying the item: for health's sake, for convenience, to make life more pleasant—or even, as Coleen says, "to save one's soul." She notes, too, that at times "you have to spend money in order to save money."

After answering the question "Do I need this?" the Masts then ask, "How badly do I need it?" or "Will I still wake up tomorrow morning if I don't have it?" Says Coleen, "This last question will really trim your budget!" She explains, "I have an attitude of nonconsumption. My bargain-hunter friends actually spend a lot more money than I do because they're always 'looking for bargains.' I have found that if you don't even read the sale flyers, you won't feel bad about missing the great bargain on something you don't really need."

The beginning of spending wisdom is knowing what is a necessity and what just seems like one, what is essential and what isn't. These distinctions can be very difficult to make. Two cars, two television sets, or two phones can seem very necessary. But if you take a minute to look around you, you will realize that many of the things in your life add to your comfort

Susie and Scott Mast provide their parents with reason enough to enjoy life.

and enjoyment but are not essential. Most of us collect a lot of extra baggage through life. Where there is a need to cut back, it's good to know what is a necessity and what isn't. The difference between the necessary and the unnecessary was brought home to me once when visiting an elderly aunt in her 100-year-old farm house. When I commented on the absence of closets in the bedrooms, she remarked that people years ago in that simple farming community had very few clothes. Each family member had two sets, a good Sunday outfit and work clothes. Pegs in the wall held the work clothes, and the one good suit or dress hung in the one communal closet.

The Test of Time

One-income families have developed many techniques to keep their spending in check. Sue Hinkle of New York reports:

A little trick I developed before I was married has saved me a lot of money. I never browse in a store among articles I can't afford. This is easy when my three children are with me. If I don't see it, I don't want it.

Also, if I think I need something, I record it on my list and wait several weeks. If I still want it and haven't figured out a way to make it, I then buy it, finances permitting.

Barbara Dick, of Washington state, says, "We are dedicated scroungers and gleaners. We just don't buy unless it is absolutely necessary."

A philosophy of "wait and see" is echoed by numerous others. Maurine Joens of Arkansas suggests "not buying anything on impulse. Wait several days, weeks, or months. Usually when time passes, the urge to buy whatever it was that seemed so important usually passes, too. My husband and I also have an agreement that neither of us will spend any money without the approval of the other one. This eliminates much spending." Ken and Maurine Joens, whose five children range in age from one to fourteen, have created a lifestyle that makes it possible for Ken to be with the family more than is usually the case for a father. They began working toward this goal some years ago. "The first step," Maurine writes, "involved getting out of debt and staying out of debt. We also made some investments in things, such as a flour mill, wood stoves, and a milk cow, which reduce the need to spend money." At the present time, the Joens family lives comfortably on $350 a month, and Ken needs to work away from home only part time.

In the Market Place

When it comes to saving money, where you shop can make almost as great a difference as what you buy. In addition to all the usual, highly visible stores, there are also all kinds of unusual nooks and crannies that make up the marketplace.

Ken and Maurine Joens have reached their goal of living on a limited income.

Discount or Outlet Stores For the most part, the families that are tightening their belts stay away from the big shopping malls. Many at-home mothers look upon a trip to the mall as an outing for the kids but not a shopping trip. They purposely take only a small amount of cash with them because they're looking for a change of scene, not an occasion to spend money. The big discount store up the highway is a more popular choice.

The prices charged for goods at the shopping mall reflect the cost of the bright lights and seasonal decor. When you shop at the discount store, you won't be paying for these extras. You also won't have the help of too many sales clerks, so you have to plan on spending some extra time to find exactly what you want.

You have to be selective when shopping at the discount

stores. They do carry good quality merchandise, even popular brand names, but they also have large quantities of poor quality items, priced very low to attract customers. Often this merchandise is a disappointment—after only a few wearings the seams rip, the zippers break, and the snaps come loose. It's the wise, selective shopper who knows how to benefit from discount shopping.

In many areas you can find outlet stores which are open to the public. These outlet stores may offer merchandise that's not up to a manufacturer's specifications—but is still quite sturdy and useful. Or an outlet store may offer items which are simply overstock—500 extra green T-shirts in size 12, for instance. If your youngster wears size 12 and doesn't hate green, you're in luck! To get the best bargains, you may have to shop these stores often as the merchandise changes almost daily.

Slightly damaged appliances can often be found in outlet stores at savings of up to $200 off the retail prices. If the scratch is on the side of the stove which will be against the wall in your kitchen, or if the dented washer will be in the basement where no one will see it anyway, you can take advantage of someone's clumsiness and save some money.

Secondhand or Resale Shops   In the middle of town, down a side street, you'll find the secondhand store—a favorite among limited-income families.

Susan Davis from California describes her situation, which is similar to that of other young mothers she knows. "When I was pregnant, Bob and I decided I would stay home and raise our baby. That first year was typical, I think, of a young family's struggles. Bob was self-employed in the construction industry, so our income fluctuated, and we were always about one jump ahead of the bill collector. A hobby for me and a means of saving money was and is thrift shopping! A friend and I and our kids pile into a car and head for our favorite three or four stores. Most of my maternity clothes and the baby's clothes and toys came from these shops. I felt my baby was better

Spending Power

Stephanie Davis enjoys her improvised bathtub seat and second-hand toys.

dressed in her lovely brand-name dresses and outfits—some bought for as little as 25¢—than she would have been if I'd bought new things. I convinced interested grannies and aunts that their best gifts would be things I seldom or never found— shoes and socks especially.''

In general, resale shops come in two kinds. Some are veritable emporiums crammed with piles and racks of merchandise that represent the good, bad, and indifferent. Prices are low. If you're discriminating and patient, you can do quite well here. Another type of establishment will be more selective, offering high quality, almost-new goods. The prices are correspondingly higher but still much less than buying new. These shops often take good, used items on consignment, giving the seller a percentage of the amount paid for them, so these shops can be the source of a few extra dollars as well as a source for clothing bargains.

Garage-Sale Shopping   At times, it seems as though half the world is giving a garage or yard sale and the other half is going to one. A garage sale or flea market holds the double attraction of very low prices and surprise finds. You may not find a thing you'd want to carry home, or you may come across exactly what you've been looking for at a fraction of what it would cost new.

Garage-sale shopping can even be therapeutic. Everyone knows that getting a new pair of shoes or a pretty scarf or a handy gadget can lift one's spirits, but when money isn't available for such new purchases, a surprise find at a garage sale can chase the doldrums. To keep such buying in check, take only as much money with you as you know you can spare. Otherwise, if the twenty dollar bill that you were planning to use for groceries is in your purse, that too may be spent. Then when you're scrounging for something to eat, it will be very hard to justify the outlay for a patio umbrella.

Sue Huml, of Illinois, has gained the reputation of being an expert garage-sale shopper. From her years of experience, she offers the following suggestions:

1. Make it a point to buy only first-class items, no junk. To get the best buys you have to be disciplined.

2. Select an affluent neighborhood. Subscribe to or borrow the local newspaper for that neighborhood and find the day when most garage sales are held.

3. Record the time each garage sale starts. If one is listed at 9:00 A.M. and another at 10:00 A.M., plan to arrive at the 9:00 A.M. sale no later than 8:15. Make the 10:00 sale by 9:15. The early bird gets the good stuff! If you've never had much luck at garage sales, it's probably because you arrive too late.

4. Try to go garage-sale shopping once a week. Go especially if it's raining. Many people are deterred by rain, but the fewer the people, the better the selection.

5. Buy quality items, brand-name clothes, hardly used appliances, furniture in good condition, etc.

6. Bargain with the sellers. Always offer less than they are asking. It's all part of the fun and saves you even more money.

Sue's success in locating good finds has prompted her neighbors and friends to place orders with her for special items. "First, I determine exactly what my 'customer' is looking for. For example, a man's bike, nearly new condition. Then we discuss price." She charges a 20 percent commission, so if the bike could be found for $45, her commission of $9 would bring the price to $54, still an excellent buy. "Since I am out once a week looking for bargains for my own family," Sue says, "it's no extra trouble to shop for others who don't have the time."

Shopping at garage sales is a very small part of Sue's life. "I view my time at home as my career," she says. "Just as my husband does the very best he can in his job, so do I."

Buying on Credit

A discussion of spending would not be complete without some mention of credit buying. For the most part, the serious savers pay cash for their purchases. If they don't have the money, they don't buy. Not that some haven't flirted with that temptation, the credit card, in the past. But later, being a little older and wiser—and poorer—serious savers are adamant about avoiding heavy credit obligations.

Shop the garage sales in an affluent area. . .

The most common advice from those who wrote in is to bury your credit cards—for a while at least—so they're unavailable except in an emergency. As Christine Hilston of Ohio says, "Credit cards can bring financial ruin, but used wisely, a general purpose card and a gasoline company card can be lifesavers at times." For the rest of the plastic in your wallet, the ceremony of "destruction by scissors" is recommended by a lot of people. It's just too easy to overspend when all one has to say is "Charge it."

Although you can get into a lot of trouble using a credit card for everyday purchases, you may find that using a credit card or some sort of payment plan is necessary for major purchases—such as a refrigerator or washing machine. Interest charges can be very high, but using credit wisely can be a way to buy some extra time at home. Paying the minimum amount each month will keep your credit rating good, and some time in the future—when your husband gets a pay increase, perhaps—larger payments can be made to pay off the balance.

It is important for a woman to establish credit in her own name. Whether we like it or not, the business world uses credit records as a basis for doing business. The person without a credit rating is at a disadvantage. Sue Arnold in Virginia tells the story of "a newly widowed friend of mine who found she had to pay steep deposits to get the utilities turned on in her new, smaller home. She had no credit history. The fact that she had actually paid the family bills for years meant nothing."

A Time to Share, a Time to Splurge

How terribly dull and drab life would be without the lift that comes with sharing and occasional splurging! For a moment, you can set aside the continuing task of economizing and choose to spend or to give something away when ordinarily you'd save. There is a time and a need for both in life. Consider sharing and splurging to be a part of The Plan. As a safeguard against the malaise of feeling poor, nothing is more effective than a generous spirit.

Half Is Better Than None Of course, it is hardly a challenge to share or to splurge when there is more than enough at hand. When such is not the case, one must be more clever. Long ago, an occasion of charity and some ingenuity was celebrated in art by the painter El Greco. He recreated the scene where the young Roman soldier, Martin (to be known later as St. Martin), in full armor and atop a spirited steed, meets a cold, ragged beggar on the road. The quick-thinking Martin divides his cloak with his sword and gives half to the needy beggar. Although it was only a half, contemporary poet, Phyllis Mc-Ginley, philosophizes, "halfway warm is better than freezing, as half a love is better than none."

Giving and accepting are both ways of reaching out. . .

The modern homemaker's gift is more likely to be a loaf of homemade bread, a visit to a shut-in neighbor, flowers or produce fresh from the garden. Barbara Dick of Washington is particularly imaginative. "I share seeds with friends," she writes. "I enjoy giving something full of life to those I love. We grow nonhybrid plants, except for my golden zucchini. Saving seeds helps save species which might otherwise die out. I collect my own seeds to plant the next year, and I encourage my friends to also save seeds."

Returns from Giving   Susan Glennon of South Dakota describes the reciprocal nature of giving and receiving. "A bumper crop of tomatoes shared may return in the form of an outgrown dress for your young daughter or a shared ride to the store on a day when you don't have the car and it is raining." Giving and accepting are both ways of reaching out, of showing that one cares about someone else, and of rediscovering goodness in the world. Martin and the beggar both felt better about themselves, though each had to pull a somewhat skimpy wrap more securely around himself.

Many of the families that contacted us speak of *tithing*, or setting aside ten percent of what they earn for church or charity. Some do so regularly; others have adopted a more flexible approach, giving nothing for a month or six months when income is very restricted but increasing their contributions when times improve. Sue and Jim Brown from North Carolina have a twofold plan. "We save money and give away money," Sue writes. "We believe in budgeting some money to savings every month, but just as important, or more so, is budgeting money to give away. No matter how little you have, if you can help someone with less or with a real need, it gives you a sense of fulfillment that is a fantastic morale builder." The Browns believe, too, that "sharing extends the helping hand that we have received from others."

The Secret of Splurging The companion to sharing, especially for a family, is the once-in-awhile treat, the respite from saving ways that can be a release valve that keeps the saving system from exploding. The secret of how to splurge on a tight budget is to look to the simple pleasures in life. Ellen Martyn from Ontario, Canada, writes that her husband has been seeking a job in his line of work for almost a year. "The word luxury has new meaning. Raisins have become a real treat to our kids. If we have cookies with nuts and carob chips in them, it's a double treat. Juice is a luxury, as are plums and bananas. And ice cream," she says, "well, ice cream is worth a celebration."

Despite the need to budget carefully, Ellen is a firm believer in the occasional splurge. "Don't become an ogre over money," she advises. "On a recent outing to a ball game, I packed lunches, but we still bought hot dogs at the park because that was a real treat for the kids. It was part of the ball game for them."

An unusually good cheeseburger at a local coffee shop is a favorite splurge of the Ricciardi family in Connecticut. "I know the usual argument—the money spent could buy two

*Being at home with her
young children allows a
mother to enjoy some
priceless moments. (Shown
here are Alexis Campanell
and baby brother Garrett.)*

meals of cheeseburgers if made at home," Cheryl admits. "But this way, no one has to prepare them and no one has to clean up afterwards. And when mom is home all day without a car, it's a boost to the spirit to be able to go out now and then."

A Healthy Balance "For too long we denied ourselves simple expenditures so we could pay more of the bills," Cheryl relates. "Then we realized that a few dollars here and there wouldn't make that much of a difference anyway." She and Ed now occasionally buy a bottle of wine on weekends. For a time they continued to feel guilty about buying anything that wasn't a necessity. "But looking around," she says, "we'd see others in the same boat treating themselves once in awhile." A healthy balance, they have found, is the key to surviving a rough financial time.

Cheryl also suggests that when your birthday is coming up, "ask loved ones for ingredients to make something special from your favorite cookbook." Hers is WHOLE FOODS FOR THE WHOLE FAMILY, a La Leche League publication. "This year my mother bought me carob powder and other ingredients for the whole wheat brownies in the League cookbook." Last year Cheryl's mother and sister surprised her with a gift of spices and shampoo as well as sponges, dish and laundry detergents, and other things that she tends to run short of.

Karen Elkins from North Dakota observes that "if through budgeting you are able to splurge now and again or save toward a specific goal—something you'll truly enjoy—you won't feel as though you're 'always doing without.' No matter how much a mother wants to stay at home with her little ones, if she feels deprived and poor because of it, it's easy to feel resentful and depressed." Her solution: "It really helps to think of budgeting and cutting corners as the challenge it is. Attitude makes a difference. I have even begun to enjoy finding ways to spend less," she says, adding, "It does take practice to live on one salary."

CHAPTER 6

The At-Home Executive

Homemaking—not to be confused with housework—is a demanding, satisfying, exciting occupation which can be second in your life only to the role of wife and mother. Homemaking involves the whole woman, physically, mentally, emotionally. As Maurine Joens of Arkansas says, "Any energy and love that I expend I choose to spend on my family, rather than on a job that can be done by someone else."

Leading, Supervising, Goal-Setting

Many of the skills necessary for homemaking are highly valued in the executive. The homemaker, like a good executive, must be sensitive to the needs and feelings of those around her. She is in a leadership role; she inspires; she oversees the activities of others. Their achievements—her children's triumphs—reflect her encouraging support. The same can be said for the executive who heads a team of workers. The homemaker must be self-disciplined, regularly setting goals for herself. Working toward those goals, more often than not proceeds at a steady though erratic pace—which is to be expected. What other executive is launching a life while running a business?

There aren't enough hours in the day for many mothers-at-home to do all the things they want to do. Because they're at home, these women have the time to be astute shoppers. Living on one income encourages them to cook with care. The mothers we hear from are busy planting gardens and preserving the bounty. They paint and patch. Many are knowledgeable about household repairs. "If I don't bring in a second income," says Linda Butler of Utah, "I feel it is my responsibility to make my husband's income, whatever it is, stretch twice as far." Says Susan Glennon of South Dakota, "This is the occupation that allows me to stay home with my kids." Homemakers are also highly motivated to conserve energy and other natural resources.

How do you manage to do all that a homemaker must do—or even some of it? What about the constant interruptions that come with mothering young children—time out to nurse the baby, to play a game of peek-a-boo, to change a diaper; time for caring for the other children; time for getting three meals on the table, and keeping up with the ever present laundry? These "interruptions," it must be remembered, are really the sum and substance of your job. Your job as a mother-at-home cannot be scheduled, or programmed to fit into a 9 to 5 five-day-a-week work schedule.

Using the Minutes Not the Hours

One of the most common complaints among mothers is, "There are so many new things I'd like to do but I just never seem to get to them." The solution is not years off, to a time when the children are grown. The answer is to select *one* project to start with—something you're eager to try—and then to develop a new work style. "The most valuable piece of advice I ever received as a homemaker," writes Joann Grohman from Maine, "was from a man I admired for his productivity. I asked him how he managed to accomplish so much. He told me, 'Learn to utilize small modules of time.' In other words, don't keep

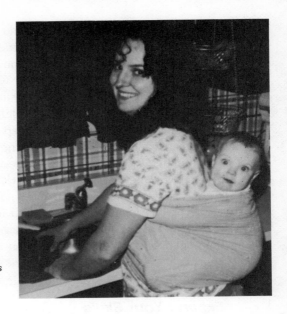

Elaine Caper washes dishes with Monica in her traditional carrier.

putting off things you want to do or should do because you are unable to clear the tracks for four uninterrupted hours."

Joann elaborates, "I stopped thinking about all the interesting and money-saving or money-making things I could do 'if I had the time' and began doing them. In those days, I didn't know a soul who made bread, but soon I was turning out about ten loaves a week and have been baking ever since." Joann wrote a book, *Born to Love: Instinct and Natural Mothering,* in little slots of time during a year when she was also feeding eight to ten people three meals a day. She advises, "the main trick is to keep your brain in gear while doing things with your hands and feet."

Tote That Baby

Elaine Caper of Illinois observes, "Saving money and stretching dollars involves a lot of time and work. If I can do this and keep my baby-toddler happy at the same time, then it's all worth it." Elaine found the way to do both by using a baby carrier. Her little one loved being carried around on mother's back, where she could observe all the activity or take a nap, as she pleased. Elaine's first carrier, which she got on loan, worked well, but she was intrigued by the methods for carrying a baby that are common to other cultures.

In Africa mothers traditionally keep their babies with them while they work. They often work in the fields with their babies snug on their backs in one of the oldest forms of baby carrier. A two-yard length of sturdy cotton cloth holds the baby securely to mother. This carrier requires no sewing. Elaine learned the technique for wrapping the cloth from a missionary and now considers her African-style carrier superior in comfort to the commercial carrier she had been using—also, it's much cheaper.

Expand Your Skills

In homemaking there is always something new to learn and try. One mother from Kansas, Cynthia Nodson, is planning to expand her knowledge of the art of homemaking much as one would concentrate on a course of study. She and her husband have two girls, ages five-and-a-half and three-and-a-half. With the youngest entering the preschool stage, Cynthia plans to use the extra time "to learn to run our home as economically as possible."

Cynthia reflects, "We feel that no one thing we do saves enough money for me to stay at home. Our whole lifestyle is what makes it possible." She explains that, among other things, she and her husband "have developed a loose framework for our family as it is now and as we hope it will become. We have chosen to leave a large gap between our first two children and future children. Using natural family planning, we feel comfortable doing this spiritually and medically." The Nodsons feel that "by spacing our children a little, we are delaying the

Hilary Rocca (shown here with her husband and children) sees herself as a professional mother.

time when we will have the full financial impact of a large family until we are into our higher earning stage." The gap time for Cynthia will be a time of preparation and learning.

Your Self-Image

The years you spend at home with small children are extremely busy ones, possibly the busiest in your life. For all the satisfaction you reap, there will be times when you feel locked in and washed out. At such moments, the thought of taking a whirl in the workworld can seem very inviting. A League member in France, Hilary Rocca, describes a scene with which many of us can identify, regardless of where we live: "Is there anything worse than sitting at your breakfast table, hair undone, no makeup, feeling like the household drudge, the baby nursing—again—and the two-and-a-half-year-old squabbling with the six-year-old because he is resting his finger on her chair? To crown it all, your employed neighbor, her children off to the day-care center, gaily waves good morning to you as she hops into her car, looking as though she's just stepped out of a fashion magazine."

Your self-esteem plummets; your self-image receives a blow. Ironically, on another similar occasion you probably waved and went about your business. Little squabblers can be quickly distracted and steered toward more enjoyable and productive pursuits. As for the baby, settling a restless infant comes naturally to you when you're feeling good about yourself—and there's the key. The woman who doesn't feel good about herself and knows she doesn't look good has two strikes against her. *Mothers need to take care of themselves.* Neglecting one's health is a form of selfishness, especially if one is a mother! Make a point of eating nutritious foods at regular intervals, and get proper rest. You needn't sleep eight hours at a stretch; rest during the day or take a catnap when your husband comes home. He'll enjoy the company of a rested wife much more than having you drag through the entire evening.

Hilary offers a tip for your morning routine: "I see myself as a professional mother," she writes, "and I get up early to organize my day and get myself ready for *my job.* I'll be forever grateful to Karima Khatib, a La Leche League Leader, for having said at a meeting that she remembered getting up at five or six o'clock in the morning to get ready for work in her premotherhood days, so why shouldn't we mothers make the same effort for our children and husbands?

"In the morning, I do a complete, fast, beauty routine. I wash my face, pat a time or two to dry, and apply a little eye cream and moisture cream. Then a quick shower—it actually only takes three minutes. By the time I'm dry and dressed, the cream is absorbed and I can make up my eyes, brush my hair, and I'm ready for the day. This routine can be accomplished entirely with the baby on my hip—except for the three minutes under the shower. I find that if I keep myself looking smart, not only do I look good, but I feel good. I am better able to give of myself to my children. My husband and family and friends respect me as a person—and I can look my glamorous neighbors in the eye!"

Part Three

Making It

CHAPTER 7

Housing

As the ultimate in inexpensive housing, the cave deserves its place in history. Perhaps the cave family had the right idea. Maintenance on their domicile was a snap, and if one of the kids wrote on the walls—well, one generation's scribbling is another's anthropology. Of course, as so often is the case, the cave family never knew how good they had it. In the intervening epochs, housing has come out from underground, and housing costs have gone sky high. For most of us today, the monthly rent or house payment takes one of the biggest—if not the biggest—bites out of our income.

Making a House a Home

When looking for ways to save, look closely at what it costs you to live where you are. This cost includes your house (or rent) payments, taxes (if they are billed separately), heating and cooling costs, and transportation costs. A reduction in any of these areas will often tip the balance of payments in the family's favor and make it possible for mother to stay home with the young children.

What makes a house a home is the people in it. There is something terribly sad about a residential street where house after house stands silent and empty during the day, heavily bolted against modern predators. The adults are out working—quite often to pay the high housing costs—and the children have been dispersed to various caretakers. Is the house serving the people, or are the people in service to the house? When parents and children are at home only in the evening and on weekends, the tab for housing, per hour of its use, is *very* high. In terms of enjoyment for the whole family, the return on the investment is truly low.

The families writing to us have found numerous ways to keep a roof over their heads and at the same time keep mom and little ones at home. Cathy and Don Cutting's early ventures into home ownership followed a familiar pattern, but their most recent move is less typical. Cathy writes from Ontario, "When we discovered that we were pregnant with our first baby, our number one priority was to buy a house. Looking back it seems silly, but at the time, we felt that a baby had to have a house and yard of its own in order to grow up properly. We saved all of my salary and borrowed from the grandparents for a down payment, but even so, the mortgage payments were enough to all but break us when I quit work."

The Cutting's baby arrived, the joy of their lives, and Don's salary increased steadily. According to Cathy, "Soon we had money to spare at the end of the month. So do you know what we did? We sold our comfortable, adequate house and moved to a bigger, newer house with more extras in a 'better' neighborhood. Once again we were strapped for money, and this time the effect on us was much more devastating. My husband and I were often grouchy and discouraged. Life seemed very hard."

Redefining Priorities

About this time, Don received a job offer in another city. "We accepted it," Cathy says. "We saw this change as an opportunity, too, to redefine our priorities and make some financial

Solar house in Arizona built by music teacher Charles Rullman.

decisions we could live with. When we moved, we looked for a house we could afford 'no matter what.' Our choice was a townhouse, a style which years earlier we had said we would never live in. It's within minutes of Don's place of work and is a very acceptable alternative."

In Wisconsin, Jj Fallick and her husband "bought an old, cheap house. When we were looking for housing three years ago, we deliberately looked for a much cheaper house than the realtor's formula said we could afford." The Fallicks have no regrets. "That decision," Jj says, "stood us in good stead when my husband was disabled for four months and then laid off for one week out of four this past year."

In 1978 the Rullmans were living in "a typical subdivision with an all-electric house and a thirty-year mortgage," a situation that Marsha and Charles describe as "folly and futility." Charles Rullman decided to build a more economical house, doing much of the work himself. "Before anyone thinks he

109

was an experienced builder, let me clarify," Marsha explains. "My husband had never built a house before or even helped in constructing one. He teaches music and tunes pianos at the local university, which does give him the option of not working in the summer."

Careful plans were made, and with starting money from the sale of their house in the subdivision, and with the help of two friends, Charles built their energy-efficient solar-envelope house in Arizona. The Rullmans see this single, substantial saving as the most important factor enabling them to remain a one-income family.

Building a Dream House

Audrey and Larry Dewey were living in a cabin in the state of Washington when their first child, David, was born. Audrey recalls, "There was no running water or electricity, but it was something we could afford on one small salary." She says that she and Larry had decided "right from the start to do just about anything so I could stay home full time with the kids."

Baby David was about one year old when they bought some wooded land and using a handsaw began the job of clearing it. "We now stand and admire our garden, lawn, and flowers," Audrey says with pride, "and plan with excitement what we'll do next." To house the family, Larry built an eight-by-twelve-foot shed and connected an old pickup truck to it. Two years later they started their "dream house," which Audrey describes as "a modest, energy-efficient two-bedroom house—a castle to us!" Jobs are scarce in the Washington area in the winter, but, Audrey says, "We don't feel burdened by owning a lot of things." This philosophy of living with less has made it possible for the Deweys to meet their regular monthly payments: mortgage, $80; telephone, $7.50; and propane, $10.

Lisa Robitaille from Ontario observes, "We have lived in both large and small houses, and there is a lot to be said for

Nadine Robitaille is not concerned about the size of the house she lives in, as long as mother's there.

small spaces. Smaller homes not only cost less in terms of mortgages, heating costs, and furnishings, they require much less time and effort to maintain, freeing mom and dad for more important pursuits." Lisa feels, too, that as a family, "Our expectations are much lower than many other people's. We have bought older homes in need of repair and worked on them as finances and time are available." She admits that new would be nice. "I cannot deny that I often wish for a newer, finished house. But then, I realize how lucky we are to have a home."

Bonnie Pfeffer of New York agrees that for a family, there are definite advantages in living in a house rather than an apartment, even though the house lacks some of the amenities. "We didn't get our dream house," she says. "The house we bought needs a lot of fixing, which we're doing slowly." The

111

effort is worthwhile, she adds, "because of the privacy we now have and the freedom the children have, which we didn't have in an apartment." As for staying at home, she says, "I love it. It's lots of fun because my emphasis is on the people around me and not on housekeeping."

The Giesels of Florida decided it was now or never when they undertook the building of their new home. They hired the contractors themselves and supervised the work. Jean recounts, "It involved a lot of studying, legwork, telephoning, and such, but I could do much of it at home or take the youngest child along. We moved in as soon as the house was habitable and kept working— sometimes diligently, other times not at all." While this project didn't bring in money, it has kept their housing costs very reasonable. Without taking an outside job, Jean was able to make a considerable contribution to the family's welfare. "Prorated, I earned perhaps $10,000 working part-time for a year," she says of her involvement in their house building.

"Babies don't wait to grow up. . ."

If the idea of building a house yourself intrigues you, you may be interested in an owner/builder school. The first such school, the Shelter Institute, was organized in Bath, Maine. Now homebuilding courses, which enroll women as well as men, can be found in locations across the United States. A session typically runs for three weeks during the summer and includes classroom presentations and on-site, hands-on experience. Some topics covered are blueprints, building-code requirements, site selection, well digging, foundation laying, rafter building, roofing, installation of insulation and heating, and installation of plumbing and electrical systems. Energy efficiency is stressed. The cost of building a house can be cut by 20 to 60 percent, depending on how much the owner/builder does directly and how much is contracted out.

Back to Basics

Judy Hatcher and her husband built a new house recently in Mississippi, putting just the bare essentials in it and on it. "Shingles and siding are a must," she writes, "inside walls aren't. We're looking at lots of sheet rock and two-by-fours." They figure they can put walls up later, but "our children are children *now*." Judy admits that she used to worry when someone was coming to the house for the first time. "I'd wonder, 'What will they think?'" But then she decided "if we really stand in danger of losing a friendship because of our different lifestyle, well, we had better re-evaluate the friendship."

The Schilkes built their own house in Georgia from salvage. In retrospect, Mary Ellen says, "It was rough living in an unfinished house, but we survived. We have five beautiful children, and I would not trade anything for the years I've been blessed by being a stay-at-home mother." Ruth Faux of Ontario refers to life in their old house, which needs extensive renovation, as "living in a muddle." Their compensation is the thousands of dollars of interest saved on a lower mortgage and the opportunity for Ruth to be with her baby. As she says, "Babies don't wait to grow up."

The location of your home will influence not only your cost of living but also your lifestyle to a surprising degree. Some people chose rural living because they felt that it had many advantages for raising small children and teaching them about gardening, raising animals, and living with nature. The children are not the only ones to benefit from a rural location. Rural living has held the not-so-obvious benefit of making people more creative and self-reliant and teaching the fine art of improvisation.

Terry Koppenheffer of Pennsylvania puts the finishing touches on a room addition.

Different needs influenced the Trombley family in their choice of a location. Mary Trombley describes their experience in New York. "By looking in the city, and on a smallish lot, we were able to buy a three-bedroom Cape Cod house for less money per month—mortgage and taxes—than rent had been." Their new location brought other savings as well. "Our home is less than a mile from where my husband works, so transportation costs and commuting time are minimal. Best of all, we are within walking distance of our church." Since there is a convenient busline, the Trombleys need only one car.

Charlene Burnett from Missouri believes, "Living in a large city makes it possible to participate in many activities. My children attend art and music classes for only a small fee."

Extending the Family

Many families give high priority to living near other family members. They see this proximity as an opportunity to help and be helped. No family is immune to crises, and it is comforting to be able to call a parent or sister or brother in the event of an emergency run to the doctor or when the refrigerator breaks down on the hottest day of the year. The Browns from North Carolina believe living near family can be an asset to all involved. Sue writes, "We decided to move back to Jim's original home town. My parents had moved there, and Jim had close relatives there, too. We wanted to be near our families. I believe that for us this has made all the difference in the world as far as enabling us to live a simpler lifestyle. We received much help from our families with meals, treats, and so on. In return, we helped them whenever they needed it and spent time with them so they could enjoy the babies." Her husband took a job very close to their home. "It was a lower-paying job and also a lower-pressure job, giving him more time and energy for the children and for us to do things together. Also, we could manage with an older car that Jim could fix himself."

"We received much help from our families. . ."

Anita Browning of Missouri lives near her mother, her sister, and her grandmother. "It's easy to help each other and talk things over with each other. In the summer, particularly, we try to do things together." Anita mentions that she and her sister are each expecting a baby about the same time, and since they have the same doctor, they arrange to have their

Alexis Campanell helps out with the family's remodeling project.

appointments on the same day. "We share the ride," she says. "Often my mother and grandmother go, too, and we pick up groceries and staples that are usually cheaper in the larger town. Lunch is at a fast food chain restaurant. Other than this, we seldom eat out. We enjoy ourselves."

Diane Grubb of Ohio has an at-home-mother's dream location. "Part of the reason I enjoy staying at home so much," she says, "is the neighborhood. My sister, who is also an LLL Leader, lives next door. The rest of our neighbors are about our age, with children our children's ages. There are seven houses in a row where the mothers have all breastfed at least one of their children." There are no fences between yards, so "the children are free to roam from yard to yard, and all a mother has to do is look out her back door to see where they are playing. We consider ourselves very fortunate."

CHAPTER 8

*E*ating *W*ell and *S*pending *W*isely

Food satisfies a wide range of needs in our lives. It fuels our bodies for the day's work, and the family meal can be one of the social highlights of a family's day. The joy of eating family style doesn't just happen, however; it involves time, thought, and money. The role of food manager—to plan, procure, and prepare the right food—is extremely important.

Food eats up a significant part of the average family's monthly income. A smart food manager, however, can maximize the amount of nutrition her family gets at the same time that she minimizes her family's food expenditures. You should avoid paying for questionable food additives and undesirable food processing. These practices break down whole, natural foods and leave only chemical-laden remnants. You and your family are robbed of needed nutrients. In the long run, these half-foods cost more than wholesome products. Keeping your family healthy through good nutrition is a smart economic move that pays long-lasting dividends.

Sharpening your sense of what's good food is similar to sharpening your money sense—you get better at it as you go along. Begin by reading up on whole-foods cooking. Although there are many good books available on this subject, naturally, we believe the La Leche League cookbook, WHOLE FOODS FOR THE WHOLE FAMILY, is among the best.

If your family has been less than enthusiastic about "health foods," proceed slowly. Don't expect to change their eating habits overnight. Concentrate on one or possibly two things at a time. You can begin by decreasing the amount of sugar you use in preparing foods. Then replace some of the customary white flour with a whole-grain flour (preferably one that is stone-ground).

Dr. Dennis P. Burkitt, one of three scientists winning the 1982 General Motors Cancer Research Foundation award, recently stated, "Americans should start eating the way their ancestors did in the early 1900s and before that. More potatoes and tubers, more grains and not so much meat, fat, sugar, and salt. Right eating prevents health from deteriorating," he points out. "The thief is the bad diet....Prevention is the most important thing. Advances in treatment are nothing, really, by comparison."

Dr. Herbert Ratner has often advised LLL mothers on good nutrition by offering the following admonition: "Eat a variety of plants and animals, in as close to their natural state as possible."

In your search for wholesome foods, start reading food labels. Peering at the fine print on cans, cartons, and bottles may seem very time-consuming at first but once you know which brands meet your standards, you can quickly zero in on these and sail past the rest.

It's important to know that the ingredients of a product are usually listed in descending order with the first one listed on the label being the major ingredient of the product.
The Supermarket Handbook by David and Nikki Goldbeck

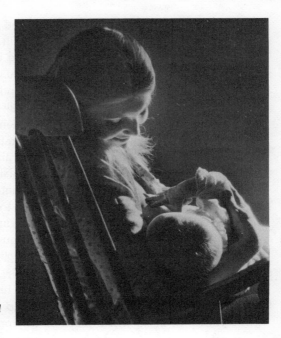

Breastfeeding gives your baby the best start to good nutrition.

has been a help to many shoppers who want to learn which products on their supermarket shelves offer the best nutritional values.

The Best Start

Of course, the best start to good nutrition is breastfeeding your baby. Mother's milk is the superior food for the infant, the one food that nature intended your baby to have. The cost, approximately 600 extra calories a day for you, is negligible compared to the considerable expense of artificial infant feeding. The estimated cost of feeding a baby for the first year of life, using formula and prepared baby foods, amounts to approximately $1,200. In contrast, the healthy, full-term baby that is breastfed does not need any foods other than breast milk—no supplemental bottles of milk, formula, or juice, no solid foods or vitamin supplements—for about the first six months of life. Mother's milk alone suffices and is, in fact, preferable to all other foods. Limiting baby to nothing but mother in the first half of that first year provides the baby with the optimum protection against the onset of allergies and is a safeguard against infection. Contending with a cow's-milk allergy (most formulas have a cow's-milk base) or other problem resulting from baby's failure to get his natural food is frustrating; when the malady requires medical attention, it is also an added expense. For breastfeeding help, read THE WOMANLY ART OF BREAST-FEEDING and contact La Leche League International for information on the LLL Group nearest to you.

The safest and easiest way to introduce other foods to your baby is to wait until the middle of your baby's first year and then offer one new food at a time, beginning with a palatable, nutritious, and easily obtained food like banana, that you can mash yourself. Once your baby has had the good start that breastfeeding provides, you'll want to follow that up with a variety of fresh, whole foods as his appetite expands. It only makes sense to establish fresh foods as regular family fare. Although relying on lots of fruit and vegetables—fresh whenever possible—may seem costly, this expense will be offset by the fact that you will not be buying or will seldom be buying the sweet pastries, candy, sugared cereals, or snacks that come in an endless and non-nutritious profusion. Mothers-at-home find that planning, procuring, and preparing the family's food is one of their most important endeavors, and they offer all kinds of practical tips for making the job easier for you.

Food Planning

Making the best use of the foods you buy calls for some advance planning. Before you don your chef's hat, put on your thinking cap and figure out your menus for the week, or even for the month. Your family will eat better, and your budget will look better.

When there were just the two of you, you may have gotten along fine with a quick trip to the market, possibly on the way home from work, to pick up something for dinner each night. When there are more people in the family, such casual eating practices will not do. Advance planning can make meal preparation cheaper and easier and can reward you with a better, more varied menu. It's impossible to come up with a nutritious, economical supper night after night when the planning starts at five o'clock in the evening. With advance planning, the time you spend in the kitchen preparing the main meal will not necessarily be longer than with spontaneous cooking; it may even be shorter. As an added bonus, you'll find that you enjoy your role as Executive Chef much more.

Menu-planning "So many times I've gone to the store and spent over $100 only to come home and say, 'There's nothing for dinner,' " Kitty Desmarteau of Oregon writes. "Now, about once a month, I sit down with my recipe file and cookbooks and make a list of about twenty different main dishes my family likes for dinner. I jot down the name of the meal on one piece of paper and, on a separate sheet of paper, list the ingredients for these meals. I check the cupboards as I go along to add anything that might be missing. The ingredients list is divided into *Meat, Dairy, Canned, Dry* (beans, rice, etc.), and *Produce.* As I write my menu list, I either pull the recipe card or make a notation on my list of the page number in the cookbook. Many times I double the recipe to get more than one meal from the one-time preparation. If, when shopping, I find an exceptional buy, I'll add other meals to my list." Kitty finds that by using this system, she can cut down on the number of vists to the grocery store—which in itself is a savings of time and gas money.

Barbara Wilson-Clay from Texas agrees. "Once a week I sit down and rough out the menu," she explains. "From this, I make my shopping list. I find that I waste much less food, and focus more on good nutrition; I have better utilization of leftovers and I no longer freak out at dinner time trying to decide what to serve."

Laura Rank, a Wisconsin mother of five, uses a rotating menu to help her plan meals and cut food costs: "In the seven days of the week, you'll find the following seven mainstays, in varying order, on the menu: beef, pork, chicken, fish, cheese, eggs, and liver." Meals at the Rank household are filled out with home-grown fruits and vegetables.

Getting a Head Start Janis McCauley of Virginia pre-browns the large package of ground meat she buys on sale and freezes it for later use. "This way I don't have to thaw the ground beef prior to finishing most recipes, and I wash the pan only one time." Janis freezes the browned beef in portions for chili, spaghetti sauce, casseroles, pizza, soup, or whatever is on the menu. She uses this method to buy in bulk, reducing her price per portion.

Joann Grohman of Maine admits that "nutritious, low-cost foods cooked from scratch don't take too much time but they do take planning ahead. When the dry beans are not put on to soak or the brown rice is not started early enough, there is the temptation to use a quick, expensive substitute." Joann suggests using odd minutes of time for planning, "for instance, when waiting at the gas pump or while weeding the garden."

Another advocate of getting a head start in meal preparation, Barbara Dick of Washington will sauté enough onions and celery to last for the month. She freezes them in amounts appropriate for use in the family's favorite dishes.

Eliminating Waste A continual challenge for the family food manager is how to get the most out of foods that are on hand and how to avoid waste. Marsha Robison of Texas discovered that "I seemed to be having a problem with food spoiling. An item—say, cottage cheese—would go to waste if we didn't feel like eating it as is. And waste is a real problem when the food budget is tight!" Marsha scoured cookbooks and other sources for taste-tempting recipes and then made a record of her finds.

Mike Tounzen and five-year-old Michael do the cooking so the family can enjoy "eating out" at home.

"I began a little notebook in which I list recipes and where to find them under a certain food heading. I find it works well with dairy products and also vegetables and saves having to go through the index of every cookbook looking for a particular recipe."

Sheena Sharp of British Columbia, Canada, regularly makes up names for the dishes she invents using the ingredients she has on hand. Garnishing can also be used to sell your latest effort in high nutrition. A smiley face can be easily made with green pepper rings and a little pimiento.

Plan for leftovers or phase them out when possible. It makes good economic sense to cook enough for more than one meal of some of the family's favorites—such as soups, stews, chili—things that taste good or better the second time around. These are planned leftovers. It's the bit-of-this and dab-of-that leftovers that clutter the refrigerator and quietly go moldy. Whenever possible, store leftovers in glass containers. You'll be able to see what's in them easily. Any wide-mouthed jar with a screw top will do—peanut butter jars work well. To avoid leftovers, pare down the portions you cook. If you're concerned about not having enough for a meal, throw a couple of extra potatoes into the pot. If these are left over, they are easy to use as hash browns or in an omelette. Another good standby which will fill empty spaces in tummies—hearty slices of whole grain bread.

Procuring Foods

Once you have your menus in hand, think of yourself as a purchasing agent and ask yourself: What are the best buys? Where can I find them?

Every mother-at-home who succeeds in keeping food costs down has a shopping plan, whether informal or formal. Five basic rules to incorporate into your shopping plan are:

1. *Be aware of prices.* Take time to compare the prices from store to store on the items you buy most frequently. Scan the newspaper ads and flyers.
2. *Get as much as you can to cover your needs in one shopping venture.* Avoid unplanned trips to pick up a few things for dinner. They're counterproductive because they use up precious time and usually extra gas. When the menu is determined at the last minute, you're more susceptible to impulse, or high-cost, buying.
3. *Have a dollar limit in mind and stick to it.* As a control measure leave your checkbook at home and carry only the amount of cash that you plan on spending. If you need to first cash a check, make it out for the predetermined amount before you set off down the aisle with your grocery cart.

When you're serious about sticking to a certain amount, you need to keep track of how prices are adding up as you place items in your basket, so consider taking a small calculator with you.

4. *Don't shop on an empty stomach.* Hunger pangs will quickly override good intentions. Eat well before leaving home.

5. *If your children come shopping with you, let them know they will receive one treat for helping mom.* Make it clear that the treat must be from an approved list. Arrange for the child to have the treat in hand as you approach the check-out counter with its multitude of candy displays. Be sure that the children are well-fed and rested when you set off on your shopping trip.

On the subject of shopping with children, Margaret Houge from Montana offers the following suggestions: "The kids get non-edibles for treats, such as balloons. These provide good rainy day activity and are helpful at any time to distract a fussy or bored child." Also, Margaret sees shopping as a way to instilling a sense of smart consumerism in her children. "We tell our kids that we don't buy certain products because of the lack of vitamins," she says. "My five-year-old is getting to be quite a good little shopper."

How Often to Shop? Many mothers-at-home who wrote to us had developed a definite shopping pattern that was geared to fit their particular circumstances and philosophy on how to save.

For Susan Akre of Oregon, the key to saving money on food "is to go to the store only once in a great while. I shop at a discount-type grocery store about once every two months." On these trips, Susan buys as many staples as she can fit in the car. Once back home, she stores her purchases "wherever there is a nook or cranny." The Akres shop for perishable foods about once a week.

Also from Oregon, Gail Kimberling, like Susan, shops at a discount store. "I've found that by doing my shopping there only once a month, my husband Dave is able to come along and help out, whereas he probably wouldn't have the time to do this if I shopped every week," Gail writes. "We usually make a family outing of it." She points out, too, that by participating in the shopping, her husband is "as aware of the prices as I am. Before we started shopping together, he would complain no end about the amount of money spent on food. Now he knows why!"

"*Sometimes items on the nonessential list are there for several weeks...*"

Jacie Coryell of Colorado advises shoppers to stock up on one or two items each week: "Allot five or ten dollars as 'stock up' money each week and spend it on one or two items that are on sale. Your first stop should be to pick out these items. Then do your regular shopping, staying within your budget, of course." Jacie looks for good buys in meat, frozen food, canned goods, paper products, anthing else that can be stored.

"Economizing on food is something that I handle a little differently than some," Sue Brown explains. "Whereas many families buy large quantities on sale and freeze or can the food, I prefer to take the opposite approach." This North Carolina mother prefers not to tie up large amounts of money in food. Because they live near the store where she shops, she says, "I can get to the store quickly, so I buy less food at a time." Sue does not feel that she pays more for food by shopping this way. "Something good is on special every week anyway; I find it easier to be selective when shopping weekly." Sue has developed a master list of the things they use regularly, "and I make my weekly list from that, although I adjust for unexpected bargains."

Define Your Scope   In New York, Bonnie Pfeffer tries to think of grocery shopping as something enjoyable. "It gets me and my child out of the house for a couple of hours; we are in contact with many people, and it is educational." Bonnie checks the weekly ads carefully for the best food buys and compares the specials at the different stores. She has also set a limit on how far she will travel in search of a bargain. "I will go to as many as four or five stores as long as they're within my three-mile radius. I save three to five dollars a week on my food bill this way."

In New Zealand, Lynley Steel relies on a shopping list that is divided into three parts. "The first list is for the essentials, and the second has things that are needed but are not strictly essential. The third is for odds and ends I'd like to have if I have enough money." Lynley observes that "sometimes items on the nonessential list are there for several weeks before I have enough money to buy them. I find that I can go for a long time without things that I might have otherwise bought on impulse. And occasionally things come off my list because I've decided I don't really need them after all."

Lynley lists items in the order in which they can be found in the supermarket to avoid wasting time crisscrossing the store looking for something. She also adds up prices as she goes along "so that I know exactly how much I can put in my trolley and have the money to pay for it."

A Helping Hand   Good neighbors can help each other save. This seems to work best when there's a real sense of concern on everyone's part. Rita Lehman, Illinois, has an easygoing yet understanding rapport with her neighbors. For one thing, they check with one another before going shopping to see if some-

Elizabeth and Laura Lehman wearing matching T-shirts that proclaim "I eat at Mom's."

one else needs something. "This often saves an unplanned trip," Rita says. "We know, too, what products each family uses and keep on the lookout for sales or coupons to clip for each other."

When stores are some distance away, several friends plus children will often go shopping together. There are pros and cons to this approach, however, as Charlene Burnett, Missouri, has found. "Car pooling is okay to a degree, but it's hard to look for bargains with six preschoolers along. I do best when I just drop by my favorite stores by myself with only my own children."

Where to Shop   Patricia Scott in Wyoming buys soybeans for about twenty cents a pound when buying a bushel bag at a nearby feed and grain store. "If sixty pounds is too much for you, find a friend or two to split them with," Patricia suggests.

She grinds up soybeans "in place of meat in soups, stews, spaghetti sauce, pizza, casseroles, quiches, hamburgers, or just by themselves."

Mary Kastendieck of Colorado, buys organically grown whole-wheat flour from a local farmer who grinds it himself and sells five pounds for eighty cents. The Kastendiecks also buy yeast (two pounds for about $4.80) at a food distributor who sells mostly to restaurants but takes some local walk-in business.

Angela Marvin of Pennsylvania recommends figuring the cost of meat in terms of *servings* rather than by the pound. "A boneless or well-trimmed piece may be a much better value." Freshness dating on meat enables the Robisons of Texas to save. "One of our local grocery stores has a section where they place meat that is at the end of its freshest period," Marsha writes. "The meat is not spoiled by any means, but it is marked down, frequently by half." Marsha says that they rewrap the meat when they get it home and keep it in the freezer. "We cook it immediately when it's thawed, and we enjoy good cuts of meat at prices we can afford. It pays to inquire at the meat department as to their policy on freshness."

Setting Goals Setting specific goals is usually more effective than a generalized good intention to cut back on the food bill. Lynne Coates of Oregon, explains that "It's easy to say, 'I'll cut back $10 a week on food money,' but to actually do it, it's much easier if you figure 'This week I'll hold my meat purchases to $5 and cut $1 off the amount of cheese I buy, and so on.) Then if it doesn't work, you know you need to try cutting something else."

"We have an occasional 'No Groceries Week,' " Claudia Barber of Indiana writes. "It's not actually NO groceries, so it's not as dire as it sounds. For one week, we limit our purchases to dairy products and fresh fruit and, in the winter, salad greens. We spend about $15 instead of our usual $50 on groceries, an easy way to 'earn' $35. And WHAT do we eat? We clean out the pantry and freezer and use up all the odd cans of tomato sauce that had been 'lost' and the liver that *somehow* kept getting overlooked. We take what we have and find or alter a recipe to fit the ingredients, rather the other way around." Claudia says that some of their new creations don't get rave reviews "but others become new standbys."

Estimating Costs   Coleen Mast of Illinois tells us her family spends about a dollar a day per person for food, excluding milk. "None of our three hungry children is ever denied nutritious food. Not one of us is overweight, and we are all healthy."

The figure of a dollar a day per person, or thereabouts, is mentioned most frequently by those who included an amount on how much they spend for food. "I feed a family of four for $25—$35 a week," writes a mother from the Midwest. "I feed a family of six for around $35—$50 a week, and that includes cleaning supplies and toilet paper," says another mother, who buys all of the groceries at "the co-op or warehouse type store." Giving one of the lowest figures, a mother in the West says she spends $25 a week on food for a family of five, and, she adds, "this includes a teenager."

With a household of hearty eaters another mother mentions, "With three adults and four children, we spend about $100 a week for food, less when garden harvest time is here."

Many factors can affect a family's outlay of money for food: access to a garden, the ability to raise some animals, the opportunity to shop at low-cost, discount markets, or the availability of a good food co-op.

Preparing Your Food

When it comes to food preparation, you'll want to have one eye on good nutrition and the other on good food value.

Starting from Scratch   For better nutrition, truer flavor, and bigger savings, *make your own*—whether it's your own mixes, main dishes, or munchies. Coleen Mast of Illinois makes "every food we can from scratch, from soup to salad dressing to biscuits."

"Memorize your family's favorite recipes," advises Joann Grohman from Maine. "Once you have that recipe in your head, it somehow seems a lot less trouble to assemble and is an excellent way to stay away from costly quickies. Muffins, cookies, pancakes, and quick breads seem to spring from your hands once you no longer have to hunt for the recipe and study it."

Along this same line, learn to estimate how much a tablespoon or a teaspoon of an item is in the palm of your hand. For example, pour a teaspoon of salt into your hand a number of times until you can judge that amount without using a measuring spoon. It's another way to speed the work along. Also, measure out the flour needed for the simple recipes you use frequently, pour it into the mixing bowl, and note how high it comes up. You'll soon find you can simply scoop the flour directly into the bowl without counting cupfuls.

When making the family's favorite nutritious muffins, Janis McCauley, Virginia, bakes a double recipe. The extras go into the freezer for lunches. To conserve energy, she bakes quick breads, such as banana nut bread, in muffin pans. "Muffins require less time in the oven—twenty minutes as opposed to an hour for the loaf size," she notes. Sometimes, too, when she's making an item such as muffins, she'll measure out enough dry ingredients for a second batch, and store in a plastic bag. Then at a later time when she wants to make a "super quick treat," she only needs to add the liquid. Having the rest premeasured saves the time of assembling and measuring all the ingredients.

Baking bread is not only economical and therapeutic, but nothing else quite matches the aroma and mouthwatering goodness of homemade bread from the oven. If you're new to bread baking, start out by making only one or two loaves at a time. A good recipe is a tremendous help, but better yet is to watch an experienced bread maker mix and knead the dough and then prepare it for the oven.

"I'm the bread baker for the family," Phyllis Nelson of Minnesota writes. "This is probably where I learned to become an experimenter in my kitchen. Once the first batch came out, I sought to improve or alter future efforts. What a grand way to use up those different, end-of-the-bin flours. From this dabbling has come a seven-grain bread that gets better with each baking."

In British Columbia, Canada, Margaret Anderson has found that "a real economy is making my own bread. I buy baking yeast from our corner bakery for $1.25 a pound, making the cost of the yeast I use per loaf literally a few cents, much less than the usual packages of granulated yeast."

Sue Brown of North Carolina has a unique way of baking her bread in the summertime that avoids heating up the house "A gas grill came with our house, so I bake bread on it in hot weather, as well as do other cooking. We get organic flour and baking yeast so cheap, I can't afford not to bake our bread," Sue says.

Maurine Joens of Arkansas has found that with a longer raising time, she needs less yeast: "I use one tablespoon of yeast per twenty-eight cups of flour. I mix the bread before going to bed, put in only one tablespoon of yeast, and by morning the dough has risen fully and can be baked first thing."

With a little encouragement, you'll probably find that other family members enjoy getting into the bread-baking act. And you have ready helpers in your preschoolers. Few toys hold more fascination than a piece of bread dough that can be pulled, poked, and made into endless shapes before going into the oven. You'll have no trouble recognizing the children's masterpieces: They take on a kind of gray look from all that kneading with those busy little fingers!

One mother-at-home found that a small styrofoam cooler works beautifully to make homemade yogurt. It keeps the milk-

Four-year-old Stephanie Brown lends a hand in shaping loaves of bread.

yogurt culture at just the right temperature and eliminates the need for an electric yogurt maker. Judy Souder of Texas makes her own yogurt and uses it in place of sour cream. "I also make salad dressing with yogurt instead of mayonnaise," she says. Another young mother, Teresa Strom of Illinois, passes on this recipe for a delicious, very fresh tasting salad dressing or vegetable dip: Mix equal parts of yogurt, buttermilk, and mayonnaise. Season with finely chopped onion, garlic, parsley, salt and pepper to taste. Blend well and enjoy.

Making the Most of Meat Meat can make one of the biggest dents in a food budget. Knowing how to prepare it to get the most out of your meat dollar can result in big savings. "The best steaks I've ever eaten came from a blade chuck roast, still one of the cheapest cuts of meat around," Angie Martin of Maryland reports. She buys the blade chuck roast on sale, and looks for a piece of meat that is thick and has a large eye.

"The blade bone divides the meat into two parts, the eye, with a circular grain and another part with a straight, diagonal grain. Using a sharp boning knife, separate the eye from the blade," she advises. "Remove any other bone or membrane. Turn the eye piece on its side and cut it into slices. To cook them, brush with oil and sprinkle with garlic and pepper. Broil a few minutes on each side until done." The remaining sections of the roast can be cut into thick slices or pieces to be cooked long and slow with liquids in Swiss steak or for a delicious stew. The bones can go into the stew or the soup pot.

Learn new skills by working with like-minded friends...

Katie Fowler of Texas buys wholesale cuts of pork, lamb, or beef and cuts them up herself: "Honestly, five years ago I had never seen a chicken whole. For that matter, I could not make yeast breads or sew, either, and now these are jobs I tackle every week and save." (Note: Always wash the knives and cutting boards used for cutting up chicken with hot, soapy water. A quick rinse will not do. Better yet, have a separate cutting board for raw meats. Most commercially processed chicken has salmonella which could cause food poisoning.) Katie learned her new skills by reading and also by working with like-minded friends. "I learned what's a really good buy, and we actually eat less meat now because I've learned how to cut it and cook it more efficiently." The fact that she is not working outside her home gives her more time for reading and learning. "I really appreciate this time of my life."

Susan Glennon of South Dakota substitutes turkey for beef in many of her meals. Susan buys the largest size turkey she can find and uses it in a variety of menus. "I freeze up bags of turkey for turkey tacos, turkey lasagna, sweet-and-sour turkey, turkey fried rice, stir-fried turkey and vegetables—the possibilities are endless and delicious." To save money, avoid the "butter-basted" variety of turkey. The bird is injected with oil, not butter—a procedure that adds to the cost of the turkey but not to the taste. You can have a juicy bird by basting it a few times when roasting it. If you cook it breast side down, the juice will drain *into* the drier white meat, instead of out of it.

Chicken is an economical choice as a main dish, for chicken sandwiches, or for salads. There is no easier way to prepare a chicken than whole and unadorned, in the oven at 400 degrees for about an hour and fifteen minutes. If you bake potatoes and vegetables along with the chicken, you can save money by making optimum use of the oven once it's turned on. To get even greater mileage out of your dinner preparations, tuck an extra chicken in the pan and bake it for delicious lunches. No lunch meat that you could buy would be as fresh and free of preservatives as this roasted chicken. If the chickens fit snugly together in the pan, be sure to rotate them midway through the cooking period in order to assure even cooking. (The sides that had been together should then be facing the outside of the pan where there is greater heat circulation).

Jill Holloran of Virginia suggests a quick way to prepare chicken livers, a healthy but inexpensive food: In a small amount of oil or butter, sauté the chicken livers for five minutes. Jill recommends that the meat still be pink inside when you spoon it out of the pan. The chicken livers can be served over rice, or with crackers. Instead of buying chicken livers, save the livers that come packaged with your whole chickens until you have enough for a meal. Liver is highly perishable, so keep it in the freezer until you are ready to prepare it.

During the hot summer months, Angela Marvin of Pennsylvania cooks pot roasts of beef or pork and turkey roasts on top of the stove in the morning when it's cooler. She cooks the meat for several meals at one time, divides the meat into meal-size portions, and freezes them for later use.

Meatless Menus   Many families are eating more meatless meals, both for health reasons and for budget reasons. Beans and rice in various combinations are popular meat substitutes. "We have gradually cut down on the amount of meat we eat, having it now only twice a week," says Colleen Houston, a mother from British Columbia, Canada. This happy transformation in eating habits is due in good part, Colleen feels, to having presented the family with satisfying and tasty meatless dishes.

Cindy George's husband, Brian, considers their family to be "half veggie." This Michigan family eats vegetarian meals about half the time. "Cheese enchiladas and kidney bean loaf are two of our all-around favorite meals now, and WHOLE FOODS FOR THE WHOLE FAMILY rapidly took its place as my favorite cookbook," Cindy writes. The La Leche League cookbook features numerous meatless dishes in addition to meat recipes. It also gives examples of which foods to combine in order to assure optimum nutrition. "I'm always trying out new recipes, so we never get bored with our meals, and none of us feels too deprived because we're not eating steak or buying soft drinks or potato chips," Cindy explains. "Feeding my family delicious, nutritious, and economical meals has become a source of pride for me!"

Linda Butler of Utah substitutes tofu for ground beef because "ground beef costs about $1.50 a pound, has a lot of fat, and serves only four to five people. In comparison, a pound of tofu costs under a dollar, has no fat, and serves eight—twice the protein for two-thirds of the cost, and fewer calories."

From Arkansas, Kathy Kotora plans her summer meals around her garden. "When our vegetable garden is ready, we become summer vegetarians—corn on the cob, lettuce salad, zucchini soup, green been casserole, and, of course, our favorite, fresh vegetables and a dip." She explains that meat becomes more of a side dish because the vegetables are free.

Foods that Stretch   One of the secrets to saving money on food is knowing how to make good food go farther. For ex-

Patty Meadows has seven good reasons to economize.

ample, a pound of soft butter can be mixed with a cup of safflower or other unsaturated oil to create a spread that tastes like butter but has less saturated fat than regular butter.

When making tacos, Mary Kastendieck of Colorado uses a half and half mixture of cooked ground beef and mashed, cooked pinto or other beans: "This makes the meat go a lot farther without changing the taste that much."

Judy Souder of Texas adds lentils or brown rice to her meat loaf. For sloppy joes or stroganoff, she mixes cooked, whole wheat with the ground beef.

At the Meadows' house, potatoes are mashed with the water they are cooked in. "Just add some butter, and you'll need little or no milk," Patty Meadows insists. Other mothers-at-home add powdered milk to the potato water. Either way, the vitamin-rich potato water is not wasted, and the potatoes stay piping hot. Patty suggests mixing leftover mashed potatoes with an egg or two to make potato cakes, which can be cooked slowly in a little butter or oil until golden brown.

Avoid buying fruit juice in cans that are labeled with the words "drink" or "ade," such as Grape Drink or Orange Ade. These mixtures are high in sugar content and contain much more water than fruit juice. If you buy frozen juice concentrate you can make it go farther by adding extra water. Angie Martin of Maryland has found that the addition of a little fresh lemon juice intensifies the flavor of most juices.

Don't overlook the thirst-quenching power and unbeatable price of plain water. "In our family, fruit juice is saved for special treats," Suzanne Parker of Georgia writes. "We use water to quench our thirst. I keep a small container of ice water in the door of the refrigerator for each child. Each one can help himself at any time directly from the container, which saves lots of dirty glasses." The Parkers also carry water on trips or picnics: "A little lemon juice squeezed into the water is very refreshing." Suzanne puts the juice of half a lemon and the rind in a thermos jug of ice water.

When Mary Kastendieck of Colorado prepares for a family outing, she washes out a gallon disposable milk container, fills it half full of water, and then freezes it. When the family is ready to leave, she adds water or juice to fill the container. "We always have an icy cold drink with us this way," Mary says.

Homemade soup can be a great food stretcher. A thick, hearty soup can be served for supper with fresh baked bread, or it can provide a quick, nourishing lunch. The secret to good soup is in the stock, which can come from foods or food parts that many people throw in the garbage.

Set aside three containers in your refrigerator or your freezer for collecting leftovers which can become soup ingredients. One container can be used for collecting the liquid left over from cooking vegetables, rice, or pasta as well as leftover gravies or meat juices.

In another tub or large plastic bag, save bones and any meat scraps— fowl and beef are best for this purpose. A turkey carcass with any leftover skin in itself represents a foundation

Susan Lebbing thinks it's fun to help mom make soup from scratch.

for a large pot of soup. When scraping dinner plates, separate any bones into a colander, rinse them quickly, and deposit them in your bone bag. Soup-maker Debbie Koppenheffer of Pennsylvania discovered that her local supermarket sells bones for the dog for five cents a pound, while the big soup bones in the meat counter cost fifty-nine cents a pound. Debbie suggests that you ask your butcher if "doggie bones" are available.

The last bag or tub in your soup-making collection is for vegetable scraps—either leftover cooked vegetables or what remains when you clean fresh vegetables (celery tops, outer leaves of lettuce, the woody ends of other vegetables). Go sparingly with strong, distinctive-tasting vegetables, such as cabbage, brussels sprouts, cauliflower, broccoli.

Early in the morning on soup-making day, empty the bone and vegetable scrap bags into a large, heavy pot. Check the refrigerator at this time for any limp stalks of celery, parsley, stray carrots, or soft tomatoes. Using such items in the soup prevents them from accumulating to the point where they must be pitched in the garbage.

Break the bones if necessary, cover all these ingredients with water, add any spices you like, and bring the mixture to a boil. Then turn the heat down to the point where the surface just quivers, with maybe an occasional bubble coming to the top, and let your soup cook all day. Long cooking is the secret to a rich broth.

After the soup has cooked sufficiently, strain it into a good-sized pot and dispose of the bones and vegetable remains. At this point, add the liquid you've been saving. After bringing it again to a boil, begin adding whatever else you want in the soup that week—barley or rice, freshly cut vegetables, onions, potatoes, carrots, or green beans—which need cook only until tender. You may also want to add a can of stewed tomatoes or tomato juice. Last add any cooked meat, such as leftover turkey.

If you prefer, you can refrigerate the stock after you've drained it and keep it on hand to use as a base for cooking rice or in casseroles or to serve as a quick and delicious broth for lunch or to start off dinner.

An advantage of making your own soup is that you can control the amount of salt in the finished product. Canned soups are high in sodium, the part of salt that causes problems. One cup of most canned soups contains more sodium than a three-ounce serving of ham, a large dill pickle, or fifty potato chips.

Preserving Foods   One way to get more food value for your money is to buy fresh foods when they are low in price and store them for later use.

In Oregon, the Desmarteau family likes to take advantage of the many opportunites in the area to get truly fresh produce for less money by going to a field or orchard and picking it themselves. Kitty's daughter Heather has been helping with the canning and freezing "since she could hold a butter knife, and I let her cut up peaches while I filled jars," Kitty says.

"I learned to can from a neighbor," says Phyllis Nelson of Minnesota. "We shared the work and kitchen space. It was an opportunity as well for letting our little ones play together. Since that first year, I've learned to work on my own and have purchased my own pressure cooker."

An old and reliable source of help in homemaking and agricultural matters is the Cooperative Extension Service. You can attend classes on food preservation, including canning, at your local Extension Service Facility.

The Hokansons in Wyoming buy fruit by the bushel, and the whole family helps can the winter's supply. Many of their vegetables come from their garden. According to Julina, "Because of our cold weather and short growing season, we go heavy on carrots, beets, peas, onions, herbs, and cabbage. We store the carrrots in a root cellar, bottle the beets, dry the onions and herbs, and turn the cabbage into the most delicious sauerkraut." The Hokansons also store in their root cellar about 800 pounds of potatoes, which they purchase from a farmer friend. "Potatoes are an everyday staple here," Julina says, "like homemade bread and milk."

Buy fresh foods and store them for later...

New Yorker Lisa Demunck writes, "I can tomatoes and tomato sauce, pickles, relishes, ketchup, and pickled beets. We try to grow mostly things that I can put up. I grate my zucchini and freeze it in bags or freezer containers in two-cup amounts. When I want to make zucchini bread or need some for quiche, it's pre-measured and handy."

In North Carolina, Jocelyn Butler prefers to purchase fresh fruits in season and freeze them for later use. "Canning tomatoes," she says, "was not a success. The weather was too hot!"

Some mothers-at-home prefer to can certain fruits without using sugar, thus saving the cost of the sugar and eliminating sugar's empty calories and bad effect on the teeth. Angie Martin of Maryland explains how she cans *ripe* peaches and pears without sugar (under-ripe fruit does not lend itself to this method): "Select good-looking fruit and lay it out in the basement, or another cool, dry spot, on newspapers. Check it every day for ripeness, taking out any pieces that have bad spots. These can be eaten that day. When the fruit is at the peak of ripeness— just starting to be soft—drop everything and can. Pack the peaches or pears into clean wide-mouth jars, pour boiling water to fill, and seal as usual. Process for the recommended amount of time." Angie says that the fruit will make its own syrup in about two weeks. "It's delicious," she says, "and healthier than the canned fruit you buy. My children love it for breakfast with homemade yogurt." Applesauce also holds up well when prepared without sugar.

Filling up a freezer is the best way to get the maximum return on the cost of owning and operating it. Phyllis Nelson of Minnesota uses her freezer to store her bulk bread, juice, and vegetable purchases, as well as a side of beef. "We've been asked how we manage to buy the meat. Each month a sum of money is automatically deducted from my husband's pay and placed in the credit union to be used for replenishing our meat supply. In January, when most budgets are strained from the holidays, we can take advantage of lower beef prices with ready money."

The freezer is also useful for storing ready-prepared meals that need only be thawed and heated for an easy supper.

Natural cheese is better for freezing than processed cheese, and can often be bought cheaper in a large block. Before freezing the cheese, cut it into portions that are right for your family and wrap them well in plastic. When thawed, the cheese will be a little more crumbly than when fresh, but freezing will not detract from its flavor. Cheese can also be grated before it's frozen. "I *hate* to measure grated cheese," Janis McCauley says. Janis has found that four ounces of cheese equals one cup grated. "When I started weighing the cheese beforehand, I didn't have to measure by the cupful. It's great."

Charity and Celeste Koppenheffer play with their baby sister Celina.

Patty Meadows of Virginia freezes ripe bananas after mashing them with a fork. Darkening does not affect their use in breads and cakes.

Dry bread can also be frozen once it has been cut into crouton size and placed in a plastic bag with a locking top. On a day you're using the oven, you can spread these croutons on a cookie sheet, sprinkle them with oil or butter mixed with a little soy sauce, garlic powder, or Italian seasoning. The croutons can be toasted when whatever else you are baking is finished and the oven is turned off. The retained heat is just enough to crisp them. Croutons can be used on salads, in soup, to top casseroles, for stuffing, or in meat loaf. Marsha Robison's little boy does not like the crust of the bread, so she cuts off the crust before fixing sandwiches for him. These crusts go into a bag in the freezer to be used for either bread crumbs or bread pudding.

Even breakfast foods, such as leftover pancakes or French toast, can be frozen in plastic bags and reheated in the toaster. Little ones don't always eat a whole piece of fruit. Debbie Koppenheffer in Pennsylvania freezes such odd pieces of fruit until she has enough to combine with milk and a little honey in the blender for a delicious fruit shake.

Karen Six, Ohio, simplifies freezing by placing a freezer bag into an appropriate size rigid container, filling the bag, and when the contents are frozen, removing the bag. The container can be used again, and, she points out, the squared bags can be stacked neatly.

Dry It   Before the canning process was discovered or the freezer was invented, people were preserving food by drying it. The sun will furnish the energy needed to dry your fruits or vegetables if you live in an area where the weather is dry and sunny in the summer rather than hot and humid. A *dehydrator*—a box-like apparatus with numerous shallow shelves—can achieve the desired result no matter what the weather. An efficient dehydrator costs about $100, but you can build your own from plans available from *The Mother Earth News*, P. O. Box 70, Hendersonville, North Carolina 28791.

Drying is the least expensive way to preserve food...

A friend built Alice Barbiere's dehydrator, which turns slices of apple or bananas that Alice's two-year-old or four-year-old might not finish into tasty long-lasting snacks. This New Jersey mother sees the dehydrator as a way to recycle food. Compared to the cost of prepackaged snacks and the loss of food that might otherwise be wasted, the cost of operating a dehydrator is negligible. Julina Hokanson built their dehydrator, which holds about one-half bushel of fruit at a time, for about $50. "By winter, we try to have ten gallon jugs filled with a variety of dried fruits and vegetables," she says.

Drying is considered the simplest and least expensive way to preserve food. Without fuss or special equipment, you can easily dry fresh herbs. Simply wrap a small bundle of parsley, chives, dill, or other herb with a string and hang in a dry place where air can circulate around it. You'll know it's dried when it crumbles between your fingers. Crush and store the dried herb in a cool, dark place, but use an empty container that has only held the same herb.

Breakfast, Lunch, and Snacks   A good way to start the day is with a hearty breakfast. It doesn't have to cost a lot to serve your family a nourishing breakfast.

Several mornings a week serve a tasty homemade granola or steaming bowls of old-fashioned oats rather than more expensive ready-to-eat cereals. (Starting oats and water together rather than waiting for water to boil before adding oats shortens the cooking time to just minutes.)

Lunches are always a challenge, especially when there are school-aged children in the family. Patty Meadows, who packs lunches for five youngsters, believes the typical lunch-meat type of sandwich, "aside from being expensive, can also get boring." Instead of sandwiches, her children "like last night's biscuits and some chunks of cheese or leftover meat or leftover homemade whole-wheat pizza."

A wholesome, economical, and good-tasting snack that everybody likes, is popcorn. Nothing beats popcorn hot off the stove, with just a hint of salt or a sprinkle of grated cheese. If you cook it in oil, you don't even need butter. Popcorn also packs well in lunches.

Special Times   Meal time is a social time for family members. The call to dinner is a call to gather round, to reassure each other that we are family and belong together. It is a traditional way, too, to entertain and enjoy the good company of others. Yes, you can entertain with fun and food even on a limited income. "It's fun to cook and fuss over company," Cindy George writes. "Even though there may not be meat on the table, there are candles and cloth napkins!" In the state of Michigan where the George family lives and where unemployment is high, young couples know how to make the most of simple fare and inexpensive entertainment. The Lozens, also from Michigan and also facing unemployment, socialize with others at potluck dinners where the whole family is included. "We rarely spend money on sitters for our children," Peggy Lozen explains.

If you host a cooperative dinner, each couple or family can bring a contribution to a multitaste delight. You might want to pick a theme for your dinner party and divide the courses among those coming. Everyone could share the cost of the main entree, which would still make the total cost per person much less than eating out at a nice restaurant. Or, if you find that dinner is more than you're up to, invite another family over to enjoy dessert with you. At any time, you could do as Helene Fowler of Washington suggests, and have friends over for hors d'oeuvres or a snack, something to drink, and conversation.

When the Parkers of California are in the mood for a romantic dinner for two but there isn't enough in the budget for an evening out, "we have discovered," Denise writes, "that we can have that steak, lobster, or shrimp dinner at home for about half or one-third the price of going out. We make a real party of it. I buy some inexpensive flowers for the table, get out the china and crystal, and fix a really special meal here at home. Early in the day, I get everything ready, making the meal as simple as possible. Then, after the kids are in bed for the night, my husband and I do the finishing touches together and have a wonderful candlelight dinner in private. Clean up afterwards just waits until the next morning. We enjoy it because there is no pressure to get the kids home from Grandma's, and no waiter is hurrying us along."

The element of surprise can turn ordinary meals into something special and is also one of the best ways to put an end to a day when everything's-gone-wrong-and-there's-nothing-ready-for supper. In fact, with a little sleight-of-hand you can turn it into a lovely evening. A mother-at-home who lives in France, Hilary Rocca, tells how to work your magic.

"If dinner isn't ready and you're looking dreadful, start with a quick beauty routine. Put on something different from what you were wearing when your husband left in the morning, preferably something a little glamorous, and spray on some perfume. Now for dinner: Set the table, using a cloth and candles. Cut up some chunks of cheese and serve with a glass of wine while you cook up something fast—an omelette accompanied by cucumber spears and fresh fruit, perhaps, and you've transformed what could have been a disastrous homecoming into a huge success!"

Invite another family over to enjoy dessert...

For even more culinary variety, Pamela Duffy, Colorado, says that her husband Duane took a French gourmet cooking class at an adult education program. "He enjoys cooking as a form of relaxation," she explains, then adds, "but I think I'm the one reaping the benefits!"

The Duffys, who have five children ranging in age from one to twelve, have become something of experts, too, on the subject of making ends meet when mom stays at home. "Our family has learned—yes, it was a learning process—to cope in a variety of ways," Pamela writes. "We garden, can, and freeze our food, clip coupons, sew, shop at garage sales and secondhand stores. We've become quite informed about simple home remedies for minor illnesses. We encourage the children to 'use it up, make do, or do without.' We've taken bill consolidation loans, and more than once, Duane has taken a temporary second job to see us through rough spots."

Is it worth it? The Duffys think so. "Family life is often difficult," Pamela concedes, "and perhaps making ends meet is one of the roughest parts. But I would be the first to state that the sacrifices are worth it, a million times worth it. In our struggles, though, it's nice to know that we aren't alone, that others too believe strongly in the value of mother being home."

Suggested Further Reading

Johnson, Roberta Bishop, ed. *Whole Foods for the Whole Family.* La Leche League International, 1981.

Goldbeck, David and Nikki. *The Supermarket Handbook.* New York: Signet Books, 1976.

Ellis, Merle. *Cutting Up in the Kitchen: A Butcher's Guide to Saving Money on Meat and Poultry.* San Francisco: Chronicle Books, 1975.

Home Canning of Fruits and Vegetables. Superintendant of Documents, U. S. Government Printing Office, Washington, D. C. 20402.

Food Safety for the Whole Family. USDA-FSIS Publications, Room 1163-S, Washington, D.C. 20250. Free.

CHAPTER 9

*C*ouponing, *C*o-oping, and *C*ultivating

Sometimes just keeping an eye out for value in the process of planning, procuring, and preparing food doesn't seem to make enough of a dent in the food budget. Some mothers-at-home have found it helpful, or even necessary, to take more drastic action in the battle against the food bill even to the point of turning an activity such as couponing, co-oping, or gardening into a small business they can run at home. The key to success in these areas, as in any business undertaking, is a combination of know-how and commitment.

Coupons and Refunds

Although one coupon or one refund may not represent a significant saving compared to your total food budget, for those who can be systematic about clipping and collecting on these small slips of paper, the savings can add up over the year to hundreds of dollars.

The first step is to set up your system. Couponing involves collecting, sorting, and redeeming coupons; refunding involves saving labels, proofs of purchase, and sales receipts and mailing these in, usually along with special refund forms.

Getting Organized   Barb McFadden of Michigan has found that although organization is essential, "equipment needs are minimal: a card table or two, empty shoe boxes for filing labels and proofs of purchase, a pen, scissors, stamps, envelopes, and a notebook."

A coupon is a certificate entitling you to a stated reduction in the price of a specified item at the time of purchase. Two coupons cannot be applied to the same item. If you have five coupons for ten cents off on frozen apple juice, for example, you can apply them to five cans of the juice in one shopping trip, but you could not apply all five coupons to one can to get fifty cents off. Coupons that have the store's name on them are not the same as manufacturer's coupons. You can apply both a store and a manufacturer's coupon to a single item.

Nancy Griffin of Illinois has found couponing and refunding to be quite profitable and offers some guidelines for those just getting started:

1. *Collect as many coupons as possible for items that you normally use, such as detergents, juice, or paper products.* Nancy had collected nineteen fifty-cent-off coupons for a certain brand of detergent when the quart size, which usually sold for $2, went on sale for 99¢. By using her coupons, she was able to buy nineteen bottles of detergent for 49¢ each.

2. *Look for coupons and refund-offer forms in newspapers, sale flyers, magazines, and in the mail.* You can also ask friends, relatives, and neighbors to save coupons for you. If you hesitate to ask them to comb through their papers for coupons, tell them that you'll be happy to pick up their old papers and magazines. Older children could conduct a neighborhood paper drive once a week. Look for coupons primarily in the food section. Save some coupons and refund forms for products that

you do not use; you may be able to trade the unwanted coupons for those you can use.

3. *On each coupon, circle the expiration date and any information on what size must be purchased.* Some coupons can be applied to any size, which makes them easier to use. If no expiration date is given, write NED for "no expiration date" on the front of the coupon. Because these conditions are often printed in very tiny type or buried in a long paragraph of instructions to the store dealer, they can be time-consuming to locate again.

4. *A simple filing system saves time in the long run.* Nancy files her coupons in a shoe box, which she takes with her when she goes shopping. The coupons are arranged by categories—*detergents, juices, frozen goods,* and so on—with each category separated by a divider.

In refunding, instead of giving a price reduction on a purchase, the manufacturer sends you money, a coupon for a free item, or some other gift in exchange for an identifying mark or proof of purchase from the product package. (These are called qualifiers.) Friends and relatives can be a major source of the labels, boxtops, or other proofs of purchase that must be collected and mailed in to get the refund. Information on what refunds are currently being offered is available through refunding columns which appear in many newspapers. Refund forms tell you what is required and can be found in stores, newspapers, and magazines. You can send away for some forms, and with other offers, you don't need the printed form— you can send the qualifiers with your name and address on a three by five card.

Serious refunders automatically save the box or label from almost any product they use that they think might someday be featured in a refund offer. Nancy Griffin of Illinois recommends designating a drawer or a box in your kitchen where you can quickly deposit any labels or packaging as well as your cash register receipts (which are often required). "It's really just as easy to put them in this drawer or box as it is to toss them into the wastebasket," Nancy points out. "Then every few weeks, you can go through your qualifiers and sort them into product type and put them into bags or envelopes marked with the type of product, such as canned goods or paper products." Labels on jars pose a special problem, since they usually come off only with soaking.

Many refunders have boxes of boxtops, labels, and wrappers...

"This can be a pain," Nancy admits, "and you may decide as I did that it's too much trouble and you're just going to forget the jars. Then a refund will come out asking for the qualifiers that you have been throwing away for the past six months, and those labels you didn't want to soak off are worth a dollar apiece! Then you start soaking!"

The big question among refunders concerns what to save: which part of the package should you keep? Often, the proof of purchase seal is enough. The Universal Product Code (UPC)—that series of lines and numbers printed on the package—may be all that is needed, but be sure to note the name of the product next to the code before cutting it off. Nancy says that some companies always ask for the same identification from the package, while others change their requirements from offer to offer. On canned goods, save the entire label. With detergents, the net weight statement is commonly what's needed. If you're in doubt on the matter, save the whole package. Flatten it so it takes up less space. You can throw out what you don't need once you get the refund form and know what is required. Many refunders have boxes upon boxes in their basements and garages of boxtops, labels, and wrappers.

If the manufacturer asks for a proof-of-purchase seal that doesn't appear on the package you have, send in the whole label. Sometimes the refund forms come out before the special packaging appears in the stores. Nancy Griffin offers the following tips for beginning refunders:

1. *Keep close tabs of refund expiration dates and mail early:* manufacturers are allowing less time now than they have in the past for sending for an offer.
2. *Use a sturdy envelope when mailing a number of bulky items, and secure the flap with a piece of tape.* Just licking it may not hold. Put a staple through the qualifiers to hold them together. If coins are included, tape them to a three by five card. If the envelope is more than one-quarter inch thick, which may be the case when you're sending a number of wrappers along with the form, this oversized envelope will need extra postage, even if the weight is under one ounce.
3. *Keep a record of the offers you've sent for* including what you sent and when it was mailed. One dedicated refunder places a piece of carbon paper and an index card inside the envelope before addressing it. As she writes the address of the company or agent giving the refund, she is also making a record for herself. She also makes a quick notation on the card of the date and what she's sending in for.

Getting the Maximum Savings People are either very enthusiastic about coupons and refunds, or they practically ignore them. Some swear that substantial amounts of money can be saved with them; others shrug their shoulders and say that they don't use the popular coupon items—the non-dairy creamers and the diet pop.

In order to save more than an occasional dollar or so on coupons and refunds, you need to know how to make these offers work to your greatest advantage. To do that, you must:

obtain coupons for items *you regularly use*;
use coupons so you're paying very little for your purchase,
  per ounce or pound.
apply five, ten, or more coupons for a particular item to bulk
  purchases.

Nancy Griffin of Illinois believes it is possible to save 25 to 75 percent on your grocery bills following a few basic procedures. Ann Sutherland of California decided to try refunding as a money-saving idea: "We found it did work for us, even though we are careful shoppers. We clipped cents-off coupons and got grandmas to save them for us, too. We looked for all kinds of refund forms and traded our extras with each other and with exchange pals through a refunding magazine."

"I dabble in refunding," Linda Greengas of Connecticut writes: "At times, I find it difficult to sit down and get organized. Even though I don't always put much time and effort into it, it does amount to a savings—from $100 to $300 a year."

In New Jersey, Cheryl Hutchinson finds that "the brand-name item is *still* more expensive, in spite of the coupon. I take carefully selected coupons to the store with me, but then compare the price of the store's own brand or a generic brand against the discounted coupon item."

"My 'home business' is couponing and refunding," says Diane Nuelsen of Kentucky. I easily made $50 to $60 in the last two months. I buy what's on sale, then use a cents-off coupon for it, and often there's a refund with it also. We eat according to sales and refund buys."

Debbie Smollen of Connecticut says that she saved "up to $50 in one month and received up to $20 in free merchandise." Debbie spends less than an hour a week on her project and involves the older children in soaking and clipping for her proof-of-purchase file.

"I'm an eager coupon clipper," Barb McFadden writes from Michigan, "For a while I belonged to a refunding club where the moms would save refund forms and swap them. It's easy to come home with a handful of forms and become obsessed with filling them out so as to get money back. I had to watch myself so I wasn't 1) spending all my time on it and neglecting the children's needs, 2) buying non-nutritious food, and 3) sending away for every little refund, in which case I'd actually lose money, considering my time and the cost of stamps and envelopes."

"When a store has a rock-bottom price on an item, take all the coupons you've been saving and buy as many as you can!" recommends Nancy Griffin. Apply your coupons to the smallest size allowable. Nancy tells of finding small tubes of toothpaste, regularly priced at 49¢ each, on sale for 29¢ each. Using her 25¢ off coupons, she was able to come home with a supply of toothpaste at 4¢ a tube. "These little tubes are especially nice," she adds, "when you have little ones who can waste a lot of toothpaste using a large tube."

"I easily made $50 to $60 in the last two months..."

Double Coupon day is a real bonus to a dedicated couponer. On such a day, a store figures coupons at double their face value, up to the cost of an item. If your double-value coupon is worth more than the product, you won't have to pay anything for it, but you won't get money back. Some stores set a certain dollar limit to the coupons that can be turned in. Even so, double coupon day is usually worth a special trip to the store. Nancy advises that get there early, since "the really great deals go fast." Also, announcement of a double coupon day may not appear in bold letters on a flyer, so scan it thoroughly for such a notice.

Baby was three months old when Karen Iwicki went back to her full-time job as a Field Systems Analyst. The company she worked for was very supportive of her desire to continue breastfeeding her daughter, but Karen says, "I cried merely because I couldn't stand being separated from my new baby."

Her husband suggested that she give staying home a try. He had just received a modest raise, but at about the same time, the Iwickis took on the care of a young nephew. Karen's reaction to being home was "Wow! Was I happy!" She was also determined to find ways to economize. The loss of her salary meant a cut of over $15,000 in their yearly income.

"I had 'played' with refunding the year before, but now I went at it with the fervor that only comes from the need to survive," she says. "I use coupons on sale items and trial sizes. I started saving my labels and boxes from all groceries. I sent for fifty-eight refunds in one month alone. Two months later, when we were really wondering if my being at home would work, the refunds began rolling in —two dollars, one dollar, a free package of juice, a free box of cereal, canned food, free samples of medicine, tissues, free eggs. It makes me feel good to go to the mailbox each day. There are more ways to help me feed and care for my family of four."

This Illinois family has learned to adjust in other ways, too, and now Karen says, "My husband and I sometimes wonder how we used to spend all that money."

The Food Co-op

Cooperative action may be the way to go in your search for nourishing foods at reasonable prices; in fact, as a member of a food co-op you could come home with superior products for less than the average supermarket price. "We save money on food by belonging to three co-ops," writes Glinda Pipkin from Texas. Once a month, Glinda splits a round of cheese with members of a cheese co-op and realizes a savings of sixty cents per pound on her twelve pound purchase. The Health Food co-op that she and twenty-five other families belong to buys brown rice in fifty pound bags, one hundred pounds of flour at a time, and peanut butter in thirty-five pound tubs. The Pipkins take turns with eight other families going to the Farmers' Market in Dallas for produce every two weeks.

The food co-op is mentioned again and again in letters from mothers-at-home as one way they economize. A Michigan mother, Cindy George, buys the bulk of her staples—flour, pasta, beans, dried fruits, grains, nuts, cheese, peanut butter, oils—at a food co-op. Eighty families belong to this co-op and each family works three times a year to purchase and distribute the food.

The ability to buy in quantity makes it possible for consumer co-ops to get wholesale prices on the things they buy. Costs are also lower because members provide the labor involved in buying and distributing the food. Only the very large co-ops have overhead expenses, and even then, profit is not a factor in setting prices. Larger co-ops have traditionally furnished their members with information on products and consumer issues. A smaller neighborhood food co-op may not have a formal educational program, but it does give people the chance to get together and learn from one another.

The idea of people working together to obtain a mutually needed product or service has been around for a long time, and the formation of the modern co-op dates from the mid 1800s. Among the most successful examples of such combined efforts are farm and union co-ops, although the credit union is probably the most widely known type of cooperative in the U.S.A.

Co-op members who are the most pleased with their experience give high points to the spirit of helpfulness among the members in their group. They also believe the variety and quality of the foods they receive are superior to food that can be purchased from the grocery store. "The flour and pasta are whole grain," Cindy George says, "and most of the food is organically grown. It's free of chemical additives, preservatives, and coloring—things that we feel it is important to avoid. We get better quality food at a better price."

Coleen Mast (far right of photo) and other co-op members meet to plan their order.

Finding The Right Co-op   In Ohio, Donna Laugle considers her membership in a neighborhood co-op to be one of their best and most successful money-saving projects. Ten nearby families are involved in the co-op. "I had previously belonged to a larger co-op," she says, "but found that I was spending too much time at meetings and with packaging."

Another advantage of co-ops is that there is no limit, other than the time involved, to the number to which you can belong. Families join together in different combinations and for various purposes in order to save money on foods. Judy Souder in Texas belongs to three co-ops, one for eggs, one for cheese, and one for produce. "The 'Egg Lady' goes to a farm that supplies eggs to stores and buys the seconds—the misshaped eggs—at a big savings. The 'Cheese Lady' gets cheese at a wholesale house, and the 'Produce Lady' goes to the Farmers' Market."

Helen Riley of Oklahoma looks upon the food co-op to which they belong as one of her pet economies. She finds that the food is fresher and usually of superior quality, but finds, too, that it pays to keep up with prices. When comparing the co-op price to the going rate at the supermarket, she found that most of the items cost somewhat less at the co-op—some considerably so—but that a few were more costly. Often, a co-op limits the kinds of food purchased. Katie Fowler's Texas co-op does not handle meat or frozen goods, for example.

In any investigation of co-ops, or buying clubs, as they are sometimes called, be aware that there is another genre of buying club that is not based on the cooperative philosophy of people joining together for their collective advantage. There are commercial, profit-making buying clubs that offer a buying service and may supply excellent merchandise but at a price that is usually considerable. They may make all kinds of promises of fabulous savings but what isn't as clearly spelled out is that they require members to pay large sums in membership fees. Stay clear of them; this is not what you want when you're trying to cut back on household expenses.

If you can't find a food co-op that meets your needs, you can, with the help of a few friends, launch your own. "The biggest money-saving project I've gotten involved in so far has been starting a food co-op with another La Leche League Leader," says Katie Fowler of Texas. "There are about thirteen other members, all with small children."

Summer Milton, a lawyer and mother-at-home in Texas, has found that "the main thing about forming a co-op is being sure everyone understands how things work and who is reponsible for what." The co-op experience can be less than rewarding if the division of labor is markedly unequal, as was the case for a family in Illinois. While one member would make the long trip to the market and load and unload the bushels and crates of produce, another member made no more of a contribution than to allow the use of a basement and unlock the door to it. Some members ordered for more than their own use and sold the surplus to nonmembers who did not share in the work in any way. This family took a second look at their involvement in the co-op.

How to Get Started   A small co-op can be set up to suit the members, but members must know what is expected of them. Sue Arnold of Virginia belongs to a fairly large co-op that uses a church as a distribution center, and provides worker members with detailed printed instructions. In a small group, one or two people at a time can handle the work with a minimum of paperwork. Of course, a small group might not get as good a price as would a larger co-op. The question to ask yourself is where you can get the right balance in food savings and time commitment.

In the Arnold's co-op, the work has been broken down into four main jobs: *Order Taker, Buyer, Sorter,* and *Cashier.* More than one person may be assigned to each job. A good-sized co-op may also use a *Coordinator* or *Manager* to oversee the operation, keep a current record of the membership, and send out notices.

The Order Taker is responsible for gathering members' orders and the approximate amount of money to cover the orders. Pre-payment is a must, as suppliers want to be paid in cash. Overpayments or shortages are settled when the members pick up their orders.

The Buyer does the actual shopping, either by phone or by going to the market, farm, or warehouse and selecting the produce, eggs, cheese, grains, or whatever. The buyer determines how much of each item to purchase by adding up the amounts from each member's order form. Some flexibility is necessary so the buyer can take advantage of the best prices. The member's order form should indicate with a plus or minus sign whether they would prefer more or less than the amount they have specified. The buyer should also be able to decide against buying something the members have ordered if the quality or price of the item is not acceptable, or to take advantage of an exceptionally good buy on another item.

The Buyer delivers the purchases to the distribution center—someone's basement or garage, perhaps—where the Sorter is ready to take over. An orderly system is needed to divide up the food according to the members' orders. A scale may be needed for weighing along with plastic bags, boxes, and tape. When more than one person acts as sorter, it's less confusing if each sorter takes a different item and fills each member's order for that item. Anything perishable should be divided last.

Next comes the job of the Cashier, who totals up the orders and figures out any amounts owed or overpayments. The cashier also determines that the total amount received covers the actual costs of the purchases. When the members arrive to pick up their orders, the cashier collects any amount due or makes a refund of overpayments.

The true co-op can be an excellent opportunity for savings and for a higher standard of living than would otherwise be possible. For more information on cooperatives, check your library for books on the subject, or write to: The Cooperative League of the United States, Inc., 1828 L Street, N.W., Suite 1100, Washington, DC 20036; or Cooperative Union of Canada, 111 Sparks Street, Ottawa, Ontario, Canada I1P 5B5.

The Farming Business

Gardening can be a source of fun and profit as well as the best eating imaginable. Commercially grown fruits and vegetables are regularly selected on the basis of how well they will hold up in shipping, not for flavor.

Gardens and the pioneering spirit naturally go together. Providing for one's family and making the earth productive are mutually compatible. For someone on a slim budget, a garden can make the difference between skimping on food and eating quite well. A survey conducted by the Gallup organization for a national nonprofit group, found that the typical home garden in 1982 yielded produce estimated to be worth $470 in retail cost.

Bountiful harvests don't just happen, of course. The very basic requirements are land and an interest in coaxing it to produce for you. If you have access to a plot somewhere, even a small space, on which to sow some seeds or set out a few plants, you'll soon know if the farming life appeals to you. Does the feel of warm earth crumbling through your fingers make you itch to start digging? Do you get a little thrill when you see the first tiny shoots poking up through the ground? If the joy of harvesting a pan full of tender green beans or a pail of berries obliterates the discomfort of a hot summer sun shining down on you and the buzzing of little things flying about you, you have green in your thumb. You just could be kin to the likes of Barbara Dick, who sees gardening as "essential." A mother in the state of Washington, Barbara says, "Watching my plants grow nourishes the soul." Certainly, anyone looking for a creative outlet and a way to save money would do well to try gardening.

How Does Your Garden Grow? The first thing you need to know is what will and will not grow on your piece of land—given your climate and soil conditions. Along with digging up facts about gardening, you'll want to consider how much time and money you can, and want to, invest in your new venture. Cathy Cutting writes from Ontario, Canada that "we spent a good amount of money on seeds, water, and manure and then found that our plot was too shady to get enough of a yield to make it worthwhile. Also, it restricted our weekend vacations, which were our major source of recreation." Cathy's parting words of advice are, "Research what you are getting into before you start."

A good way to begin learning is to talk to another gardener. The local garden club, if you have one, can undoubtedly put you in touch with someone who knows what is best suited to your area. Dedicated gardeners readily share helpful hints. If it's the season for things to be blooming, take a walking tour of your neighborhood and check out other gardens. When you

*Steve, Linda, and Jessica
Butler find gardening
worthwhile.*

find one that looks particularly good, make a point of striking up a conversation with the proud grower. You'll uncover a wealth of information. The Cooperative Extension Service is a dependable source. The Extension Service is well-known for its work with young people in 4H groups, which are more popular in rural areas, but it is every bit as ready to serve the urban gardener as well. They have gardening bulletins and booklets available for little or no cost and will also test soil samples for you, answer questions about garden planning, and advise on insect control. The control that the home gardener has over the use and the choice of insecticides is another recommendation for growing your own. You can make your part of the world and what you eat a little less polluted.

If this garden is your first attempt, think small rather than large. You can always expand next year and the year after that. If space is limited, you may not have much of a choice, but don't let the absence of a definite garden spot deter you. A salad garden can be managed in very little space and can be quite rewarding. Sallie Diamond of New Hampshire recalls that, "Even when we lived in apartments while my husband was in school, a little ingenuity generally provided us with at least a small gardening space. Once, in downtown Cleveland, the apartment manager gave me permission to beautify the yard by putting flowers and plants in front of the building. We alternated flowers with salad materials and had herbs in decorative arrangements.''

Kathleen Ever of California has always had a garden: "One flower pot on a sunny window sill is all that is needed to grow leaf lettuce.'' Kathleen notes that if only the leaves are cut for eating and the root is not pulled, this kind of lettuce continues to produce for months.

Claudia Barber of Indiana has a larger area of land available to her: "We grow 80 percent of the vegetables our family of five eats and some of the fruit in a little over 600 square feet of space.'' The Giesels in Florida garden intensively on about 2400 square feet. "We try to have something growing over most of the garden most of the time. This is economical and helps keep weeds from being a problem,'' Jean writes.

Gardening becomes more rewarding with planning, and the Giesels have found that by keeping records of the number and kind of plants grown, they have a fairly good idea of what will be about the right amount for successive plantings. Why have numerous cucumber plants when only a few will take care of the family's needs?

In Ontario, Canada, Mikell Billoki considers maintaining a substantial garden and orchard to be one way to reduce the amount of money they spend and at the same time live comfortably. Mikell admits that some careful planning and record keeping is required to make it a truly money-saving venture. "Each year we improve our skills,'' she says, and they now manage "to make our efforts pay off in year-round food supplies at a minimal cost.'' Since they live in a rural area, they are able to supplement garden fare with fish, game birds, or animals, fruits, plants, and mushrooms.

Christy Stamps of Illinois looks upon gardening as a business venture. In their first year, "We stopped counting as we passed $500 worth of food from our garden,'' Christy says. As the garden plot gets bigger, however, there's a greater need for specialized equipment, such as a tiller. With a bountiful harvest comes the need to preserve the surplus, which requires a freezer or canning equipment. One way to raise the necessary capital for these items, Christy notes, is to set aside the money saved in the first year or two of gardening and to reinvest it in supplies. Christy says she doesn't mind the hours she must put into her "business," because she can work planting and harvesting into convenient time slots. "The kids can get in on the fun and good eating as soon as they're old enough to know where not to step," she says.

Building up the soil and keeping it rich and fertile is necessary for any successful gardening. Composting can help return organic matter back to the soil and increase its yield. Another multiplying technique is double planting, which is particularly useful when garden space is limited. As the first crop is ripening, a second can often be planted in the same space. Yield can also be increased by selecting seeds that are described as being "jumbo" or "prolific" bearers. Many gardeners get a head start on spring by starting plants from seeds indoors in a sunny window.

Elaine Caper of Illinois reports that the strawberries in her patch are transplants from her neighbor's yard. When the neighbor decided to put flowers where the strawberries were growing, Elaine offered to dig them up for her. Many kinds of plants frequently need thinning to thrive, and the person who is willing to do a little spade work for the owner will be rewarded with some lovely additions to his or her own garden.

Harvesting ripe fruit that is weighing down trees and bushes can be a lot of work to owners. Many are happy to make the fruit available to anyone who wants to help with the harvesting. Ready with ladders and pails, the Koppenheffers in Pennsylvania spent Saturday afternoons one fall checking whether people wanted help picking their grapes. Debbie Koppenheffer reports that from what they picked they made twenty-five gallons of wine and many quarts of grape juice.

Even little ones like Jessica Butler enjoy helping in the garden.

Reciprocal arrangements can also be made for sharing specialized equipment for gardening and canning or even land. The Fallicks in Wisconsin have a large garden behind their house and also work other plots at times, at their church or on a friend's land. They borrow equipment and also loan their equipment to others.

Given some early exposure, many kids develop a lifelong fascination with growing things. Jj Fallick's six-year-old daughter Katy supplied all their parsley for the past two years from her own garden. Carol Barshack of Illinois reports, "Last year, my son Rob planted his garden in the *sandbox.* His choice was pumpkins seeds, and they overran the sandbox, but yielded four big pumpkins. He was so proud!" In Pennsylvania, the Koppenheffers planted blueberry bushes, "which, in the future, our daughters can pick to earn money," Debbie says. "We also grow and sell strawberries, earing between $50 and $150 a year, depending on the harvest."

Sandy Woolf's large garden in Ohio has a sand pile at one end for the children to play in while she works. With such an arrangement, little ones can be happily occupied and within mom's sight.

Raising Livestock In recent years, modern-day pioneers have re-established old ties with food-producing animals and are again finding room for them on the homestead. Of course, where you live and the amount of space available are important considerations in the matter (not to mention the neighbors), but don't automatically rule out the possibility of keeping some livestock.

According to Joann Grohman of Maine, "If you've been able to keep dogs, cats, hampsters, and goldfish alive, why not put that time and money into something that helps feed you? Six hens are less trouble than a cat and cost next to nothing to feed. While few municipalities forbid hens, there are restrictions on some farm animals. To me, a sheep tethered on the lawn is far less offensive than most dogs. So is a suitably housed pig. Rabbits provide more quality protein for less feed, work, and space than any other domestic animal." She says a milk goat is a little more trouble and less profitable than other animals, but is a good starter animal for people who want to keep livestock, while a cow can be highly profitable. "On as little as a quarter acre, not only can a cow save money; it can truly generate income."

Jerri Forsyth of Nova Scotia decided to get a cow because she didn't drive and they live several miles from town: "I milk her in the morning before the children are up, and a neighbor milks her in the evenings. The children go with me to the barn in the late afternoon to do chores. They learn to care for and to respect an animal. I make my own butter, cheese, and yogurt. We also have plenty of whipping cream and sour cream."

"We all have allergies to cow's milk, and so we raise milk goats," explains Mary Ellen Schilke of Georgia." A goat costs less than a dog and gives a wholesome food in return, not to mention what a great pet she is."

The Koppenheffers of Pennsylvania keep twelve chickens and have added two goats to their homestead. "We feed them spent plants from the garden—lettuce, broccoli, cabbage leaves, cauliflower leaves, corn stalks—and any clover and weeds growing around," Debbie says. "The chickens get all the table scraps as well as egg shells, which provide calcium. The sale of surplus eggs pays for any additional feed. From our beehives we get honey—much cheaper and ten times better tasting than honey from the store!"

Sue Sperry of Missouri raises cows on a twelve-acre farm: "The cows are range fed, which allows us to have fairly chemical-free meat and milk. We butcher our own meat, not only for the tremendous savings, but also for the satisfaction of knowing we can do it. And we get just what we want. Our bacon, sausage, and hams are cut and smoked right here. I take the lard and make soap. I haven't bought a bar of soap in three years now. The milk from the Holstein heifer we raised provides us with cheese, butter, yogurt, buttermilk, and all the milk we can drink, plus an allowance for the children from selling the excess."

In planning to keep such animals, you'll want to read up on their care. You'll need to know what they eat and the type of shelter they'll need. You'll also need to check into local ordinances restricting the type of livestock which can be kept.

From this chapter, you can see that pioneer families use a multitude of techniques to stretch their food dollars. Whether it's couponing, co-oping, or cultivating, they've all found a way that suits their own family's needs—allowing mother to spend those precious early years at home with her little ones.

CHAPTER 10

Clothes Magic

Like food, clothing is a part of our daily lives, and early on, we have to decide how much time, thought, and money we can, or want to, devote to it.

Few of us want to be totally uninvolved with our appearance. A comfortable outfit in an attractive color can make a person feel good about himself or herself. You don't need to spend a fortune, however, to keep yourself and your family looking good.

As you may have surmised, there's a certain philosophy and, yes, a plan, that makes it possible for the family on a very tight budget to work this clothes magic. It isn't as spectacular as the wand that enabled Cinderella's fairy godmother to turn rags into the finery that caught the eye of the prince, but there's every bit as happy an ending to the story.

Mothers-at-home have found at least seven basic ways to keep their families well-dressed on a limited budget:

1. They buy quality clothes that will wear well.
2. They choose classic styles that will not move quickly out of fashion.

3. They choose an attractive color around which to build each family member's wardrobe.
4. They shop at discount stores and at off-season sales.
5. They find secondhand clothing and hand-me-downs that are still in good condition.
6. They keep their mending and darning skills sharp to save clothes that would otherwise be discarded.
7. They make clothes for themselves and their families.

Quality Not Quantity

Again and again, saving mothers-at-home recommend buying fewer clothes but insisting on good fabric and workmanship. Quality is not necessarily found only in the exclusive shop featuring dear little togs for tots all admittedly well-made but also high-priced. Nor is quality restricted to the latest trends or clothing with a designer's label. Quality clothing can be middle-of-the-road in price and can be a long established brand known for wearing well. "Buy quality brands, especially if things are going to be handed down," Angela Marvin of Pennsylvania advises. "You'll get better fit, longer use, and a better value in the long run. Often cheap clothes are misproportioned and don't wash well." Hilary Rocca from France comments on buying good quality children's clothes, "My present baby is wearing clothes that still look good after five children."

Classics Are Always in Fashion   Basic styles can continue to look good year after year. These classics won't look dated after only a few years; they have staying power. "I'm still wearing clothes from high school and I'm now twenty-eight," writes Barbara Dick of Washington. "Except for fabric to make maternity dresses, I haven't purchased anything new in years. Our clothing costs are minimal." Angela Marvin has found that it's a better idea to buy basic, good quality clothing that can be worn for years rather than to get fad styles that "I'd feel silly wearing a year or two later."

Clothes Magic

Kay Wallin bartered homemade bread and rolls for her son's good coat.

Holli Rovitti of New York points out that the more unisex clothing you invest in for children, the more hand-me-downs you'll be assured of. According to Cynthia Nodson of Kansas, "Elastic waist pants can be worn equally well by either little girls or boys, so buy neutral colored pants and make the transition with a change of top." Coats can also be switched successfully. A classic double-breasted coat will look good on big brother and little sister.

Regarding clothes selection for mother, Hilary Rocca advises: "Don't be tempted to buy cheap clothes to wear around the house. It's better to buy medium to good quality for everyday—say, two medium quality outfits rather than three or four cheap ones. And don't be tempted by too many bits and pieces—belts, socks, scarves, costume jewelry, and such that 'hardly cost anything.' These buys can add up to the cost of an entire ensemble."

Colors that Coordinate As you consider style and quality, give some thought, too, to color selection. It costs no more to

171

choose a garment in a color that will bring compliments your way than it does to choose a less attractive shade. Once you've found the color that is most attractive on you, you can build your wardrobe around it. (The same applies to your husband and children, of course, but probably more so to women's clothing.) A color plan affords greater versatility with fewer clothes, giving you the opportunity to mix and match the same blouses, pants, sweaters, and skirts in a greater number of combinations. Shopping becomes simpler, because you won't be looking at things in colors that you know you don't want.

"My wardrobe is in basic colors, based on blue," writes Janice Hartman of Delaware. "Things mix and match well. I try to plan around one color with the children, too." Janice suggests that people taking this approach explain their strategy and their color preference to those who are likely to give them clothing as a gift on birthdays or other occasions. A different color scheme for each family member will also make it easier to sort clothes, such as socks.

You and a group of friends can color analyze each other...

Determining the best color for each person may take a little doing. A color analyst or consultant will give you a pronouncement on the matter for a fee, usually in the $35 range, but some analysts charge as little as $10 or as high as $300.

At little or no cost, you and a group of friends can color analyze each other. Get a copy of one of the books on the subject (you can probably find one at your library) and a selection of materials to use in testing different shades on each person. Solid-colored pieces work best, in a size that is large enough to be effective—ten by twelve inches is a good size. If possible, get together during the day so that you can take advantage of natural light.

Where and When to Shop

Many cost-conscious mothers have found that saving money on clothes requires learning how to be not only a careful shopper, but in many ways a "non-shopper" as well.

Many mothers-at-home try to restrict their new purchases to shoes, socks, and underwear. "The new clothes we do purchase are only things we need, and never faddish items," says Peggy Lozen of Michigan. "Our major clothing items are coats, boots, and shoes. Here we may spend more money for a quality item which is then often worn for four or five years. Our clothes buying is kept to a minimum." Patty Meadows of Virginia explains, "We buy good shoes and underwear so they'll fit right and last. We just try to get them on sale. Otherwise, we *never* buy new clothing, except for special T-shirts or jeans as gifts for the older kids on birthdays, Christmas, and such occasions."

Buying new shoes for children can be a costly event for the parents. The little one who is just beginning to walk does not need hard-soled shoes; in fact he will be better off without them. If soft shoes are on hand from another child and the length and width is right, there's no reason why these soft shoes can't be used again. Toddlers normally aren't hard on shoes, and they do well in the inexpensive models that are often available at discount houses. Be sure to avoid shoes that have the upper part made of plastic, unless they are sandals. Encasing a child's foot—or anyone's foot for that matter—in a material that does not breathe and allow air circulation is asking for trouble.

As for the older, school-aged child, the most expensive route in shoe buying is the "inexpensive" shoe. One mother describes how she and her husband were aghast at the $25 price tag on children's tennis shoes at a shoe store that they had always considered to be in the medium price range. When they found a very similar-looking pair for half the money at a discount house, she says "we were quite pleased with ourselves." Their enthusiasm for their purchase was tested, however, a few days later when their nine-year-old son complained that the end of the sole on his new tennis shoe was flapping. Strong glue was applied, but after two days, the sole was again loose. When, after a short time, an eyelet ripped open, the disgusted mother was again shopping for new shoes for her son.

Whenever possible, new purchases should be made with an eye to seasons and sale patterns. "Name brands can be had at tremendous savings during the off seasons," Peggy Lozen observes. "I never pay full price for new children's clothing." Angela Marvin of Pennsylvania advises, "Learn the sales with good reputations in your area. There are usually some with very good brand names available." These mothers buy ahead for the next year, basing their choice of sizes on how quickly their children have moved up the size charts in the past. This practice gets more difficult as youngsters get older and develop very definite clothes tastes of their own (which are seldom the same as their mother's) or when they add inches to their stature overnight. Charlene Burnett of Missouri buys ahead and stows her purchases for the future in boxes labeled by sizes. "The end of the season is the best time to find bargains," she says. "And, no matter what store I'm in, I go only for the clearance rack."

Recycled Clothing   Using secondhand clothing is not only a way to cut clothing bills drastically; it also serves another worthwhile purpose: that of conservation. Many young parents value usefulness more than newness, and they care little about the fact that they are the second or perhaps even the third party to wear something. "Recycling is ecologically sound, and we feel virtuous," says Mikell Billoki of Ontario, Canada. "We recycle with a passion that has made it almost an occupation."

The thrift shop and the good rummage sale can be oases in what often looks like a desert of high clothing prices. Not only are prices appealing, quality can be found, too, with a bit of searching. Designer items and lovely little outfits that first

The Wallins wear matching pajamas their mother obtained in exchange for babysitting.

appeared in the exclusive children's shop are now affordable buys, once you've tracked them down. Even diapers may be obtained at bargain prices. Le Anne Fay from Michigan, writes: "I purchased cloth diapers from our local diaper service. They use them for only a certain period of time, then sell them at a very low price. There's lots of wear left in them."

Tess Ware in Alabama found three high-quality used-clothing stores in her area that offer her a good selection of women's, babies', and children's clothing. "I don't sew very well," Mikell Billoki admits. "What I do best is thrift shopping. Since kids often outgrow clothing before it even looks worn, you can often find great deals on quality used clothing for children. I've come home with a shopping bag full of pants,

T-shirts, and sweaters for our boys for under $10." Another thrift shopper, Glinda Pipkin in Texas, keeps an eye open for clothing finds at garage sales, too: "We buy almost all our clothes from garage sales or thrift stores." At one garage sale, she came upon a windfall of like-new baby dresses, socks, booties, and a diaper bag and "I didn't pay over twenty-five cents for anything," she reports.

Before shopping at a thrift store or rummage sale, write down family members' measurements—chest, waist, dress and pants inseam length—on a small card and keep a tape measure in your purse. Often size tags are torn out of used clothing. By measuring garments, you'll know if it is something that will fit.

A rummage sale offers greater variety than a garage sale. These sales are usually held at a set time of the year, and are often run by church or community groups. A good rummage sale will attract a crowd, so you should arrive early on the day of the sale for the best buys.

If at all possible, consider contributing some time to helping set up such a sale. It's traditional for the workers to be given the opportunity to make purchases before the door is opened to the public, so you'll have a better chance of finding the things you can use. Phyllis Nelson of Minnesota first took on the job of running the rummage sale at her church because "I was 'volunteered' to head it up." Now when asked to take the position, she says she wouldn't turn it down. For Phyllis, there is an added pleasure from giving something a new lease on life. She relates, "I was doubly thrilled when I bought a much wanted mixer (the price was $5) and the woman told me how happy she was to see her mother's mixer go to a good home."

With thrift purchases, as with any shopping, don't buy more than you can put to use, even if the price is only pennies. If you don't need something, it isn't a bargain.

As outlets for your own used clothing or other items, thrift stores and charities can also be a way to bring in a few extra dollars. Many churches and charitable organizations welcome donations, and gifts to them are tax deductible. Many thrift shops buy used clothing or take it on consignment, paying a percentage of the selling price. "I've sold used clothes at a clothing consignment shop in town," writes Lori Dow of Iowa, "for more than I spent to make them."

In many ways, the message coming through letters from mothers-at-home is to de-emphasize clothes. Large amounts of clothing are looked upon as impractical. "Stuffing kids' drawers with clothes costs more and produces more work for mom," writes Holli Rovitti of New York. Holli reasons that if you do the laundry at least once a week you need only enough clothes for that length of time. With many more outfits on hand, family members are constantly changing, and more washing, folding, and putting clothes away has to be done.

Maurine Joens of Arkansas keeps a box for nonmatching socks. It's amazing how many pairs one can eventually make, and even nonmatching pairs can be worn around the house. "I love tube socks," says Kathy Kotora of Arkansas. "The same size can be used as knee socks for a small child and anklets for the older child. They're unisex, easy to sort, and no heels to darn!" Large-size T-shirts that have been passed down or picked up at rummage sales can be worn to bed at night according to Helene Fowler of Washington.

If you don't need something, it isn't a bargain...

Hand-me-downs have a couple of advantages over new clothing. First, they usually come free. Second, those things that circulate within your own family are associated with numerous memories of the original wearer or wearers, although hand-me-downs can also come from neighbors, friends, and more distant relatives.

Mothers who appreciate hand-me-downs are also careful to observe the rules of etiquette. They make a point of graciously thanking the people who pass things down to them, no matter how many or few of the items can be used. The surplus can always be passed on, perhaps to a large agency reaching many people. "We value hand-me-downs," Jj Fallick writes from Wisconsin. Jj remembers back to her own childhood and to the happy thoughts that she associated with the things that she had handed down to her from much-loved family members. "When kids are little, especially," she says, "I think they really enjoy wearing things that used to belong to an older friend or sister or cousin."

Mothers find ways, too, to highlight the business of going through the clothes cache, of trying things on and deciding what stays and what goes. "My kids can't wait until we bring down the seasonal clothes from the attic," writes Linda Greengas, Connecticut. "We make a special event of it, with private dressing rooms and all. The younger ones get to pick and choose their favorites from things that an older brother or sister has outgrown," Linda says that when a child has trouble finding something that seems right, she comes to the rescue with a little strategy of her own. "I always have a story to go along with the clothes," she says. "I tell of something funny or different that their brother or sister did when they wore an item." Phyllis Nelson of Minnesota is another master at reminiscing. "We remember when Jenna first wore a dress to school," she writes, "how Dana received a certain outfit from Papa, or how nice a child looked in a picture wearing a particular coat." These little stories are greatly enjoyed (after all, the children themselves are the main characters), and they add extra appeal to familiar garments. And what about the new things that were bought the season before at the special clearance sales? These, too, are stored with the outgrown clothing, and everything is brought out at one time. The emphasis is on outfitting each child in decent clothes, not on the newness or oldness of a thing.

Clothes Magic

Felicity Nguyen outfits her two boys with hand-me-downs.

One popular variation on the hand-me-down is the clothes exchange. It's a mutual sharing of outgrown or no longer used clothing among families with children of stair-step ages. After each usage, the item is returned to the original owner. Carol Barshack of Illinois says that clothes swaps with friends and family are one of her pet economies. "Winter dress coats are really nice to swap because, how often are they worn? And it's always nice to have an extra jacket on hand for play while one is in the wash." Carol explains that for ease in returning them, each mother puts her initials on the tags of the articles that belong to her. A breastfeeding mother herself, Carol says that she can always tell her baby things in a lineup of clothing. "There are no formula stains," she notes.

Repair and Renovate

If you team up thrift-buying with a sewing machine, you can make a clean sweep of saving on clothes. You don't need a machine that is loaded with gadgets. The straight stitch, forward and reverse, zig zag, and a buttonholer are basic and should not be too expensive. With your sewing machine set

Charity, Celeste, and Celina Koppenheffer wear pretty dresses made by their mother, Debbie.

up where it's handy to use, you can quickly sew up the inevitable tear and, in general, repair and renovate rather than buying new clothing.

Suzanne Neff of Ohio has used her sewing skills to update fashions and put new life into worn garments. She has found that wide-legged pants can be transformed to the slimmer look by taking in the excess width at the seams.

Take out the hems, turn the pants inside out and lay them flat. Measure them against a pair that is the desired width. if you want them four inches narrrower, you'd measure *one* inch in from each side, which will reduce the width by two inches front and back, for a total of four inches. Draw a line with tailor's chalk from the knee to your mark. This will be your stitching line. Pin so that front and back don't shift, and allowing 5/8 inch for seam allowance, cut off the excess material. Sew up both seams, and re-hem the bottom.

Maurine Joens of Arkansas says that she turns the old flare pants into styles with a cuff or elastic at the ankle. She also recycles clothing by taking collars off and adding contrasting stitching. "Many of my clothes and shoes are from my high-school and college days, either recycled or waiting for the style to come back," Maurine says.

Suzanne Neff has been successful, too, in extending the life of a man's shirt. "My husband's dress shirts were getting very worn-looking around the neck," she says, but "I discovered that a single line of stitching could be taken out and the collar removed and turned." (The side of the collar that shows when the shirt is buttoned would then be underneath where the worn part would not show.) Suzanne restitched the collar and had a new-looking shirt. "This same procedure can be done, too, with the cuffs," she points out. "Take them off, turn the side facing in to the outside, and sew them on opposite sleeves."

Colleen Houston of British Columbia, Canada tells of her introduction to some old forms of the art of clothes mainte-nance. "My grandmother was horrified when I said I was going to throw out my two-year-old Shannon's almost new tights because of a hole in the knee," Colleen says. "She immedi-ately set to teaching me how to mend and patch. I can now keep clothes lasting much, much longer. A year ago I would have discarded them and bought something new."

Patching can be done by hand, but machine sewing usually holds better and is, of course, faster to do. Darning, which is used to mend knitted things such as socks and mittens, is done by hand. You'll need a darning needle, a long, strong needle with a large eye, and darning thread in the appropriate color.

To darn a sock:
Trim around the hole, making it a more even shape and cutting away any frayed or thin material. Using a running stitch, sew all the way around at the edge of the hole. (Slip the sock over

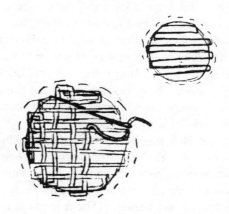

one hand, with the hole spread between your fingers to make darning easier.) You'll now be doing what amounts to a lattice work design. Starting at one side, make a small stitch and draw the thread straight across to the other side, securing it with another small stitch. Moving your needle over a bit, take another small stitch, bring the thread across, and to the other side and anchor with a small stitch again. Continue doing this until you have threads a small distance apart across the entire hole. Now, beginning at one end, go over and under the bands of thread in a weaving pattern, again taking a small stitch. Reverse your direction and also the weaving pattern, going under with your needle where you went over on the previous row. As you go along, straighten the rows with the tip of your needle. Draw the thread across smoothly, but not too tight. In short order, you will have filled in the hole.

To patch a hole:
Patching involves filling in a hole or reinforcing a worn spot with a piece of good material. You can often find enough matching fabric in a seam or pocket to make the patch. If there's a hole, you'll trim around it to give it a uniform shape. Cut the patch large enough to cover the hole and extend somewhat beyond it.

With right sides up, place the patch under the hole, pinning it at the corners to hold it in place. Turn under the raw edge

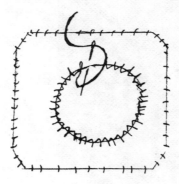

around the hole, pinning it as you go along, and stitch it to the patch with your machine (or sew it by hand, using what is known as a blanket stitch.) Now, machine or hand stitch around the outer edge of the patch, and—no more hole!

Debbie Britton of Colorado says that she appliques animals, flowers, or some other attractive design cut from scraps onto shirts or pants with holes in them. "Often, these become favorites," she says, "since they are personalized."

Making Your Own Originals

It isn't all that difficult to make clothing, especially if you begin by sewing something simple. A child's pair of pants, for instance, can be made from two pieces of material—a front and a back—and some elastic. Little people are very tolerant of a few imperfections, and little garments take hardly any time to stitch up. "I've often been amazed at how easily and inexpensively I can make overalls for a toddler," Denise Parker of California writes. "One hour from start to finish, and they're done."

Jan King of Ohio observes, "It takes so little material to make a child's outfit—only one-and-a-half yards for a pair of coveralls, and the price of children's ready-made wear is out-

*The Laugle family
members wear mom-made
shirts.*

rageous!" Like many other mothers, Jan also enjoys making "those dressy outfits for Christmas, Easter, and the like. It makes them so much more special." The cash outlay for making a simple item for a child can be reduced to practically nothing when the material is left over from another sewing project. A third of a yard of leftover denim was all Mary Kastendieck of Colorado needed to make shorts with an elastic waist for her three-year-old boy. She was able to make a sunsuit for her daughter from a dress that had seen better days: "I recut the material and used the buttons off the dress for the sunsuit." Sue Neff remade an old miniskirt into a skirt for her daughter.

Thrifty seamstresses save all reusable parts from clothing that is ready to be discarded—buttons, hooks and eyes, zippers, trim that is not worn. Panty hose that has runs or tears are a source of elastic. Store these notions together in one place—such as a shoe box.

If a garment is worth making, make it out of good material. Your time is too valuable to be spent on something that isn't going to hold up. Although good material that comes straight from the bolt at the regular price can be expensive, you can buy quality pieces when they're on sale or off the remnant table. A high percentage of a natural fiber, such as cotton, is always preferable especially for children's clothing.

"I buy material when it's on sale," Jan King of Ohio says, "for instance, corduroy in the spring, and squirrel it away until fall." Be forewarned, though, that a fabric collection has a way of growing. Your stash of material can represent quite an investment. I have a sister-in-law who has a trunk that she has been stocking for years and from which I swear, she can extract just the right piece of material to make anything from a coat to an evening dress.

Patterns, too, represent an expense but here again, there are ways to cut costs. You can swap patterns with friends, buy patterns at thrift outlets (for ten to twenty cents) or obtain them from the public library. You can often find patterns at garage or rummage sales, too. An experienced seamstress can often alter the size on a simple pattern. One pattern can also be used for several different looking outfits as they often include several variations along with the basic pattern. Debbie Kohenzy of Illinois sews most of her daughter's clothes and passes on the tip that pattern sizes run larger than store-purchased sizes and have more ease.

With your sewing machine and a fortuitous purchase of soft material, you can even save by making your own diapers. Joann Grohman of Maine offers some suggestions for keeping baby dry and comfortable. "Cloth diapers aren't cheap, and years ago I discovered that an old-fashioned cotton flannel sheet, cut into diaper-sized pieces, works fine. The edges can be zig-zagged on the sewing machine." She notes that "ancient cotton flannel" is highly absorbent, and recommends that you look for good specimens at garage sales and rummage sales. "The last one I bought was a double length, 216-inch size sheet, and I paid twenty-five cents for it." In place of plastic pants for baby, Joann suggests using "soakers" made of wool.

"Old wool sweaters (it must be wool) can be easily machine stitched into panty soakers to go over the diapers," she says. "These do not predispose to diaper rash as do plastic pants."

Homemade diapers, an old wool sweater made into a soaker—"But that's extreme!" a woman responded when I mentioned the idea to her. Her reaction is not all that uncommon in our world today. Yet it can be said unequivocally that there is no evidence that a child suffers any mental or physical trauma from wearing secondhand or handmade clothes; the same cannot be said when substitutes are made for mother-at-home.

CHAPTER *11*

*S*aving on *E*nergy *C*osts

Love, it is said, makes the world go round, and love, we know, warms the heart. Now, if only some inventive person would find a way to harness this tremendous source of energy, what a simple matter it'd be for fathers and mothers to keep things running! Parents have love in abundance; it is money for oil, gas, and electricity that is often in short supply.

So much for whimsical thoughts. Since technology is not that advanced, the prudent course of action is to think of more down-to-earth and mundane ways to cut energy costs. Energy saved means funds available for the many other things you need. Also, many forms of commonly used energy are a limited resource, so we all have an obligation to conserve. The future could literally be brighter for our children if we are conservative users of our natural resources today. This saving outlook becomes a way of life for many families. It is definitely part of the pioneering package that can make it possible to live on one income.

Clemence Ravaçon-Mershon of Pennsylvania writes, "When I stopped working to stay home with our children, we dropped the thermostat one to two degrees each year. People are hor-

Sharing bathtime can be fun—and save hot water, too!

rified that the overall house is sixty degrees, but we, including the one- and four-year-olds, have adjusted by moving around more and dressing more warmly. Lowering the thermostat has resulted in less illness and fewer medical bills. We cover windows with thick curtains and outside walls with extra styrofoam sheets. Of course the family bed keeps us warmer at night when the temperature drops even lower. It also means less laundry. Family baths save time and water. We slow cook things overnight. On a cold winter morning, a hot, ready breakfast warms hands and insides. With baby in a carrier, mother and little one keep each other warmer and happier."

Charlene Burnett of Missouri says, "The whole family must cooperate. We haven't used our central air conditioning for six years. In the winter, we keep the temperature in the house at fifty-five degrees." Charlene does note that at times visitors tend to keep their visits short. She says the family stays comfortable "by wearing sweaters in the winter and as little as possible in the summer."

In Georgia, The Schilke family count themselves among a growing number of people who are borrowing a page from the past. Mary Ellen Schilke writes, "We heat with wood in winter. In summer, an overhead fan circulates the air."

Heating and Cooling Your Home

Since heating and cooling are major uses of energy in the home and often very costly ones, they have received considerable scrutiny in recent years. For starters, there's the question of how tightly your house is put together, the means by which you heat or cool, and even whether the sun can shine in during colder seasons to warm you but is judiciously blocked when the weather is hot. In areas where there are long periods of severely hot or cold weather, there's all the more reason to find ways to make staying at home pleasant from an environmental point of view. A drafty house at seventy degrees can be less comfortable than a snug house with a temperature between fifty-five and sixty degrees. Air conditioning which can be a blessing in very hot regions can be made much more effective and less costly to operate with a few simple measures. When funds are limited, you'll want to make careful choices.

Those of us who are mainly concerned with staying warm in the long months of winter can look for a cheap fuel, such as wood. There may also be the option to remodel so as to take advantage of solar energy. Putting in more insulation is often helpful, but the cost can be considerable. With fewer dollars and some detective work, you can reduce the heat loss from your home by up to fifty percent. It has to do with caulk and weatherstripping, with keeping warm air from escaping and cold air from sneaking into the house. On a cold, windy day, run your hands along the walls of your house, around the window and door frames, past the electrical outlets, wherever two pieces come together—or almost together. You're looking for holes to plug. They may seem minor, but when the North Wind blows, they rob you of warmth and your hard-earned money. According to *Home Energy Savings*, a booklet put out by the University of Illinois at Urbana-Champaign, a 1/32-inch crack (thinner than a dime) around the edges of an exterior door is equivalent to having a hole 2½ by 3 inches in the wall.

Electrical outlets on outside walls are notorious for allowing air leakage. Neat little insulating seals which fit on the back of the switchplate can be obtained from most hardware stores. Besides being inexpensive, they're easy to install.

Another spot that brings in cold air is that crack that often appears along the foundation between the wooden framework and the top of the masonry. Close it up with caulk; your house will be more comfortable and easier to heat.

When looking for prime areas to insulate, look to the glass windows and doors in your house. Glass has poor insulating qualities, so extra storm windows or doors may be a good investment. If you cannot afford permanent storm windows, cover the windows with polyethylene film, at least 6-mil thick. Shutters made of a rigid, board type of insulation (available at building supply stores) can be placed in the windows at night and stored under the beds during the day. Shades of a non-porous material are helpful in keeping out chill winds, especially if they're placed inside the window jambs. Shades of this type can be more effective than insulated draperies. If drapes are not boxed in at the top and sides, warm air can move behind them and be lost out the window. Warm air always moves toward cooler air. And as the warm air goes out, cooler air comes in.

If too much heat is your problem and your big energy bills are for cooling rather than heating, you can take some fairly simple steps here, too, to lessen nature's impact. A somewhat different approach seems to be in order. Infiltration, the passage of air from the outside in, is not as important a factor in controlling heat as it is with cold. Heat radiating from the roof

Charity and Celeste Koppenheffer warm up after their bath in front of the cookstove in their kitchen.

is usually the greater problem. One solution is to fasten aluminum foil to the rafters. (It comes in big rolls for this purpose.) The foil serves as a shield against the sun, blocking out the radiant heat.

Here, too, protecting your windows makes good sense. Awnings on the outside, or sun-shading screens, and drapes or shades on the inside are a good combination. Plugging up air leaks will be worthwhile especially if they're leaks of cool air from the air conditioning system. This often happens when duct tape loosens or there is a gap between the duct and the register in the wall or ceiling. Search and seal, and you'll save money.

There's much more, of course, to the business of climate control in the house. The winning combination depends upon many things. Check the periodicals at your library for helpful articles. Rodale Press publications and *The Mother Earth News* are two sources of practical information.

You can find out how your house specifically measures up in energy matters by getting an energy audit. A trained person checks your house from measuring the amount of insulation in the attic to checking for air leaks around the foundation and taking a reading on the efficiency of your furnace or boiler. The information is fed into a computer on the spot and you are given a print-out of what improvements can be made, how much they are likely to cost, and how soon they would pay for themselves. The charge for such an audit in Illinois is $15. Check with the Department of Energy and Natural Resources in your state or province or with your local utility company for more information. An area frequently has its own conservation program which puts out helpful information dealing with local conditions. The Illinois booklet, *More for your Money...Home Energy Savings*, is excellent. It is available from the Energy Information Clearinghouse, Illinois Department of Energy and Natural Resources, 325 W. Adams Street, Springfield, IL 62706, or from National Technical Information Service, Springfield, Virginia.

Some Alternatives The space heater is back. Burning wood is again in style, with Franklin stoves featured in the latest home decorating magazines. Ben would love it; people are buying stoves bearing his name and others like them because they're economical to operate. "Our heating bill went way down when we started heating with wood six years ago, even when we buy all the wood," says Sallie Diamond of New Hampshire. Writing from the frozen environs of nothern Minnesota, Phyllis Nelson states, "Dollar-wise, our greatest savings annually has been in heating." The Nelsons burn wood, which they can cut from county-owned lots. Phyllis points out that in their situation, they would be forced to burn the more expensive oil if she were working outside the home. " Because of the fact that I am home all day, we are able to rely on wood as our sole fuel source," she says. "I tend the fire in our add-on furnace." (An add-on is a wood burning unit that is attached to the central heating system.)

Using wood for fuel won't be practical or even cost-efficient

Jonathan Sanders helps his
dad start the first fire of the
season.

for everyone, but for those living near wooded land, it offers
the advantage of being a renewable resource as well as economical. There are abundant supplies of wood at the present
time in the U.S. and Canada. And since good forest management calls for removing the less desirable cull trees, permission
is often giving to cut on publicly owned land. Once you have
the necessary equipment for cutting and hauling, you can usually find other free sources—trees that were downed in storms
or cleared from a new construction site.

Getting in a supply of wood for the winter truly seems to
be a family affair. Phyllis describes the routine at their house:
"We tend to view the cutting, chopping, hauling, and stacking
as a family project. There are opportunities for even the two-
year-old to join in. For husband and wife, there is the com-
panionship of working together on a job that visibly shows
results. What satisfaction as the wood pile grows! And because
the whole family is willing to pitch in, it's less of a chore."

Le Anne Fay tells of her husband, Ron, building a flat-bed
trailer for hauling the wood that keeps them warm during cold
Michigan winters. Their chain saw and wood splitter were bought
at a farm auction. Le Anne describes the splitter as a "noisy,

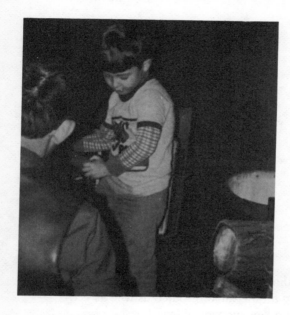

Lucas Sanders adds some kindling to the fire in the family's wood stove.

hydraulic machine," that was sure to lull her toddler Noah to sleep when in operation, while his seven-year-old sister was busy carrying the wood into the shed.

And who can deny the esthetics of a fire burning cheerily in the stove in the heart of the home? Somehow, there just isn't the same romance about starting up the furnace come a cold snap in the fall as there is in building the first fire in the wood burner. "Starting the first fire of the season has become a real ritual," Mary Sanders writes from Kansas. "The boys, almost five and two years old, enjoy bringing in small pieces of wood and kindling to hand to dad or mom. Excitement runs high when the fire finally 'takes off' and begins to warm us. Then it's time for everyone to sit down around the stove and drink hot cocoa!"

There's an extremely serious side to heating with wood that must not be overlooked. Wood burners must be installed properly, a safe distance from combustible materials. The chimney must be in good repair, and chimney and flue pipes must be kept clear of the creosote that builds up as a result of wood burning. The creosote itself can start burning in the chimney and take the house down with it. Remember, even though you install your wood burner properly and operate it carefully, it is still more dangerous than any other kind of heating system. You *cannot* just set it and forget it.

Often, too, stoves and space heaters become hot to the touch and as such pose a problem for small children especially. Jj Fallick of Wisconsin says that "for the sake of the baby this year, we put our wooden playpen around the heater to keep tiny hands away and allow baby the run of the room."

Small portable heaters such as a kerosene heater can be useful in keeping the room where the family is gathered cozy while the temperature in the rest of the house is kept at a lower temperature, but these heaters, too, require special attention. Ventilation is extremely important; in fact, some authorities believe a window should be open whenever the heater is in use. Your best defense lies in knowing of possible dangers and guarding against them each time you use a kerosene heater.

Other Energy Savings

Mothers-at-home pay attention to anything which, when turned on, starts a meter going. The hot water heater and clothes dryer are high on the list of appliances which are energy hungry and which, with a little effort, can frequently by bypassed. After home heating, the water heater probably uses more energy than any other appliance in your home.

First of all, check the thermostat setting on your hot water heater. Commonly, these are set at 140 to 145 degrees, which is *hot*. Scalding can occur from hot water directly from the tap. Contact with water 140 degrees for five seconds or less can cause serious burns. Set your water heater at 120 degrees and see how that works. If you have a dishwasher, you may have to turn it up a bit as hot water is necessary to dissolve the detergent. Incidentally, it takes more energy to heat the water used in the dishwasher than it does to run the dishwasher. The same is true of the clothes washer, which brings us to the next point—when practical, wash the clothes in cold water. Whites come out looking better when washed in hot water, but even these can be rinsed in cold water. Don't ever let the hot water just run, as when rinsing dishes. (This is a poor practice at any time, of course, even with cold water.) Leaky faucets can really waste water. It has been figured that a faucet that leaks one drop per second wastes 650 gallons of water in a year!

People commonly turn down the thermostat on their heating system at night, but have you considered doing the same with your hot water heater? Lucy Saturnino of California says this is just part of her nighttime routine, along with turning off all the lights. "My favorite money-saving thing is turning down the water heater at night after doing the dishes," Lucy writes. "No sense in heating water when it's not necessary." She explains that she turns it back up "as soon as I get up in the morning so there's hot water for showers and such."

It takes thousands of reminders and years of growing up...

The clothes dryer, now, is a marvelous invention, particularly when there is a baby in the family, the weather is wet, and there is little room inside for drying clothes. But for all its appeal, modern mothers at home are not addicted to their clothes dryers. Those who have access to an outdoor drying area are rediscovering the many splendors of the clothesline and clothespin. "I only use the dryer when I absolutely have to," says Colleen Houston of British Columbia, Canada. She mentions, too, that when she hangs or folds the clothes as soon as she takes them off the line or out of the dryer, "there is usually no need to iron them"—another energy savings.

A mother in California, Lynn Hicks, hung out the family's laundry instead of using the dryer as she had in the past and found that her bill "was reduced by *half*." "From $83 to $41," she writes. "The *only* change in our usage has been using the dryer," she stresses.

Lynn decided to look into a clothesline, she says, with the arrival of spring "and another utility rate hike." Her search led her to "retractable, compact-able, umbrella, pulley, and various other elaborate clotheslines ranging from $15 to $48." She settled on "your basic clothesline, one-hundred feet of line and a few packages of clothespins for under $5." Solar energy at her fingertips, she was ready to give the new venture a try. "The only good thing I had ever heard about sun-dried laundry is that it smells good," she says, so she was pleasantly surprised to find that the time it takes to hang up and take down the clothes compares favorably with the dryer. An added bonus is that, "It's easy to fold and sort the clothes as I go along, saving me the task of rummaging through a pile of clothes looking for something."

Lynn particularly notes that she "hasn't lost a sock" since putting the new method in operation, or more correctly, since gaining a new helper, three-year-old Sarah. "She sorts and hangs and matches all the socks, her special job. She hands pins to me, arranges them around the bucket, doles a few out to her ten-month-old sister, Anna, and generally has a great time with this whole set-up." Soaking up the sunshine, watching the clothes billow out in the wind, it hardly seems like work. Lynn and baby Anna are pleased, too, that the sun makes the diapers fresher. And, oh yes, "the laundry really *does* smell better!"

"Turn Off the Light"   If you sometimes feel as though you've made that statement a thousand times, no, ten thousand times, you're undoubtedly right. Keep saying it. It takes thousands of such reminders and years of growing up for the message to really stick with the children, but in the end it does. (For some, however, the light comes through on the wisdom of the matter only when they're paying their own utility bills.)

Many of the letter writers mentioned that as a family they conscientiously turn off lights, radios, television sets when not in use. Claudia Barber of Indiana mentions that they worked out a plan to help them stay on their toes—and turn out the lights. "When our seven- and five-year-olds had trouble remembering to turn off lights," Claudia writes, "I instituted a five-cent fine for each 'offense.' The money went into the vacation fund, which made it less painful." All was not grim, though. She adds that "there was the fun of watching papa and mama, too, pay up occasionally."

Sometimes, too, we may simply get into the habit of routinely turning lights on. Alice Barbiere of New Jersey says that they take a different approach. "We do many things either outdoors or sitting near windows to take advantage of natural lighting," she says. It's a lovely custom. As Alice notes, "There's something really special about sitting on the floor with the kids, their toys surrounding them, and warm sunshine flooding over us."

Anne Harvey and her family in Kansas pass on a simple and very practical little hint that is energy saving and mother saving. "We keep night lights on in the bathroom and bedroom in the evenings," writes Anne. "You can see well enough to do a lot of things without turning on the overhead lights." And just think—you won't have to drop everything to turn on a light for a child who is too small to reach the switch.

Transportation Costs

The car you drive—or do not drive—affects your energy balance and your bank balance. One-car families are not a thing of the past. They're doing just fine with a mother-at-home who manages to get places and do things without the everyday use of a second car.

Fran Menzel with her children buckled into their passenger carrier.

Walking is popular, if for no other reason than the pleasure to be found in seeing a part of the world in the slow motion of a walk. The same holds true for biking—it's fun. Biking is also a practical form of transportation when several small children can be included on the bike trip, as is the case with Fran Menzel and her youngsters in the state of Washington. Fran hooks up her passenger carrier and secures the children with lap and shoulder straps, and can take off for a trip to the store, the library, the park, or even a movie. The distance is about a mile or two, which Fran says is "no problem." When they bike to a shopping center three miles away, her husband pulls the passenger carrier, "as there are some hills," Fran says. It's a way to promote physical fitness as well as save on transportation costs.

Fran and her husband feel that such a carrier has a lot of potential for a young family. "Ours has a rear facing seat position, which is safer in the event the bicycle must make a panic stop," Fran explains.

In New Zealand, Lynley Steel's husband has faced unemployment twice in the past year, and experience that has made them conclude that "when one has to make the money stretch, there are ways to get results."

Lynley says that when their old car broke down, rather than put money into fixing it, they sold it. They now use a minibike and a motorcycle to get around. Lynley shops twice a week, carrying the groceries home in a box that is attached to the bike carrier. She says that friends have been helpful, too, with offers of rides. Regarding their social life, Lynley says that "with four children, the price of Public Transport makes a family outing an expense that is not often affordable." So are they becoming recluses? Not at all. Says Lynley, "At the moment we're working on getting people to come visiting us more often."

CHAPTER 12

Have Fun!

It's a must. There is a time to work, and a time to set work aside and relax, do something that doesn't *have* to be done and have fun. Recreation is not in the realm of an elective; it's essential. The word recreation is itself a clue to its importance—to re-create, bring a renewal and resurgence of life. You can't afford to miss it!

And what do money-poor families do for entertainment? The list is long, but mainly, they have a zest for the active life and are more likely to run out of steam or time before running out of ideas for low-cost things to do. Their enthusiasm and interest are perhaps more impressive than the activities themselves, but then, the same can be said of the high-priced variety of fun. What's left when enthusiasm and interest are lacking?

From their letters, it is amply evident that saving families can have a good time, in fact an excellent time—

> Visiting with family and friends
> Reading, often aloud to nonreaders
> Listening to music, making their own
> Walking, hiking, biking
> Swimming
> Sledding, skating, cross-country skiing
> Taking advantage of cultural events that are free or low cost

Visiting museums and other places of interest that are
known for their roominess
Going to the movies for free or at a reduced price
Camping, backpacking
Making an indoor tent using sheets and a card table or
the backs of chairs
Picnicking, near or far from home
Planting an indoor garden in anticipation of spring
Celebrating all holidays, birthdays, half-birthdays
Dining "in house," occasionally dining out
Forming a fitness class
Playing games
Doing volunteer work
Feeding the birds
Organizing a preschool play group
Working with paper, cloth, anything that can be cut, col-
ored, pasted
Calling on shut-ins
Planning next season's activities
Making things together, learning things together

"We love to have friends over," writes Cherly Hutchinson
of New Jersey, "and I always accept guests' offers to contribute
a dish to the meal." Cherly says that she keeps "a special
recipe file of menus that are economical yet company-special."
Candles and a centerpiece on the table lift these occasions out
of the class of an everyday meal.

In Ohio, the Hilstons are Great Lakes shipping buffs and
enjoy visiting ports, boat watching, and photographing the scene,
"cheap entertainment, costing only the price of gasoline and
film for the camera," says Christine Hilston. When it's the Festival of Flowers in their town, they make sure they catch the
parade, "but we bypass the carnival," she says.

Coleen Mast, Illinois, says "a fun morning for us is 'park
hopping.' We spend about twenty minutes at each playground
we find on the map and then move on to the next." They also

Have Fun!

Kite-flying is a favorite and inexpensive family activity for the Keelers.

try to take advantage of free activities in the community— "parades, exhibits, art fairs, special events at the local shopping center."

"We may take a drive, swim, fly kites on the beach, or splurge on a pizza," writes Gail Kimberling from Oregon regarding their recreation choices. "All are relatively inexpensive and involve the whole family. Also, we are fortunate that we live near both of our extended families, so a lot of our free time is spent with them, which costs nothing but love!"

Kathleen Emerson of California recalls how she and her husband, when they first met, enjoyed going to stage musicals in the large city where they live. Now, this is a form of entertainment that they find too costly. Kathleen says, "With the coming of our first baby and the change in our finances, we realized it was out of the question for at least a while." But on a positive note, she says, "We are fortunate enough to own a piano and both of us can play and carry a tune. Show tunes are popular enough to be available in most music stores, and so we now enjoy our own 'shows.' We take turns playing and singing and dancing around, and the kids, needless to say, love it as much as we do! We really enjoy sharing our enthusiasm with our children.'' The Emersons figure that when their children are older, "perhaps we can go to shows again and bring them, too. But meanwhile, we can recapture the pleasure without the cost in dollars or the anxiety of leaving a young child.''

Attitudes Make the Difference

Donna Laugle, Ohio, reflects on children and money spent on entertainment. "When I was a child," she says, "my father earned very little. However, I never felt poor or deprived, nor did my mother go out to work. Of all my childhood memories, the best ones are those that didn't involve money at all. The times our family spent together going on picnics or hiking were by far the most fun. I want my children to have those same kind of memories and to feel rich in love, not money.''

As you no doubt know, the success of a venture depends to a great extent on the attitude of the people involved. Says Katy Lebbing, Illinois, "It's important during saving times to have fun. Perhaps this is easy for me because I had a mother who made a game out of so many of the things we did, and I find myself doing the same with my children. When mother is happy and positive, the whole family feels and radiates this.'' Of course fathers are equally important in setting the tone of family fun. In the Dow family from Iowa, Steven lost his job due to the poor economy. Lori Dow writes, "One afternoon, Steve and the kids—Amy is four and Eric is twenty-one months old—sifted all of the rocks out of the sandbox. It took over an hour and the kids loved it!'' She explains, "There is no money left for entertainment. We used to love going out for pizza once a week, but now we make our own. Even Eric can help spread all the stuff on top. Exploring the city parks is a lot of fun, and family walks are great. A good imagination is always a help, and as long as we do things together, we seem to survive, keep our sanity, and avoid boredom.''

Steve, Eric, and Amy Dow enjoy an afternoon sifting sand.

Family Night

The Ficks of Illinois feel strongly that it's important for a family to have fun together because it's "what makes us all want to keep on going." The Ficks treasure the "special loving feelings that we get from doing things together and being together." A "loving time" is not something that can be readily planned, Carol Fick explains, but a planned activity that brings the family together on a regular basis can be the impetus for family unity. For the Ficks, this revolves around a weekly "family night" and, as often as not, Carol says, "We spend lots of time playing different ball games." When relatives ask them what the children would like for a gift, the answer is usually "a ball." They have received the appropriate balls for soccer, volleyball, basketball, and football. As for their playing style, Carol says, "We seldom if ever have rules except those that fit the ages of our family at the time. We laugh a lot, and if someone tries, but misses, a catch, a hit, or a basket, we always say 'almost.' " As a family, they stress trying again, rather than winning. "By playing together, by participating, we are *all* winners," Carol maintains.

The Myers family enjoys a game of softball.

Their "family night," which Carol considers important to name and hold regularly, is "a very simple two hours that we take to do things together. What we do is not what has made our family nights special," Carol explains. "It's that we take the time for *us.*" A great deal of learning and maturing can take place at such times, as Carol notes when she says, "Some of our family nights have seemed like disasters, and then we adults try to keep our cool and give the angry person or persons a chance to regroup and get on with what it is we are doing. We are not asking for perfection; we just all do the best we can."

TV or not TV?   The Hutchinsons of New Jersey are one of a number of families who do not rely on television for entertainment; in fact, Cherly writes, "We have no television set at all." She says they figure they've saved the price of the initial investment, repair bills are nonexistent, there's no ongoing charge to power it, and "no drain on brain cells." Writes an ex-television watcher from Louisiana, Caroline Triplett:

We got rid of both television sets about five months ago. Oh, the benefits we have experienced without the distraction of that noisy box! Our evenings are no longer planned around the TV schedule, and now that we are not being tempted by the lure of easy entertainment, we are discovering new talents. You should see our six-year-old Billy draw. He's really good! And daddy (Bill) organized a cooking committee after dinner last night. He and the kids made a delicious banana cake while tired mommy went to bed at 7:15! We are doing much more reading. Bill sits down regularly with two eager little boys and reads to them until eventually they are all asleep. Our sleeping habits have changed. Now we all go to sleep when we're tired. There's no staying up to see an old rerun. It's exciting to think how much more we can grow together in the years to come, using our own creative abilities to entertain ourselves and each other.

Rachel Diener, Minnesota, would be another to refute the claim that women at home spend most of their time in front of the television set. "One of the best decisions we have made was to sell our television set," Rachel declares. "After going through about three weeks of 'withdrawal pains'—automatically sitting down in the living room and staring blankly at the spot where the set had been—we learned to find other entertainment. Number one with us is taking the whole family to the public library. The children are learning to love reading as much as their parents do."

Ode to the Library

"Never underestimate the value of your local library," states Elaine Caper, Illinois. Elaine voices a sentiment that is shared by many. Some examples: "A how-to-book *did* show us how to reupholster the sofa—fix the car—cut hair." The list goes on: "I love to read, but magazine subscriptions strain the budget. I find I can check out many magazines from the library." "Even paperbacks are getting expensive, so we now check our library for the latest fiction." "You can get just about any book by asking your librarian. I've gotten books from church and college libraries through the interlibrary loan system," Elaine says.

Nor is that all. From firsthand experience, letter writers point out that besides being repositories of the printed word, the public library dispenses information and pleasure through records, tapes, games, puzzles, films, art—paintings, photos, statues—and in at least one library in Minnesota, "a block-building area that enthralls the youngsters." And if that isn't enough, there are programs for children and adults, from puppet shows to kite-making clinics. "I always come back from the library feeling that I've been on a free shopping spree," says Elaine.

Among the free events held at the library in Elaine's community is the Family Movie Night held twice a month. The films can be counted on to be acceptable family fare, often classics, and there's no worry that coming attractions of a decidedly undesirable film will lead off the evening's entertainment. Elaine says that their children often bring a friend, making this a nice way for them to be the ones to treat while the only cost to mom and dad is picking up and taking the little friends home. "And since the library movies are very informal," Elaine points out, "it's easy to take the baby and walk along the side or back of the room."

Movies courtesy of the library, this time shown at home, are an entertainment favorite with the Worzers of Texas. "Our public library has a media section with a great selection of Super 8 cartoons and other movies, *Star Wars,* for one," Linda writes. "We check out the quota, pop up a bowl of popcorn, and Voilà! movie time at home, free of charge! We often invite neighborhood children and have quite a party, with everyone having a great time."

A Wealth of Learning   Primarily, libraries are books, and reading material can bring fun and tremendous learning experiences to young preschoolers and their mothers-at-home. Nori

Reinert, New Jersey, tells of her favorite section in their local library.

> Best of all is the wealth of possibilities in nonfiction books. An introductory book on rocks and minerals can lead to much happy exploring and identifying rocks in the yard, neighborhood, and park. We use empty egg cartons for collecting and labelling our finds.
>
> In warm weather, a book about insects can lead to a "bug zoo." Books from the library can inspire a leaf collection or labelling the trees in the yard. Our children have enjoyed our bird watching log. We add names as newcomers show up at our feeder.
>
> Another good choice is how-it-works type books. They're a big hit at our house (and I'm glad to have explanations of some of these things for myself!). The sciences are very appealing to most preschoolers, since they're all little detectives anyway. There are myriad elementary books about the properties of water, air, and electricity, about weather, the stars, etc., with answers to those endless questions small children ask. Easy science experiments are good indoor fun during bad weather, and most require only household items. Sure, it takes time on mom's part, but doesn't everything really worthwhile?

The combination of a child, an interesting idea, and an interested mother is an unbeatable combination for imparting the beginnings of wisdom.

Preschool at Home

Preschool learning is included in this section because, unless it's fun for the preschooler, little learning takes place. Of course, a tremendous amount of teaching and learning of a vital kind transpires between mother and child in a happy, secure relationship, much of it unplanned. But given the young child's eagerness to explore and do things, suddenly all the world is waiting to be rediscovered. Learning will never again be such an adventure. It's a priceless time in the lives of parents and children that is too precious to be squandered. While a good preschool program can offer numerous opportunities to a child, plus the chance to socialize with other children, such programs do not come cheaply. And, mothers writing to us stress, an interested mother or group of mothers armed with some good books on the subject and a few craft materials can be every bit as effective in providing a child with a stimulating environment. These mothers feel strongly about the matter, with a number of them writing primarily on this point. Some comments and suggestions follow:

> *No* way can a nursery school compete with a really dedicated mother. I am a primary school teacher, and contrary to what many think, one does not need to be a teacher to teach one's own child. My tips on things for you to do with your child: Painting—even once a month is worth the effort. Gluing—Let your child smear it and stick it the way he wants it. (Most of the creations brought home by Johnny from nursery school have been designed by teachers to impress mother.) Flash card words, large and red—I am not very consistent about this, but would recommend that you take it very seriously if you have poor spellers in the family, yet always with a spark of fun. Your efforts could save the cost of many extra lessons. Puzzles—Try just about any type of children's puzzle you can get, but look for the inlay type. The frame seems to be essential with children starting out on puzzles. Old radios and tape recorders can be taken apart. The public library for books, books, books—nothing can beat the morning "read" in bed.
>
> One thing that nursery school does offer is companionship with other children. In three towns I have solved this by organizing a play group in which we mothers get together with our children in the garden, weather permitting, and a basket of toys and perhaps a planned activity. These two days a week are a real highlight for us all. It spurs me to get on with the housework, though we all have a turn to be hostess. Maximum, six to seven moms with children.
>
> *Marion Lewis from the Republic of South Africa*

Have Fun!

We now have three children in grade school and can count several thousand dollars saved through keeping them at home with me instead of sending them to nursery school. My husband and I believe that by waiting until our children are five or six to put them into the competition and tension of a classroom, they have been much better able to cope with this often stressful situation. We have taken our children on field trips. Some of our destinations have been the zoo, a fire station, an apple orchard, the ever popular library, an animal farm, the airport, a college including the TV station on campus, a bakery, and hands-on museums.

LeAnne Fay of Michigan

We chose to organize our own small preschool for each child. The year before kindergarten, one day a week, we met with several friends—six to ten is a good size. We mothers took turns teaching—numbers, letters, colors, seasons, songs, and games— and planning a simple craft, nutritious snacks, and free play for the children. You need not be professionally trained as a teacher in order to undertake a project such as this. Ideas abound at your local public library or bookstore. Just relying on ideas gleaned from each mother may be sufficient, but a couple of good reference books can go a long way in generating new ideas.

Marilyn Hein, Kansas

The more closely I look at schools for the three- or four-year-old, even the Montessori environment, the more I am convinced that I could teach as much or more (and have) at home. I've always worked with my kids, but it took looking at the schools to convince me how effective I am and to realize that by setting aside school time at home, I am actually saving money that I might otherwise have felt was necessary to spend on my rapidly learning little ones. I grow excited as we learn together, and indeed, who else *does* care about their development as much as I do?

Martha Sterrett, Texas

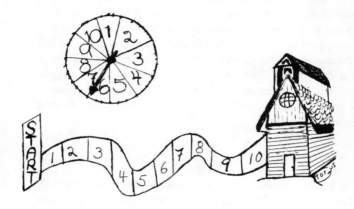

My four-year-old spends "hours"—well, many minutes—playing with her favorite words printed on small cards backed with masking tape. She matches these with pictures, colors, shapes, etc., which also have masking tape on the back, and sticks them to a wall. Her favorite books are the ones she makes up herself. I write down her stories, and sometimes use picture flash cards with her favorite words. Children's games are so expensive, and little ones tire of them quickly. By using the spinners and movers from a store-bought game, or making your own, you can design countless new games. For example, numbers, letters, colors, animals "Going to School."

Sheryl Ferris, Vermont

I've not had to worry and wonder and hope that my children's needs were being met for attention, affection, and stimulation. I've been close by with special feelings a mother has for her own child and I have known that my daughters were in a loving, stable environment which was sensitive to the unique needs of each. Being with them has brought me a peace of mind that no amount of money could buy.

Cathy Rose, Missouri

The Outdoor Life

Step out the door on a nice day and suddenly the stage on which to do things and have fun includes the earth and sky and everything in between. Eat an ordinary meal outdoors and it's a picnic—summer or winter, as long as the sun is shining. When the weather is warm enough, let the kids splash and play with water in the backyard to their heart's content, and yours, too, as there are no puddles to mop up. Take a walk, keeping the pace slow enough for the youngest and varying it enough to please big brothers or sisters with short races and stretches of hopping and skipping. Outfit your bike with a child's safety seat, obtain and use a protective helmet for your little one, and make biking more than a once-in-a while thing. Bike to the store or to visit a friend. Bike to save money and stay in shape.

How long has it been since you've "gone fishin'?" As Karen Elkins of North Dakota says, "Even a beginner can drop a line in the water. All it takes is a couple of poles, some bait, and a family fishing license (ours cost us $8 this year)." Karen notes that an afternoon of fishing "combines well with a picnic lunch."

The prospect of taking home a stringer of fresh fish for supper can be quite appealing, but even if the fish outwit the fishermen—"we often come home empty-handed," Karen says—a day near the river or lake is sure to hold a good many attractions. Water is endlessly fascinating to children. Drop a pebble into a body of water and watch the ripples dance out in perfect formation. Off there to one side, you're apt to see a little eddy, the nonconformist spirit in the grand stream of things. And here is a school of minnows, "baby fishes," in constant motion but seemingly going nowhere. Then quick, look, there goes Mr. Frog jumping off a lily pad. Chances are if the sun is high and bright and there's a half-submerged log in the vicinity, you'll see a family of turtles sunning themselves. Surrounding

Vic and Susan Keeler take the whole family on outings to search for arrowheads.

you is the smell of water and of growing things and the sounds of the outdoors and the children playing. And you won't have to run to answer a phone. As Karen says, "The fun comes from being together with no other distractions." A day out of doors could be just the change of pace that a busy mother and father as well as the kids need.

A Walk by Any Name Consider, too, the simple hike. There's nothing like walking to help you really see the fine details of the world around you. It could be a town walk, to the post office or the library, perhaps, or you may want to go on a nature walk. From the time their children were born, the Harns of Connecticut have made a practice of doing things together as a family, and over the years hiking has become one of their favorite forms of diversion. "Planning the all-day hikes now seems to be so much fun for the girls," Jackie Harns says of her ten- and twelve-year-old daughters. "They read the maps, get out the walk books, and such. We have already planned half a dozen walks for this spring." She says that each family member, including the four-year-old, has a backpack and canteen for use on their outings in the woods.

"Our special love" is how Christine Hilston, Ohio, de-

Have Fun!

The Keelers also enjoy fishing together.

scribes their fondness for the outdoor life and backpacking in particular. "We've backpacked with a baby in a carrier and a four-year-old and two-year-old," Christine says. "We keep our treks short and tailor them to the capabilities of the children."

For a collector, a nature walk is often incorporated with a search, the hunt for a cherished something—rocks, driftwood, leaves, or possibly ancient remains, as is the case with the Keelers in Ohio. Susan Keeler writes, "Our most exciting hobby started three years ago when my husband, Vic, brought home an arrowhead he found while on a hunting trip." The next weekend, Susan says, the whole family was out, "walking up and down the rows of plowed fields looking for artifacts. I thought it was the most boring thing I had ever done," Susan reports, "until I found a perfect 10,000-year-old (Paleo) spearhead! How exciting it is to hold something that old in your hand and look around trying to imagine what things were like when the original owner was standing where you are!" Since then, the Keelers have found over 100 pieces, "including birdpoints, spearheads, celts, and axes, all within fifty miles of home," says Susan. Their outings are made with the baby in the backpack and the five-year-old, "tagging along looking for 'pretty rocks.' " Over the past winter, some friends interested them in butterflies, and Susan says "we have our field guide ready and have made our net. We're anxious to get started on another new venture."

Camping Anyone? When an excursion takes a family away from home overnight, food and lodging often go along with them. Camping is the popular mode, and many of those who wrote to us offer tips for camping on a budget. "Whenever we travel, unless it is extremely cold, we camp, but not with an expensive camper or trailer," writes Jean Giesel, Florida. "We have always just used a large tent and even manage without air mattresses if there's no room to pack them." Jean says that they avoid the interstate highways, whenever possible, and usually camp at state, county, or national parks. "We like the surroundings better," she says. "They are less expensive than franchised roadside 'parks.' We have also found the lesser used roads to be more interesting, cooler in the summer (we have no air conditioning), and almost as fast." Jean adds that they "try to plan a leisurely trip and not be in a hurry."

On the question of how much equipment you need for camping, Karen Elkins says, "In reality, you probably have most everything you'd need in your home already." The Elkins have found that a little innovation can carry one quite a way. In lieu of sleeping bags, take sheets and blankets. Air mattresses are not necessary. "We take the mattress from our sofa bed and sleep in real comfort," Karen says. An old shower curtain does fine as a ground cover. Laundry baskets, boxes, or large plastic bags may not be stylish, but they hold clothing and other supplies as well as suitcases. A cardboard box lined with multi-layers of newspapers will serve as an ice chest. Water frozen in milk cartons eliminates the need to buy ice the first day or so and doesn't leak. The baby's plastic bathtub can double as a traveling sink or dishpan. Dishes and a flashlight are common household items. "You will need a shelter," Karen notes and explains that they were able "to borrow a tent at first. We then bought one cheaply secondhand." For beginning

Have Fun!

The Duffy family takes a hike in the mountains.

campers, Karen recommends a "rehearsal campout" in the backyard. Besides being fun, she points out that, "You really learn what you need and what you don't. And you can sneak back in the house for the can opener you forgot!"

Where to Camp   By all means make use of the information on camping sites available through government publications, often the department of conservation or tourism. Many areas even offer an inexpensive introduction to camping that includes the use of camping equipment as well as the campgrounds. In Illinois, such a program is called Rent-A-Camp. Fees range from $8 to $16 for the camping equipment and $3 to $6 for the site. In Texas, where the Pipkin family often vacations, the state parks have screened shelters for campers that are equipped with water and electric outlets for about $6 a night. The Pipkins use their electric skillet for cooking. Glinda Pipkin writes, "We usually stay in three or four state parks during a week's vacation. Using canned foods cuts down on the expense of buying ice for the ice chest." She says that they've camped with all of their babies, "as young as six weeks old." Glinda adds, "Of course, this is easier with a breastfed baby, but when we were camping with our eight-month-old adopted son, we used powdered formula and water from home and made up fresh bottles as we needed them."

In order to keep costs down when camping, the Harveys in Kansas keep their trips short. "Camping is our number one choice of entertainment," Anne Harvey writes, "and many times we travel to a campsite just a few miles from home for a weekend. A lot of the fun is the sharing—even washing dishes can be fun!" A longer jaunt for the Harvey family could be a trip to meet friends at a campsite halfway from where the two families live or to visit relatives who live out of state. Traveling as a family is "easier and more economical" when camping, Anne says. "And the trip home doesn't seem so bad when you know you can stop for a night and set up camp. The rewards have been tremendous for all of us."

Another Kansas family discovered a "whole different type of camping" when they met up with friends in Colorado. "Here in Kansas," Janis Cox says, "it's boating, swimming, fishing." The two families spent a considerable amount of time, but very little money, exploring the back roads. "We went in search of ghost towns, old mine sites, beaver ponds, wild flowers, and other scenery," Janis says. When she compares this uncommercial venture to the "tourist traps" they had previously visited, she states, "We really enjoyed ourselves more the days we camped and we spent a lot less doing it."

With camping, a good part of the fun and excitement lies in the fact of "going somewhere." Charlene Burnett of Missouri writes about just such an experience with their children. "When 'everybody' was going on a ski trip over spring break, we went on a camping trip to visit some old neighbors who now live 200 miles away." Charlene says they have found that many times the children are "just as happy with small trips as big ones. A trip is a trip."

Vacation Fun Of course, camping isn't for everybody. People's daydreams of what constitutes a vacation are as different as, well, as people are. No two families think alike on the matter, nor do individuals within a family. For Anne Grider "a vacation means not having to cook or do dishes." As for the rest of the Grider family, a vacation is the opportunity to go places "we don't normally go." But to this, Anne adds, "hotels and restaurant fare can be out of the question financially." Undaunted, this Hawaii family came up with a formula to satisfy everyone. "Our answer has been at-home vacations," Anne explains. "We look through the newspaper, brochures, and maps and list the things we'd like to see or do that are out of our neighborhood but within about an hour's drive of home. Then, several weeks ahead of time, we begin making a list of everyone's favorite foods. A little at a time, we get it all cooked up, sealed in boilable plastic pouches, and frozen. We also lay in a supply of paper plates, cups, and such. We eat like kings with a minimum of preparation and clean-up time and have a ball for a fraction of what it would cost to go away."

No two families think alike when it comes to planning a vacation...

Recently Anne and her family took a more conventional vacation, their first "real" vacation in ten years. Of their experience, Anne says, "It was not nearly as satisfying as we had anticipated. We ate in many restaurants and only once came away feeling that we'd gotten what we paid for. And all of us missed our own comfortable beds and pillows!"

Families who have to watch their pennies often find simple ways to accumulate a vacation fund, a special nest egg or "sugar bowl account" that may build slowly but always holds great promise. Jill Halloran of Virginia writes. "Occasionally the children and I go on a 'recycling adventure.' We look for aluminum on the side of the road or at parks and take it to the recycling center." Jill says the money goes to buy "a little treat or is saved for a family outing." Babara Dick in Washington is one of those in the rank of "change savers." "One thing I do to save money for something special is to save coins," Barbara writes. "After a year of saving coins and some baby-sitting money, I had round-trip trainfare from Ohio to Connecticut for two adults and a two-year-old. Imagine that! Pennies, nickles, dimes, and quarters add up fast!"

Sure Cures for Cabin Fever

There's no place like home, but sometimes, especially during long spells of bad weather, the four walls seem to close in and the "grumpies" set in—recognizable by grumpy children and grumpy parents. "Whenever there's a two or three day spell of bad weather, things can get pretty hairy," Donna MacFarlane of New Mexico concedes. "The two boys, ages seven and five, can get into some pretty wicked fights." Donna says, but "On those days, I make a point to read to them and play with them more than I usually do." As for children's bickering, she says she usually lets them "try to work it out," but she says, too, "sometimes I intervene."

It happens—mother and the kids are confined to the house for days at a time, and everyone gets on each other's nerves. Sometimes a short low cost expedition can work wonders to restore spirits and make home seem better than ever. For anyone with a grandmother nearby, Lisa Robitaille has the perfect solution for chasing that down and out, closed in feeling that sometimes affects mothers of young children. "I find there is nothing like a visit to Grandma's to cure cabin fever," Lisa writes. "Having someone else dote over the kids for a few hours gives me a new perspective on life."

Visit the Mall Do you live near a shopping mall? If you do, you and your little ones can take a spur-of-the-moment break and "do the shopping mall." Mind you, this has nothing to do with serious shopping. "Kids get tired of that fast," mothers

Have Fun!

Jason and Jennifer Kastendieck enjoy coloring Easter eggs with their aunt, Andrea Foshe.

unanimously agree. Your stroll through the mall is a diversion, a chance to visit the animals in the pet shop, browse in the toy store, and people watch, chatting a bit with the older folks and other mothers and youngsters who frequent the malls during the day. Joyce Bartels, New York, gives a cost accounting of this indoor sport.

The three kids and I start at the end with the lockers (twenty-five cents) so we can wander unencumbered. The three horse merry-go-round is a must (twenty-five cents for all three to ride). To make throwing pennies in the fountain last longer, we sit on a bench nearby, and one child at a time walks up to the fountain and tosses in a penny, while the rest of us sit and watch (three cents). A large glass of orange juice at the booth where it's fresh squeezed is sixty cents and satisfies all three. Along the way, someone is sure to comment about the kids, which pleases everyone. If lunch is in order, we can stop at the yogurt bar or the cafeteria which carries hard-boiled eggs, applesauce, salads, fruits, and cottage cheese. Lunch usually totals $2.50 at the most. Wandering through the toy store saves lots of money because the kids get a realistic idea of what the toys in the television commercials really do, and mom gets a realistic idea of what not to buy the kids for Christmas. Our last stop is usually the photo booth. For one dollar, they get to spend as much time setting up their pose as they want and then have a keepsake of our adventure. A whole day of doing something together, meeting people, eating out, and having fun things to do costs us anywhere from $1.53 to $4.53, depending on whether we have lunch.

Bend and Stretch If you're a mother at home, at times you feel the need for some expansion room, but at other times, when looking in the mirror perhaps, you may see some expansion that you could do without! You're probably thinking, "If only I could join a fitness program." Organizing a home exercise group can be a way to get you out of the house and keep you trim. Besides yourself and a couple of other interested moms (not too many because, remember, you'll be sharing space with the young participants), you'll want a couple of exercise records and perhaps a book or two. Most important, of course, is your commitment to meet regularly. It's a break in the routine, you'll have fun, and you may soon look fabulous!

Family Outings Some old favorites with kids and parents alike are museums, preferably those that are *not* known for their subdued atmosphere. The Laugle family in Ohio has found the best of such a museum world in an airplane hangar. "At the Air Force Museum," Donna Laugle writes, "the boys can do lots of running around without worrying about damaging anything or anyone." She says that the children also enjoy the Natural History museum, but "we usually stay away from the Art Institute. The boys tend to be too rambunctious at this point for the serious art enthusiasts."

"One of our favorite outings is a trip to the Indianapolis Children's Museum, the largest in the world and absolutely free," writes Claudia Barber, Indiana. "In nice weather we pack a picnic lunch, so our only expense is gas. We have a day's entertainment for five people for less than $5." Claudia suggests that you check your local papers for news of free and inexpensive recreation, such as concerts, recitals, productions of the local drama clubs, and new museum exhibits.

Linda Lesniewski enjoys visiting the petting zoo with her little ones.

In Utah, the Butlers look forward to occasionally going to a drive-in movie, which holds a twofold appeal for a family with young children. Linda Butler notes that their fifteen-month-old daughter "is at an age where she finds it hard to sit still on my lap in a regular theater. The drive-ins around here have little playgrounds under the screen for the kids. We arrive an hour early and play with Jessica, which wears her out. She then sits still in the car for a while and usually falls asleep within the hour." At five dollars per car, the drive-in can be "an inexpensive and entertaining evening," Linda says.

What's Important

Families with limited incomes may have to expand their horizons to look for low-cost ways to find enjoyment. For most of them, though, much of their fun comes from being together as a family, no matter what activities they pursue.

The consensus is that families with mother-at-home aren't missing out on the really important things in life. Observes Donna MacFarlane of New Mexico. "I enjoy the freedom that being at home affords me. I can take the children to parks, go on bike rides, to museums, the zoo, or just plain go for a walk around the block with an ever-curious two-year-old. I am home to notice the adorable little things my children do and the interesting ways in which they perceive the world as they grow older and try to understand life more logically. I feel more secure in knowing where my children are, what they are doing, and that they are being cared for in the way that I feel is best."

CHAPTER 13

Saving Ways

There are 1,001 household tips that can save you time and money. We think our pioneer families have come up with a few that are quite unique. As you read through this chapter, you're sure to find some useful ideas.

Use Less

This could be called the age of the disposable. "Use it once and throw it away" can be convenient but expensive. There are ways to avoid this "throw away" lifestyle. Here are just a few ideas:

Reserve paper napkins for picnics. Follow the style of the finest restaurants—use cloth napkins at home, but do it the easy way: "I bought cheap washcloths on sale which we use rather than paper napkins," writes Claudia Barber of Indiana. "With a different color for each person, it isn't necessary to have a clean one for each meal. (Napkin rings would work well, too.) They're so absorbent, and with children creating continuous laundry, who notices a few extra napkins in the wash?"

Reach for a substitute for paper toweling. The humble rag is making a big comeback. Anne Harvey of Kansas is only one of many mothers-at-home who speak of keeping a supply of rags in the kitchen and bathroom. They're handy to wipe up spills, clean a baby's bottom (toss in diaper pail to be washed and reused), or use for scrubbing and scouring. Jill Halloran of Virginia bought "a dozen restaurant quality linen towels, and use them to do it all, from window washing to dish drying or wiping up spills, draining lettuce, and even draining tuna."

Recycle plastic bags and aluminum foil.

Use large brown bags as is to line wastebaskets; decorate them to hold odd-shaped gifts (stuff colored tissue inside to separate things); split them open to use as sturdy wrapping paper for packages to be mailed; add an opening for the head and arms, and use as a Halloween costume for a small child—a large, yellow circle added front and back for a pumpkin, some foil for the Tin Man.

Use crushed newspaper dampened under the faucet to mop up a spill almost as quickly as a paper towel. Newspaper is the product of choice for many when washing windows. It helps clean the windows, shines them, doesn't leave lint, and the supply is plentiful.

Save incoming junk mail that is blank on one side and use for scrap paper.

Put unused return envelopes to use—send money to school with the kids; write out your shopping list on the envelope and tuck coupons, bills, and receipts inside.

Use masking tape in place of cellophane tape. "I only buy masking tape—on large rolls in the paint department of a store," writes Maurine Joens of Arkansas. "It can be used in place of cellophane tape (doubled over and concealed under an edge) and it works well as freezer tape and even to hold bandages."

Laundry Tips

Soaps, detergents, and other laundry products come in a variety of brands and types, many of which are labeled "New and Improved" at least once a year. Families on limited incomes often take a look at simpler ways to handle laundry problems.

David Lebbing finds the best toys don't have to cost any extra money.

Remember Grandma's Wringer Washer? It's on the job in Wisconsin, washing clothes and saving water and soap. "I save about $10 a month on the water bill since giving up my automatic washer and starting to use a wringer washer," writes Noreen Knepel. "And a gallon of laundry detergent now lasts three months instead of one." While she's washing the clothes, Noreen's youngest child, a three-year-old, plays in the sandbox that was set up in the basement. "The first time I used the wringer washer, my whole body ached because I was using muscles that I usually didn't use; now it doesn't bother me at all."

Jj Fallick, also of Wisconsin, says that she washes "eight large loads a week with a wringer washer and rinse tubs, all on one day, and I use no more than six tubs full of water, as opposed to a minimum of sixteen with an automatic washer." Adds Jj, "I even double rinse the diapers. And yes, the clothes DO get clean." (A tub full of soapy water can be used for more than one load of clothes in a wringer washer. The washer can be filled with hot water to wash the first load of white clothes;

then the clothes are transferred to a rinse tub and a load of colored clothes are washed in the same tub full of soapy water.)

Don't Throw Out those wooden clothespins that leave a stain on clothes because they've darkened from the rain. Boil them for a few minutes in water and a little bleach. Dry them well.

Super-Duper Laundry Spot Remover "One gallon hot water, one cup *dishwasher* detergent, one-quarter cup chlorine bleach. Mix until completely dissolved. Do NOT store in a metal container. Soak washable things at least thirty minutes, preferably overnight. For use with synthetic materials, let the solution cool before adding the clothes." (Anne Harvey, Kansas.) As with any such products, RINSE THOROUGHLY, especially when used on baby clothes.

Indoor Lines or Drying Racks will cut down on the number of loads that go into the dryer in the wintertime and also add needed moisture to the air during the heating season. Sheets are favorites for line drying, as are other heavy items. "I use two drying racks for all the jeans because they'd cost a fortune to do in the dryer," writes Claudia Barber of Indiana. In Wyoming, Judi Myers' two teenage sons do their own laundry "and hang it on the line, too," writes Judi.

Other Cleaning Projects

Clean Away Save by using alternatives to high-priced commercial cleaning products. Many thrifty homemakers make their own. Simple mixtures are best; don't combine too many things. BAKING SODA (sodium bicarbonate) is a tried and true cleaning product, either mixed with water or sprinkled directly on a surface.

WHITE VINEGAR can safely be used full strength or somewhat diluted with water to clean kitchen counters, windows, and mirrors. One cup vinegar to one-half gallon of water will clean "no-wax" floors without dulling them. "Make a paste of vinegar and salt to clean brass and copper," says Anne Harvey of Kansas. AMMONIA mixed with water is a popular window cleaner, but be careful when using ammonia, especially in a spray.

Avoid using commercial sprays. They pollute the air as much as they clean, polish, or deodorize.

CAUTION: NEVER MIX VINEGAR OR AMMONIA WITH CHLORINE BLEACH. The resulting fumes can be deadly.

"HOT, HOT WATER used with rubber gloves to protect your hands," is Elaine Caper's tip for intensifying your cleaning efforts, on sinks, floors, walls, and such. "Disinfectants, cleaners, and polishing products are very costly," notes this Illinois mother. Elaine regularly uses "a damp rag for dusting, a dry one for polishing." To occasionally put a bright shine on furniture, try olive oil and beeswax.

Dilute, Dilute, Dilute Many cleaning products perform well when diluted. Shampoos, conditioners, liquid dish detergents can often be cut by half or more with water. Experiment until you find the right proportion. Beauty salons frequently dilute the shampoo since it's more easily distributed through the hair.

Scouring Compound "Make a cleansing powder out of sifted SAND and WOOD ASHES. Equal portions make a fine combination for cleaning sinks. All sand is good for scouring pots." (Maurine Joens, Arkansas.)

Shine stainless steel and chrome with WITCH HAZEL or ALCOHOL.

Upholstery and Rug Shampoo "Combine one-quarter cup detergent for dishes with one cup water in a large bowl. Beat to a dry, sudsy foam. Use immediately to clean upholstery or rugs." (Marilyn Yoder, Indiana.)

Soft Soap "I save soap chips, cover them with boiling water to soak, and then put them in a pump container for my own 'soft soap.'" (Anne Harvey, Kansas.)

Health and Beauty Aids

Skin Care   "Break open a vitamin E capsule for a good oil to use on dry skin areas. Apply sparingly when your face is still moist from cleansing, and blot off any excess. A rose geranium facial will chase away dry skin and wrinkles. Steep several leaves of a rose geranium plant in rose water or plain water. Shake the leaves and apply to face while lying down for fifteen minutes. Do not rinse." (Linda Lawrence, Ontario, Canada.)

Beautiful Hair   Shampoos do not differ all that much, except in price. Those designated "for oily hair" are generally stronger and clean more thoroughly. If you have normal or dry hair, you'll probably do fine buying the cheapest shampoo you can find.

Smell Sweet   "We haven't used a commercial deodorant in seven years," writes Marlene Cullen of Louisiana. "Instead, we use rubbing alcohol (isopropyl). Apply with a cotton ball."

Buy New Toothbrushes!   Buy them on sale, but by all means replace brushes that have limp, bent bristles. A tired old brush will not do the job it should for you in keeping teeth clean and gums healthy. Buy new ones for your teeth, but don't throw the old ones out! Worn toothbrushes are the perfect tool for scouring around faucets in the kitchen and bathroom. (And an old broom will make it easier for you to scrub out the bathtub, especially when you're pregnant.)

About Toothpaste   A little goes a long way—use just a dab on your brush and teach your children to do likewise. The brushing action is much more beneficial than what is on the brush.

Be a Home Barber   If you wince at the thought of using pointed shears near your child's head (let alone at the thought of doing a credible job of cutting his or her hair), Kathy Siddons of Connecticut offers some suggestions:

To start, I used a pair of long-bladed *blunt point* scissors, available in any stationery store. As my confidence and skill grew, I used real hair shears purchased from a discount beauty supply house. (A good pair of real barber shears are an absolute necessity to achieve the best results. They must be sharp and maintained that way.)

On hair-cutting day, shampoo hair. Seat child on a high step stool in the middle of a rugless floor. Turn on a record player and sing along, or let your child look at a book, or tell him a story. Your little one may enjoy holding a mirror and watching you. Cover him with a piece of sheeting—plastic wraps are too sticky and uncomfortable for children's skin.

For valuable specifics on what and how to cut the hair, get a copy of *How To Cut Children's Hair* by Bob Bent (Simon and Schuster). It contains step-by-step illustrations and ideas for boys', girls', and unisex hair styles. *Just remember always to cut off less than you think you need to at first.*

Kathy says that in the summer, she washes and cuts the children's hair outdoors. A garden hose stretched out in the sunny part of the lawn for a couple of hours supplies "buckets of hot water for sudsing and rinsing."

More than one husband has been initially reluctant to place his head, or more specifically, his hair, in his wife's hands. Before the family emigrated to Canada, Dave Harding was accustomed to getting his hair trimmed regularly by the company's barber for three shillings (approximately 75 cents). The shock of a much higher charge for haircuts in their new location prompted him to tell Sandra, his wife, "You do it, but be jolly careful how much you chop off—and let me have a mirror so I can see what you're doing."

Cutting hair is now a regular routine for Sandra, who also keeps her two young sons looking neat and trim. She has found that after about five minutes, the smaller members of the family have trouble sitting still, and it helps to "pose them in front of the bathroom mirror or in front of the television set." Her husband, she says, doesn't mind combining a haircut with watching a hockey game on television. But Sandra warns, "It is difficult to emulate a master barber when your customer is apt to leap out of the chair shouting encouragement or otherwise, depending on the way the game is going."

Auto Savings

One Minute Rule   When driving, keep in mind the one-minute rule: If you are stopped, for instance by a long slow train, *for more than one minute*, you'll use less fuel by turning off the engine and restarting it later than by keeping it idling.

Easy Does It   Your car uses fuel most efficiently when traveling non-stop at a steady speed. At 50 mph, your car uses fuel almost as efficiently as at 40 mph; if you drive 70 mph instead of 50 mph, there's a loss of about 25 percent in mileage per gallon (*Home Energy for the Eighties*, Wolfe and Clegg).

Half and Half   "We have a twelve-year-old car that should take high-test gasoline. We found that by alternating purchases of high-test and regular gas, the car runs fine." (Cheryl Ricciardi, Connecticut.)

Kid Stuff

Do the Kids Get Bored   when the weather keeps them indoors for long stretches? Do you have a basement or garage? "We cleaned out part of the cellar and have the riding toys and small slide down there. The children can run off *excess* energy while I fold clothes. It gives us a change of scenery, and I don't have to spend a lot of time cleaning up. This has been a real lifesaver in winter." (Patti Clark, Maine.)

"We purchased five pairs of roller skates last year (marked down from $25 to $5) so the kids could skate indoors on rainy days in the garage or basement." (Betty Aviles, Maryland.)

Erick and Brett Nuelsen have fun in the tub.

Fun in the Tub A plastic laundry basket is a common sight in the Nuelsen's bathtub. The basket, with the baby in it, keeps baby and toys together and out of the way of the four-year-old who also joins the fun. Mom is always nearby, yet the arrangement makes it possible for her to do other things as the children play. "I can wash and get ready for bed, clean the bathroom, or even write a letter—just so I'm there. The children love to play together, and this way, the baby and toys don't go far away from each other and the four-year-old still has his space." (Diane Nuelsen, Kentucky.)

Play Recipes To make your own play dough you'll need: 2 cups flour; 1 cup salt; 2 tbls. alum; 1 3/4 cups boiling water; 2 tbls. salad oil. Mix dry ingredients. Add boiling water and stir until it forms a ball. Add oil and knead. (Do *not* add flour after the dough has been made; it ruins the consistency.) Store in a covered container. (Karen Six, Ohio.)

Finger Paint To make finger paint, beat together until smooth equal parts of *liquid starch* and *mild soap flakes* Add powdered tempera paint for color. For a preservative, add 1/4 tsp. oil of cloves or 1 tbls. benzoate of soda. How much will you need? Figure about one tablespoon per child per picture. (Karen Six, Ohio.)

Toys from Trash Collect caps from aerosol cans. Look for different colors and sizes. The caps make great stacking toys for children, and since they are easier to stack than their commercial counterpart, they appeal to younger children. Of course, they may be nested, too—a good way to store them. Ask soda pop drinkers to save empty two liter plastic bottles for you. The empty drink bottles are great for a game of bowling. Line them up, and have small bowlers knock them down with a plastic ball. (Wilda Webber, Louisiana.)

Endless Hours of Fun—Wallpaper Books, Newsprint Rolls Let the clerk at the wallpaper store know that you'll happily take any wallpaper books that are ready to be discarded. Use the wallpaper samples to color on, for collages, gift wrap, paper chains, paper "balloons" (cut a shape out of double thickness, staple together leaving room to stuff with paper, and hang for a mobile). Check your newspaper office for leftover end rolls of newsprint. They can often be obtained at low cost or free and are perfect for large paper projects. (Lynne Sancken, Indiana.)

A Toy Exchange "Get together with several moms and their children for a toy exchange. Each family brings three or four toys to trade, and each can take three or four home for fresh play ideas." (Cathy Rose, Missouri.)

Gifts and Greetings

Nifty Gift Ideas "One year we made soap for gift-giving (we make all of our own soap), and the next year our gift was fruitcake, the next year, sachet pillows," writes Barbara Dick of Washington.

"We've sent pictures of the kids placed in construction paper envelopes. A homemade or store-bought T-shirt can be decorated with appliques, embroidery, or fabric paint." writes Joan Ellison of Minnesota.

"I've made hand-monogrammed handkerchiefs, knee socks

with a name sewn on the cuff, yardstick holders. Last year, I made matching nightshirts for my brothers and sisters, their spouses, and my parents, all with their first names mono-grammed on the pocket. I bought material on sale the year before, and I spent about three dollars per shirt." (Coleen Mast, Illinois.)

"Both my sons received their sturdy green canvas back-packs, which have served for school books, camping, and 'suit-cases,' as gifts from their Auntie Lynn. Auntie Lynn obtained them through sharp garage-sale shopping. My sister and I don't think of this in terms of 'being cheap,' rather we see it as being *creative*." (Elaine Caper, Illinois.)

For the person living alone, give proportionately sized gifts of food: "My mother-in-law, who was recently widowed, was pleased by the foodstuffs I'd specially canned in smaller con-tainers and wrapped as part of her Christmas gift this year." (Phyllis Nelson, Minnesota.)

Precious Little Time to Make Things? "Lots of moms with small children have little extra money or hand-crafting time available," states Mary Lou Pease of Minnesota. Numerous other mothers agree and offer some delightful alternatives. Mary Lou suggests, "Extend an invitation to a family meal, spend an afternoon together, give a memory album of snapshots or a promise to babysit. Find gifts that don't cost and ones that offer a cheerful, positive attitude about things."

Says Kay Wallin of Illinois, "We give gift coupons. Sounds corny? Perhaps, but what great gifts! A coupon from me to my daughter might read: 'This coupon entitles you to a walk with me alone after supper. You are free to discuss whatever you want—boys, sex, food, even your dirty room.' Another coupon might even say that I'll clean that dirty room, or that I'll give her a backrub on a day that she's had a rough time. One of the older children's favorites is that I offer to do their paper route for them for a certain period of time. The ideas are end-less, and the one who gives the gift has almost as much fun

A toy exchange provides new fun for the Wallin children.

coming up with something different as the person receiving it. We love to give them and love getting them. Also, they are cheap and full of love."

Mother's "Gift Closet"   A "gift closet" is a supply of assorted things which you purchase on sale and which prove to be lifesavers for upcoming occasions—a family member's birthday or the party which your child tells you about on the day before. "I never spend more than three dollars on gifts for children's birthday parties," writes Charlene Burnett of Missouri. "This means that when I see something on a closeout table, I often buy several of the same item."

Says Patty Meadows of Virginia, "I keep a 'goodie bag' of small gifts which I pick up on sale so I'm always prepared for those last minute invitations. Cute notepads and novelty pens and erasers, bookmarks, and records make good birthday gifts for young children. So do homemade playdough and handmade smock aprons and purses which can be made from scrap material. A little embroidery makes them really special."

Rather than give toys that will break quickly and disappoint a child, Peggy Lozen of Michigan prefers to give a book. Books are easy to have on hand, suitable for either boys or girls, and can be suited to different reading levels.

Barbara Wilson-Clay of Texas likes to spread out her gift purchases. "I try to shop at the rate of a present per month so that it doesn't all seem so overwhelming, particularly at Christmas time," she says. Barbara handles a breast pump depot which, although it doesn't produce a steady income, does "provide a windfall of a few dollars now and then," she says. "I save this money for birthdays and holidays. It perks me up to be able to buy something special for my husband, David, or the girls from time to time."

Phone Bill High? "We just cut down our phone bill by changing our 'call pak' to one with fewer units," says Carol Barshack of Illinois. Just about everybody suggests saving long-distance calls for emergencies or special occasions. Write frequently to stay in touch with family and friends. Keep a supply of postcards on hand. They're low cost and the perfect medium for short messages—probably the only kind you have time to write. It takes but a minute and a postcard to let grandparents know that "Baby cut her first tooth." "We planted the garden today." "Pray for the sun to shine! It's been raining for three days!" An exchange of address labels with frequent correspondents will speed up addressing your mail. And with postcards, you need never look for a stamp!

Encourage the children, too, to send cards. You, or an older child, can write the message for a preschooler. They'll enjoy receiving an answering card in the mail; often more so than they would talking on the phone.

The Posh Postcard With a little dressing up, the postcard becomes a lovely greeting card, and the cost is a fraction of what you would have to pay for printed cards and the first-class postage to mail them. The Spalding family of New York has combined talent and postcards in producing their own personal holiday greeting cards. In early fall, "We purchase the desired number of postcards from the post office," Cathy Spalding writes. "We then decide upon a printed design to decorate the cards." The Spaldings make their own block prints by cutting seasonal designs out of spongy pads sold for sore feet, and gluing them to small blocks of wood. "We glue the 'cloth' side to the wood. This leaves the spongy side as the printing surface," explains Cathy. The design may be a stylized Christmas tree, holly leaves, and little heart—or whatever is the inspiration of the moment. It may include letters to spell a greeting such as "JOY." For stamping, the Spaldings have a supply of standard stamp pads in red, green, and blue colors. "We stamp a one or two color design on the blank side of the postcard," Cathy says. The reverse side is divided, with the address on the right beneath the postage mark and a short personal message to the left. With the Christmas tree motif, Cathy writes, "A gentle season, Evergreen for everyday—Our wishes for you." A circle of hearts interspersed with figures of children bears the message, "May the spirit of Christmas encircle you with love."

Save on Gift Wrap   The "Foot Pad Stamps" afford more fun in decorating gift wrap. "We obtain an end roll of paper from our local pennysaver office," Cathy writes. "One roll lasts us for three years! We wrap the gift and then have great fun creating custom paper." Since the background is white, the Spaldings can write "To _____" and "From _____" in a coordinating marker directly on the package. No gift tags to fall off and be lost. A cut potato or sponge can also be used for stamping designs.

"I save wrapping paper and gift cards from the gifts we receive," says Linda Lawrence of Ontario, Canada. "I also save my youngsters' art work and use this as wrapping paper for gifts for other children and family members. We team this very colourful paper with bindings of bright yarn instead of expensive ribbon, and the whole effect is lovely. I save the colourful parts of all gift cards, Christmas cards and such, punch a hole in one corner in order to tie it onto the parcel, and write a greeting and sign on the reverse side. It's far cheaper than buying new cards."

Baby's Own Calendar What baby gift is unique, satisfies your desire to give a handmade item, is easy to make, and is inexpensive? A baby's first year calendar, according to Cathy Spalding! This New York mother writes:

I purchase a blank spiral ring sketch pad, size 8 1/2 × 11 inches, and glue fabric to the front and back covers. On the first page I write this explanation: "A calendar especially for you! This special calendar marks the beginning of each month with your birth date. Your mom, dad, and (*names of brothers and sisters*) will be able to record those daily important events for you to enjoy as you grow older. Wishing you joyful years of growth."

Opening the pad flat, I write a favorite quotation related to parenting—many of which come from La Leche League NEWS—on the top page. I illustrate the quote with my "primitive" artwork, or I have my four-year-old decorate around the words. Then, I rule the bottom page with 35 rectangles. (I have made so many calendars that I have made a cardboard template so I can more quickly rule the pages.) I label each month— Baby's first month, second month, third month. The parents begin each month on the same day as their child's birthday. They fill in the dates.

I have received very appreciative and enthusiastic comments from the recipients of my gifts. I have even been asked to make these calendars for subsequent children.

House Beautiful

Blooming Beauties   "Four to five weeks after every holiday, we start driving up and down streets on trash day looking for discarded potted plants—you know the kind, with fancy foil and a big bow wrapped around the pot. We take them home, plant them in the garden, cut them back, give them a little fertilizer, and then wait. At the appropriate time, the plants start to grow and flower, and my garden is full of color. We have cut flowers in the house that we could never afford to buy." (Kathy Warmbier, California.)

Furniture Kits   "My husband and I assemble furniture from kits. There are some very beautiful pieces being made today at very low prices this way. We've been able to fill out several rooms in our home with kits," writes Katie Fowler of Texas. Katie suggests, "Start out small with a shelf or something just to prove to yourself how simple the finishing process is."

Furniture by Way of Want Ads   "It seemed as though I'd have to go to work for a while at least to pay for furniture," Anne Grider of Hawaii says of their situation on returning with little usable furniture after spending years in Europe in the military. "We ran around for weeks looking for a few decent pieces that would be sturdy enough to survive our many moves and four young children. It was very depressing." Anne decided then to try the want ads offering furniture for sale. "I soon learned all the right questions to ask on the phone so I didn't waste a lot of time. Gradually we ended up with everything we needed at a price we could afford. That was eight years ago, and the furniture is still serving us well."

Place a Want Ad   If you're in the market to buy something used but can't find what you want in your tour of secondhand sales (or don't have the time to canvass the area in search of it) place an ad in the "Wanted" section of your neighborhood paper. Make it eye-catching—"Little girl dreams of having a bike of her own"—and include specifics such as size. One mother said that she found the perfect little bike for her daughter by doing this.

A Special Effect "Our dining room chairs are beautiful old pressed-back chairs, acquired one at a time over the years and refinished. They don't exactly match, but we each have our own special chair, and they are all beautiful," (Joan Ellison, Minnesota.)

An Inexpensive Tablecloth "I can get sixty-inch wide polyester fabric for one dollar a yard at my local fabric store. For three dollars, I made a lovely tablecloth that's big enough for my dining room table with the three leaves in it. The selvage took care of the long sides, and I turned under and stitched the two ends." (Elaine Caper, Illinois.)

Coffee Can Canisters Empty coffee cans of different sizes covered with adhesive backed paper make attractive and very low-cost storage pieces.

Window Treatment. "Bed sheets, on sale, can be made into cheap, attractive curtains," says Linda Lawrence of Ontario, Canada. Homey-looking tie-back curtains in the bedroom are pretty, as are matching handmade pillows tossed about.

Barter Is Booming

The Lehman family in Illinois acquired a much needed bed in trade for end tables which were no longer needed. Tutoring put meat on the table for another Illinois family. Mary Hurt tutored a neighbor's son. The little boy's parents operate a food store and were happy to compensate Mary for her efforts with tasty cuts of meat.

In Connecticut, Susie Dutcher teaches two infant swimming classes at the local YMCA once a week. "Although I don't make much money, I do get a substantial discount on our yearly membership and on classes and summer camp," she writes. Best of all, she adds, the arrangement "gets the children and me down there to swim at least once a week."

Elaine Caper's husband can get all the dog food he wants, "the dry crunchy kind," free for the shoveling and transporting from the place where he works. Employees are also welcome to take outdated stationery for use as scrap paper. Dog food and scrap paper were the means for paying off a doctor's bill for this Illinois family.

Sue Scott-Hinkle of New York tells of a neighbor helping "with electrical work in exchange for the use of our pasture."

Baby's first pair of shoes, size triple E, were priced at almost $30 and "that one little pair of walking shoes set our budget upside down," writes Kay Wallin of Illinois. With the prospect of her little guy needing shoes every three months or so, Kay made an offer—homemade baked goods for shoes at cost. The woman at the store "jumped at the chance," Kay says. With working full time, she had no time for baking and was delighted with the arrangement.

From a simple swap to a sophisticated exchange, trading services and things has become a burgeoning business. Some call it the "informal economy." Saving families see bartering as a way to add luster to life when money is scarce. There's an element of challenge and fun to a satisfying swap which makes it doubly attractive, so it's no surprise that enterprising homemakers have organized the bartering concept into an on-going exchange of goods and services. Gloria Turnbull of Nebraska has been instrumental in founding three such cooperatives. Here's how the latest, known as The Exchange, operates:

Credits, rather than money, are the medium of exchange. The approximate monetary value is $1 per credit. Members list the ways in which they can contribute; they also indicate their needs.

Example: WILL DO—Sewing, sewing instructions, help with yard work, consultation on new lawn installation, research of recipes, food, nutrition, set up household ac-

Kay Wallin bartered
homemade bread and rolls
for her son's raincoat.

counts, typing and other secretarial work or record keeping, weight control and exercise consultation, help with wallpapering, teach bridge, housecleaning help, child care, storage ideas and projects, house and kitchen design.

FOR LOAN—Card table, folding chairs, cake pans (bell, round, sheet, oval, star), 30-cup coffee pot, portable typewriter, newspaper log roller, portable sewing machine, roll-away bed, softball equipment, sewing patterns, magazines, freezer space, silver tea service, craft patterns, gardening tools, electric ice cream maker, binoculars.

NEED—Hair care, garden produce, help to can and freeze, mending, transportation, piano lessons, use of stroller, child care.

Some examples of exchange rates are: Child care per hour, 75¢; consultation fee, $3.50 an hour; garden produce, current retail price; haircut, $4; permanent (materials supplied, haircut extra) $12.50; electrical or plumbing work, $6 an hour minimum; light housework,

$3.50 an hour; heavy housework, $4.50 an hour; equipment rental by day, week, or month according to the item, 10% of original cost; freezer or other storage space, negotiable.

"The beauty of the arrangement is that as a member you are your own manager and can take or reject jobs at your convenience," Gloria explains. The Exchange limits its membership to fifteen members. For those who do not have family nearby, The Exchange functions as would an extended family, "helping each other with canning or freezing, borrowing tools, lending a hand here and there. Unlike the babysitting co-ops which are popular in some areas, child care accounts for less than one-fourth of the total volume of transactions in The Exchange."

A three-month trial period gives a new member and The Exchange a chance to find out if it's a compatible relationship. The new member is encouraged to use The Exchange several times in each month. Members meet bimonthly, with the Secretary keeping tabs on the overall operation.

"We don't always charge each other for everything," Gloria says. "We just do some things because we want to. But we wouldn't have gotten to know these particular people in the first place if it hadn't been through the vehicle of The Exchange."

CHAPTER 14

Earning at Home

Saving ways and a pioneering spirit can be tremendously helpful, but sometimes, despite your and your husband's best efforts, you can't seem to make ends meet. For one reason or another, outgo consistently exceeds income, and the resulting gap has you very concerned. You begin to seriously consider an outside job. But wait! Don't give up yet! The solution may lie in getting a job, but it can be one that allows you to be the full-time mother you want to be and a wage-earner as well.

And what kind of work might that be? And how do you go about finding it? The letters from mothers-at-home tell of a variety of ways—some common, others quite extraordinary—that the writers have found for supplementing the family income. These women are just as tenacious in developing or utilizing saleable skills as they are in finding sale prices on things that the family must purchase. It's another challenge, and meeting it can bring its own sweet feeling of satisfaction, besides making day-to-day living a little easier. At all times, though, mothers warn that it's important to keep your priorities straight. Most of all, your family needs you, you being there *and* involved with them, more than they need any amount of money you can bring in. It all goes back to The Plan and your determination to keep "People First." But within those parameters, there is potential for earning extra money.

Home Day-Care—A Popular Choice

It's really no surprise that mothers who are at home with their young children for most of the day would be attracted to child-care as a job possibility. After all, they have an intimate knowledge of the kind of care a small child needs and they know they can provide it—as well, that is, as any caregiver other than the child's own mother. Although their letters are often sprinkled with the term "babysitting" to describe what they do, they would be the first to say that very little sitting is involved. Unlike the teenager who "sits" for an evening with a sleeping child, these mothers are involved in the daytime care of children—feeding them, keeping them dry and comfortable, providing a safe yet stimulating environment, and to the best of their ability, meeting the child's needs for emotional security.

Unfortunately, the wages to be earned do not come close to reflecting the importance of what a good child-care provider does. In a money-conscious world, caring for a small child unfortunately commands but a paltry sum. Mothers-at-home usually go into child-care because of the high value they place on being able to remain at home with their own children. Those who stay with the work—some even after their own families are grown—speak of another kind of return. First of all, they delight in the things that children do, and secondly, they see their efforts as making a greater contribution to the world in the long run than they could in most other paying jobs.

Then too, if you look beyond the money—sometimes less than a dollar an hour—you'll find there are other compensations. Lee Hatala of Illinois says of day-care in the home: "It makes you your own boss, eliminates leaving your baby, and eliminates the costs of transportation and clothing purchases for your job. And, you are not owned by anyone, though you can be at the mercy of other parents unless you are firm in your requirements of them." Sue Beachy of Indiana says that child-care at their house is a family affair; "everyone is involved with some phase of entertainment or caregiving." The result, she says, is that her boys gain new playmates, learn about infant care, and see the differences in the personalities of other children. For all of them, there are "lots of lessons in getting along with others." For herself, Sue likes the fact that she has the "freedom to set the pace of work and play."

Barb Federspiel, also from Indiana, calls day-care "demanding work," but she, too, prizes the togetherness it allows her with her own children. "I was there to see their joy at their many new accomplishments as they grew. I've been able to be home when my children come home from school, eager to tell me about their day. When they got sick at school, I was able to bring them home right away, and I've been able to go on some school trips and see school programs during the day. It may not sound like much, but children want their parents to be able to participate and are proud when they do so."

A home day-care mother for four years, Debbie Sheets of Colorado points out that the family that opens its home to other children as a child-care site is entitled to certain tax advantages according to U. S. laws. Among them are deductions for a percentage of the house payment, utilities, home insurance, some major repairs, toys and equipment, car mileage for field trips with the children and for some grocery shopping, and also the cost of food for the children. It's a matter worth checking into carefully.

Day-care is a business venture, with its own set of do's and don'ts, and a certain amount of organization and preparation is necessary if it is to be successful. The absolutely most important factor, of course, cannot be regulated—a caring heart. With that to fortify you, the rest can be quickly set in place.

About Licensing Find out about the requirements in your locale for day-care. Depending on the number of children you

Children play dress-up at Betty Aviles' home day-care center.

take and their ages, you may have to be licensed. From all that mothers say, it's a simple procedure and the requirements are not out-of-line. Mostly, they're basic, common sense safety and health matters, such as the installation of smoke detectors, having a fire extinquisher in the cooking area of the kitchen and a closure on a basement door to keep little ones from inadvertently tumbling down the stairs.

Of course, all cleaning products must be out of small people's reach and all medications must be secured in a locked cabinet. Inflammable products and sharp cutting objects need to be carefully stored. You'll be checking to see that stairways are clear and that there are no scatter rugs that could cause a nasty spill—the kind of everyday safety precautions that mothers and fathers are constantly on the alert for. Also, each child would have his or her own towel; nappers their own linens.

For a small fee ($6 a year, approximately) the U.S. Governmental Child Development Services will approve your home for child-care purposes and list it with their referral service. They also hold training workshops in child development.

As a day-care provider in the U.S.A., you can take advantage of the Child-Care Food Program. You plan and serve nutritious, balanced meals and snacks to the children in your care and are reimbursed for a portion of the cost, up to $2.15 a day per child at the present time. The program is funded by the U.S. Department of Agriculture. The child-care provider is required to submit menus and attendance records on a monthly basis.

If you know other women who are caring for children in their homes, check with them for information on how to contact the various child-care departments and agencies. And check the ad section in your local newspaper to get an idea of how much to charge for your services. You may want to place a small ad yourself in the paper announcing that you will be taking children. A notice posted in the teachers' lounge of a nearby school can be very effective, and so can word left with the church or temple that you attend.

Other Preparations   Most of the home day-care mothers designate certain spaces in the house as play areas and set aside others as "off limits." Make these arrangements known when the child arrives and then cheerfully and consistently adhere to them thereafter. Anita Browning, Missouri, advises, "In the winter, it helps to have a place for the children to play that you don't need to keep clean all the time." She says she usually "banned the living room." At least one room was intact, and since her husband came home at noontime, it was nice to have a quiet spot where he could relax.

You'll need a good supply of toys that are appropriate to the ages of the children in your care. You may already have all you need in this regard, but with more children on the scene, you'll want to be prepared. Duplicates can cut down on squabbles. Take a second look at your stock, and keep an eye open at garage sales in your area for inexpensive (but well-made) additions. Pass up anything that has a lot of small pieces. You may also need extras in the line of cribs, high chairs, or booster seats.

Establishing Ground Rules   When dealing with the parents, it's important that they know you have their child's welfare at heart, but they will also respect you for being an able business woman. Patricia Scott of West Virginia had been in direct sales—jewelry, natural cosmetics, household products—yet says, "My most successful business has been a home day-care center." She offers the following tips on handling the business side of being a child-care provider:

1. Establish a set fee. You can charge by the hour or by the day, in which case indicate the number of hours that will be covered.
2. Be specific as to drop off and pick up times, and record these daily for each child.
3. Charge extra for overtime—time beyond the agreed upon period. Pat says this is necessary to discourage parents from leaving children for eleven or twelve hour stretches.
4. Consult with your family and set your "business hours." For their sake and your own, do not go beyond this time. Of course, let parents know what your hours are right from the start. Be clear as to vacation time.
5. Obtain written permission to administer any medication to a child, also have the parent write out the instructions (frequency and amount) and keep this information on file. Patricia insists on seeing the medicine bottle.
6. If you will be taking the children anywhere outside your home and yard, have written permission from the parents to do so. This should include everything from a walk around the block to a trip in the car.
7. Unless you know the parents well, ask for payment in advance.

8. When accepting a new child, discuss with the parents what to do in the event the child becomes ill. Will you be willing to care for a child who is not up to par—has the symptoms of an ordinary cold, for instance? What about a fever? Or the child who is vomiting or has diarrhea? If the child becomes ill while in your care, you would, of course, contact a parent. Would you finish out the day or do you want the parent to come for the child, as is the usual policy in schools? You'll want a clear understanding about these things before the fact.

A number of care providers make the point, too, that when a child is cared for on a regular weekly basis, the parent is charged for a full week even though the child misses a day. Exceptions can always be made, of course, and generally are when advance notice is given of when the child will not be coming. The rationale for this is that the care provider has had to keep her day open, and in the case of someone who is limited as to the number of children she can have in her care, could have possibly taken another child on that day. The care provider is losing an opportunity to earn, which is bad in any business. Care providers tell of numerous instances of receiving a call in the morning from a parent announcing that the child is not coming because the parent decided to take the day off of work, or the child is going to grandma's house, or to play with a neighbor. You will have to explain your situation to the parents and enlist their understanding and help in the matter.

In the same vein, the reliable child-care provider is conscious of her responsibility to the parents. They have a right to count on you. When you work on your own, no one is there to take your place should you wake up ill one morning. Some care providers, often those who have a child only part-time, ask the parents to have their own back-up person. Others work out a reciprocal plan with another child-care provider or two to cover for them in case of such an emergency. As for terminating the child-care arrangement, it's in the best interests of all concerned to know that notice will be given a reasonable time in advance.

There is value to putting the most common and important information that parents need to know down in writing. An ordinary sheet of paper folded in half will make a neat little brochure that you can give to new parents. Make note in it, too, of the many positive qualities that you have to offer— your careful attention to giving the children nutritious food and your affiliation with child-oriented organizations such as La Leche League, which help broaden your understanding of children's needs.

A home day-care service presents a number of advantages that cannot be found in a large day-care operation. The "home-like" environment and the fewer number of children involved are highly desirable features when working with little people. Also, in home day-care, children who are away from their mothers a good part of the time need to adjust to only one other mother-figure, whereas those in the big day-care places have to cope with two, three, or more caregivers. To a little child, this means a lot.

Another Possibility   A variation on the theme of doing day-care in your home is conducting an agency for child-care providers. Donna Bivaletz, herself a day-care mother, is associated with such an agency where she lives in New Jersey—Monday Morning: A Family Day-Care Referral Sevice. Its purpose is to provide a referral service for parents who are looking for good, reliable caregivers, and also give assistance to mothers who are providing day-care in their homes. Founded and directed by a woman who had sixteen years of experience in day-care work, Monday Morning now has thirty-three care providers on its referral list. Some of its features:

1. The agency bills the parents and pays the care providers every two weeks. Typical wage: Infant care— $60 a week for up to a ten-hour day.

2. The agency furnishes some toys, including large equipment such as slide and balance beam, which are circulated among the providers and change every two weeks.

3. If a care provider becomes ill, another qualified day-care mother, someone the parents and child have already met, will fill in for her.

4. Books on child rearing, craft-making ideas, and related subjects are available to care providers through the agency. The director herself is a valuable source of help on the ins and outs of day-care work.

5. During the tax season, an accountant will answer questions on tax exemptions allowable for child-care work.

6. The agency provides the caregivers with $300,000 liability insurance on each child. It also furnishes permit slips that parents sign authorizing the care provider to transport the child on field trips, etc.

7. Parents are attracted to the agency through advertising and by its reputation for having well-qualified care providers. The director maintains standards by soliciting evaluations from parents on care providers and by making home visits.

8. The agency interviews interested parents and matches their needs with three prospective care providers. The father, mother, and child meet with each of the three care providers and choose one. Terms are agreed upon, and if, after a two-week trial period, all parties want the arrangement to continue, a contract is signed. A four-week notice must be given to terminate the contract.

Donna believes that the organization of such an agency could be a natural follow-up for an enterprising mother-at-home with some day-care experience. To lessen the work involved and split the responsibility, two or three women could join together in running the business.

Some Child-Care Experiences

When Shirley Collins, Wisconsin, started in day-care work, she cared for three or four children at the most. She now operates Shi Shi Family Day Care with an enrollment of eleven children, five of whom come full-time and the rest part-time. Since the Collins' have five children of their own, Shirley started with a good collection of toys and other children's things. Even so, as the day-care grew, she saw the need for some additional large toys, child-size table and chairs, "housekeeping" pieces— sink, stove, refrigerator—and a good, sturdy storage unit. "To purchase these items," she says, "I applied for 'Start Up Funds' from the state and was granted $750."

Regarding her day with the children, Shirley states, "It's easiest to operate on some sort of schedule." At Shi Shi's, periods of planned group activity are interspersed with free play time and outdoor time. Youngsters under the age of five nap in the afternoon from 12:45 to 3:00, with a snack after naptime. Shirley says, "The children like the security of a schedule. It helps them to know what comes next." Shirley reflects, "I like to be around children. I get a sense of fulfillment from raising children and watching them grow." With each new child, she makes a collage of twelve to twenty pictures and entitles it "What do we do at Shirley's all day?" It's informative for the parents and a nice keepsake for the child.

Debbie Sheets of Colorado majored in early childhood development in school and was involved in private preschools and day-care centers for six years before she had children of her own. "After the birth of our first child, I went back to work, with the baby, at two months," she says. "I worked for six weeks and quit. My priorities had changed." When it became apparent that a second income was "an absolute necessity," Debbie decided to start a day-care center in her home. She says she now earns about $600 a month in her work and feels she clears more "actual money" this way than she would taking a job outside the home.

From her years of contact with parents and working with their offspring, Debbie says she has found that parents want good care for their children, yet "they are anxious about the provider usurping the parent's role. Kids commonly call the provider 'mama,' " she points out. Almost without realizing it, a parent may become jealous of the provider's place in the child's affections, with the result that there is soon a change of care provider.

In Maryland, Betty Aviles has been a "day-care mom" for several years now, and during that time, she says, "Most of the things I learned at League meetings I'm using all day long. I try to provide a good environment. We play games, listen to music, read stories, play outdoors." A large cooler with a push spout is used by the children in getting their own drinks of water. In the summertime, when there is more outdoor play, the cooler goes out with the children. To further facilitate her work, she says, "I've gotten very organized in the kitchen." She doubles meals prepared for the family and freezes the leftovers. Lunches for school-aged children are made the night before. She has fresh fruit on hand for snacking, also cut-up raw vegetables and yogurt dips, whole grain crackers, peanut butter, and cheese.

"I worked for six months and quit. My priorities had changed..."

From her day-to-day observations of children, she explains, "I am firmly convinced that older children, those who are at least three years old, are far better able to cope with the experience of prolonged and regular separation from mother that day-care entails." Like so many other mothers who opt for an at-home job, Betty places high priority on "seeing my own small children grow everyday, being there for an enthusiastic teenager, and being there when any of the children get hurt or sick.''

Cecile Harris of Illinois says she has been "looking after children since the age of eleven.'' Her home is now licensed for day-care and is equipped with four cribs, a high chair and several booster chairs for meal time, a fountain spout or bubbler in the bathroom for thirsty little ones getting their own drinks, and "lots of play equipment.''

Cecile, who earns $1.25 to $1.50 an hour per child, advises anyone starting out in day-care work to choose the age group carefully. She suggests working first with children who have developed some verbal skills. "You can talk to the older children,'' she says. "You're more anxious with a little baby.'' When a child joins the group at Cecile's house, she pays special attention to getting to know the newcomer. "You have to stand back and watch the child for a time,'' she says, adding that it often takes up to six months for a child "to fit in.''

These women know what works best for them and the children in their care...

A simple, caring philosophy pervades Cecile's house and her care of the children who are left with her. She encourages her little charges in learning to respect each other, though she cautions against ever forcing a child to give up something to another child. "Try to distract,'' she encourages. This technique is helpful, too, when a child cries or is upset. Cecile likes to promote a routine that is based on ordinary, day-to-day household activities, and she has such rules as "No roughhouse play in the living room, no jumping on furniture, and no eating except at the table.'' She mentions too, that over the years, she has learned not to become attached to the children. Cecile says she can't imagine spending her time at some run-of-the-mill job that couldn't be "nearly as interesting and rewarding."

Cynthia Nodson in Kansas likes day-care work for its flexibility. "When we needed more money, I became a licensed day-care mother," she writes. "I took in children mostly on a drop-in basis or for a limited period of time, during Christmas vacation for instance." Cynthia says she charged per child "and slightly higher than the going rate. This arrangement kept me busy enough, yet not so busy that I felt my own children suffered." At one time she cared for two neighborhood children, one for an hour before school and three hours after school, and the other child for a half day three times a week. "Whenever I took a child of a working parent, I insisted that the parent have a back-up in case I should need to cancel," she explains. Cynthia states, too, "I formed a small clientele of children whom we grew to love and looked forward to having with us."

Glinda Pipkin of Texas has been doing day-care "off and on" for fourteen years and, like many another child-care provider, has become selective over the years. These women know what works best for them and the children in their care, and so they may accept children of only a certain age or sex or for a particular time of the day. Some women supervise only school-aged children, either before or after school hours.

For full-time care, Glinda accepts only girls under the age of three, and will not take two children from the same family.

Glinda also mentions a matter that is extremely important to any child-care operation—the need for a back-up provider in case illness or some other unavoidable need arises. "I have always had a friend who also babysits," she says, "so we could trade if one of us had a doctor's appointment or had somewhere we had to go." Since she has two teenage daughters, Glinda can figure on some help from them after school hours. She says she has on occasion left an older girl in charge, "but only with the mothers' permission," she emphasizes.

Elisa Gagnon, Alabama, is one of a number of care providers who take school-aged children whose parents' workday does not end until two or three hours after school lets out. "I open my home to 'after school children' each day," Elisa writes. Since her working hours are from three to six o'clock in the afternoon, her day is intact for the most part, something that makes this type of child-care particularly attractive to her. Also, these older children are more self-sufficient than younger children are. Still, they need a home base and a mother figure to come home to. The care provider plays an important role.

"When the children arrive, I prepare a nutritious snack and we discuss the schoolday," she says. "Then they play or do their homework. It's a relaxed, unstructured time, and I try to make them feel at home." Elisa's children, a six-month-old and four-year-old, look forward to the older kids' company, and Elisa says, "I love having older children around for a couple of hours a day." Her fee is "a flat fee of $10 a week" for each child.

When Cindy George of Michigan thinks about her first at-home moneymaking venture, that of a child-care provider, she says, "I did bring in extra income, but I had a lot to learn!" Cindy says that she loves children and was sure that a few extra kids around the house would be no problem. "Why I'd treat them as my own," she says, "and grow to love them." What she learned, and what would be her first words of advice, is that the day-care children "are not your own kids."

For all that child-care falls under the heading of a business, there is no avoiding the fact that feelings and emotions, particularly those of the child and the care provider, must be reckoned with.

Looking back, Cindy can say, "I was a very good babysitter. I tried my hardest to give the kids I sat for all the time, love, patience, understanding, and nurturing they needed. It just didn't come as easily as it does with my own kids."

From Ontario, Canada, Brenda Murray relates, "When I quit child-care in the fall of 1981, I was making $55 a week per child." Brenda had the best of reasons for quitting; shortly thereafter she gave birth to twins, bringing the number of children in the Murray family to five. In regard to her child-care experience, one of the things that stands out in Brenda's mind is the duality and, in a sense, contradiction, in the role. It's a disparity that cannot be resolved. "I would cuddle the babies, kiss the 'ow-ies' and scratches to make them better, and use my pet words, 'love,' 'sweetie,' and the like when talking to them," she says. "But isn't it odd that I felt free to mother these children in this way in my home, yet I honestly would feel strange doing these things for these children in their home or when mom and dad were around. And the parents would probably wonder if I did it!"

Of course, the children, too, live in a double world, as is noted by another day-care provider, Susan Keeler of Ohio. Susan cares for two little boys, brothers, whose mother is a teacher. Both have been with her from the age of six months. Sue makes the observation that during the day, "The boys do things the way they are done at our house, but this is not always the way they are done at home. This can be very confusing to them." She speaks, too, to a point that is not often mentioned. "If two children are crying at the same time, my child and a child I'm caring for, I'll readily admit that I pick up my own child first," says Susan. "The other baby spends much more time in the playpen than mine ever did. I always held him to give him his bottle until I was visiting in his home when he was eight months old and saw that his parents lay him down and let him hold his own bottle. Now, I do that, too." Susan conscientiously feeds the children good lunches, reads stories and plays games with them, and has "enjoyed a lot of first discoveries with them, but there just isn't the same feeling," she adds, "the 'cuddling' that comes when mothering one's own children."

For Barry O'Brien of Texas, picking up the children after school means collecting eleven or twelve youngsters in her big van, dropping five off at their own homes and bringing the rest

After school, Barry O'Brien picks up a van full of youngsters.

to the O'Brien house where they study or play, rest or snack, until picked up by their parents at 5:30 PM. Barry has a routine—the children park all their belongings on a table near the door where they're ready when it's time to go home. "Anything special, an art project for instance, I put up high for safe keeping," she says.

Children at this age are easy to care for, Barry finds. "They understand the rules," she says, and with so many, there's no problem finding someone to play with. Play equipment is plentiful, and for snacks, the children down large amounts of crackers and peanut butter and drink "copious amounts of ice water."

Barry charges two dollars an hour for picking up and keeping a child after school hours. This is higher than the going rate at a commercial day-care facility, and she says it took her a long time "to realize that I'm worth more than a day-care center." The parents coming to her are looking for something other than day-care. "They want a home atmosphere," Barry realized, and she tells other conscientious mothers caring for children "to feel good about what you can offer."

Even though she has been involved in child-care for a number of years, there is always something new to learn. "I will never again let a bill slide," she says. She lost over a hundred dollars when a family moved without paying her. Offsetting this unfortunate experience was that of a young boy, a third-grader, who was very withdrawn—"he never looked up"—when he first stayed with her. As time went by, Barry says, "He would look me directly in the eye and he interacted happily with the other children."

Foster Mothering

As a variation on providing part-time day-care for school-aged children, there are those at-home mothers who derive the greatest satisfaction from caring for the very young—newborns who need full-time mothering. These women serve as foster mothers for babies who, in a matter of weeks or months, will be placed with their adoptive parents in a new family. Foster parenting is really a family involvement, since all members of the family—mother, father, and their own children—contribute to the babies' good start.

A foster mother in Virginia, Lorraine Gilbreth, writes: "For the past five years, my husband and I have been approved foster parents for an adoption agency. We usually receive the babies when they are four days old and have them until they are adopted, most often at about three months." Lorraine decided to become a foster mother because, she says, "I felt that after having four children of my own, I had something positive to offer these babies." Adding, too, to her confidence as well as her qualifications is "the knowledge I have gained from the League and related sources." In general, Lorraine sees foster care as "more of an outlet for motherly feelings" than can be found in day-care work. Some of the babies staying with the Gilbreth family were even partially breastfed by their foster mother "with the approval of the agency," Lorraine explains. One little girl, born prematurely, "was almost totally breastfed *at the agency's request*," she writes. "I feel proud that these babies get quality mothering in a family."

Over the years, the Gilbreths have cared for seven babies, and the question most frequently asked of Lorraine is, "How can you bear to give them up?" To this she replies that "deep down, for the baby's sake" she is anxious that a little one be placed in a permanent home as soon as possible. Also, she has learned to think of the care she gives the babies as a worthwhile job, one that "I enjoy and can take pride in," she says. The good she can do, she is convinced, outweighs any negative aspects.

As for compensation, the Gilbreths were paid $120 a month when caring for the last baby. The agency supplies some clothing, diapers, formula, and pays for all medical expenses. As wages go, these are exceedingly low if figured on an hourly rate, but Lorraine appreciates the fact, too, that foster care is less restrictive to family activities than day-care.

A Connecticut mother, Mary Campbell Hirsch, also has good things to say about foster parenting as a way for a mother-at-home to supplement the family's income. Mary stresses, "This was certainly not our motivation for going into foster care, but the monthly allowance more than pays for the baby's needs." In the Hirsch's case, the monthly allowance is $180. And Mary explains "the WIC program provides free food." When talking about foster care to other mothers, Mary emphasizes, "The experience is *fantastic*, you feel great about your 'job,' and it helps pay for fuel oil in chilly New England."

Less common than child-care is care of the elderly, the at-home job that Cheryl Hutchinson of New Jersey had "plopped in my lap." Cheryl relates that a friend was looking for someone to care for her elderly mother while she's at work, "and so we have Bessie with us from 7 AM to 4:30 PM Mondays through Fridays." Bessie's pension check covers the cost of her care, $400 a month. "The dear lady is mentally confused," Cheryl says, "but even so, she can teach us a lot with her stories of her past." The Hutchinson's children, a six- and three-year-old, have lived in a suburb all their lives, and "really enjoy the tales about the olden days in Texas, of rattlesnakes, farm work, and one-room schools." Cheryl says, too, "It's good for them to learn kindness and consideration for old people. And they feel good about doing things for Bessie."

Finding a Balance

The fact is, of course, that mothers who take a job outside the home often do so for the contact it affords with other adults and the change in routine, as well as the promise of extra money. Being a child-care provider in the home seems like more of the same: mother spending most of her day with little kids with no respite from the demands of parenting. A mother in Connecticut, Jackie Harris, tells of coming to grips with such feelings in her own life.

Thinking back some years to the birth of her second child— her oldest daughter was then two—Jackie recalls, "There I sat, feeling sorry for myself and thinking my husband was having all the fun in the outside world. I thought I was the only mother who felt lonely, lost, uncreative, unsophisticated, and just plain dull." In the hopes of bringing about a change, Jackie says, "I even took an evening job to find myself." What she found, she says, was that more than anything she was exhausted at the end of the day. "That really wasn't what I needed." As her girls got older, Jackie found she was able to get out of the house more, and "by the time they were in school, I was working at our public library," a job "I thoroughly enjoyed."

And then she learned she was again pregnant. "I was not totally thrilled," she says of her feelings at the time. As so often happens, motherly sentiment did come to the fore, and with the new baby's arrival, Jackie was determined to be a breast-feeding mother. Her efforts to breastfeed her two older children had ended all too soon. This time, breastfeeding progressed well. "Baby Jonathan turned our whole feelings about family, parenthood, and mothering around," Jackie recalls. "I guess nursing him and finding La Leche League were our turning points. I found I could enjoy my family and not feel guilty about not being out in the 'real' world."

Of that first year or so, Jackie says, "Being home with my baby was the most rewarding experience I've ever encountered. I truly feel I gave of myself totally and lovingly. And mothering was then so much easier." Before long, Jonathan was no longer a baby in arms, he needed less constant care, and Jackie again felt the need for "a job or a position where I could meet people, make friendships, and not feel cooped up." She found it, as many other mothers-at-home do, in volunteer work. Not surprisingly, Jackie became more involved with La Leche League, first as a Leader in her local League Group and then as treasurer for the Area organization (in this case, the state-wide League).

As for a paying job, she now has a job 7:30 AM to 4:30 PM Monday through Friday. "I have started a home day-care center," she says, "caring for three to four children, each on a part-time basis. Jon, now four, has other children his age to play with, I'm here when the girls come home from school, and I earn $60 to $100 a week."

When Jackie thinks about her life now, she says, "I don't need a career, although I do think about the future and what kind of job I'd like as my children reach young adulthood. I feel right now I'm doing what is best for me, my children, my husband, my family in general. And it's a good feeling."

Other Avenues for Increasing Your Income

Bake Bread Who can resist freshly baked, good, hearty bread? If you bake a fine loaf of bread, using choice ingredients, you have a proven moneymaker according to many of the mothers who have written to us.

With job opportunities for her husband severely limited, Ginger Hastings approached the proprietor of a deli in their area whom she heard was interested in using homemade bread. "It was scary," Ginger writes. "I knew my bread was good, but was it good enough to sell to a restaurant for a price that would make it worthwhile?" Ginger explained to them that she would make the bread in her home, but since she did not have transportation at that time, she would not be able to deliver it. Says Ginger, "I quoted a price and waited for a response. They accepted!

"Starting up required only more of the bread-baking ingredients I had on hand and a couple more loaf pans," she relates. "I baked six loaves of bread a day, four whole wheat and two rye, five days a week. In the beginning, I was doing the entire process by hand. It was time-consuming, which was a source of frustration for all of us. But I was still there with my family. I could play a game with the kids while the bread rose, nurse Sarah while it baked, and clean up while it cooled. My price was two dollars a loaf. My cost, not including labor, was seventy-five cents a loaf, and my profit was between $150 and $175 a month."

Ginger says that in three month's time, she had saved enough to invest in a grain mill ($240). "Grinding the grain myself cut down my cost, as buying grain is a good deal less expensive than buying flour.

"The boys, John, twelve, and Jamie, ten, got involved by operating the mill for me. They earn thirty cents for each mill full of flour they grind. It gives them the opportunity to earn a little extra money, and it's something we do together. Another three months of daily kneading (often with an impatient little one wanting me) elapsed, and I had saved enough money to invest in a bread-making machine ($290). That machine literally cut my time investment by half. I simply place all the ingredients in the bowl and turn it on—for ten minutes we can do whatever we like! The machine also means that the dough only needs to rise once, so I spend less time waiting around for it to rise."

Unfortunately, the deli Ginger had been working for closed. But she says, "I did not want to fold my business, so I checked several other local delis, but there was no interest in good, homebaked bread. At that point I began telling my neighbors and friends that I would be glad to bake for them. In six weeks, I have acquired ten customers. With only three or four more customers, my income will be back to what it was when the deli was buying, so I'm still marketing with that as a goal."

Ginger says that her total income for bread baking in 1981 was $1680. She says, too, "I have also paid off various doctor bills with bread. My obstetrician, chiropractor, and dentist all were willing to take bread in exchange for their services."

When Jane Morford of Idaho tells of her small money-making business, bread baking, she notes that while she works at home, it is "not in my spare time, because I do not have any. I just make time for whatever comes along." Jane makes whole wheat bread, which she sells to the people in the neighborhood. "I know them all because we belong to the same church," she writes. Her usual output is eighty to one hundred loaves a week. Jane says she clears about 63% of the selling price of her bread. "I take 30% off the gross and put it right back into staples for the bread," she explains. "Then I take 10% of the remaining 70% as a tithe to the Lord," a practice which Jane credits with "keeping the family afloat."

When her husband was down to only one part-time job recently, she "began to panic" she says, and so investigated taking a job in her field of training, medical technology. "The job did not come through, and I am *so* thankful," she writes. After adding up the expenses that would have been involved and taking into consideration that she would have to give up her home business, "it just wouldn't be worth it!" she decided. "I make about $240 a month profit from my bread alone."

Another bread baker, Debbie Brown of Virginia writes, "I have always enjoyed making bread, and when we moved to Central America (Debbie's husband was with the U.S. Embassy in Guatemala for three years) we found the commercial bread so appalling that I began to make all of our bread." An acquaintance suggested that she go into the business of selling homemade bread and so Debbie approached the Embassy Commissary. They were willing to give it a try. The bread would be left on consignment, priced at $1.50 a loaf, and Debbie was "thinking along the lines of a dozen loaves a week."

She writes that the homemade bread soon became a major attraction at the commissary. She gradually worked out a system for producing in greater quantities, and when they left Guatemala, she was making 250 to 300 loaves a month, all by hand. She began giving lessons in bread-making to one or two students at a time. "By the time we had to move, I had taught over thirty people. The first year's bread baking in Guatemala grossed about $2500," Debbie says, "and almost $3400 the second year."

When the Browns moved back to the States, it was "an adjustment getting used to life here, especially the prices!" Debbie says. She has again started making bread, "this time as a formal business." As part of the requirements, she had her kitchen inspected by the Health Department and she designed an attractive label showing the ingredients used in her bread. She has also applied for a tax number from the Virginia Tax Commission and plans to incorporate her business. "All this, the labels, incorporation, business cards, plus ingredients, takes some capital to start," Debbie notes, and so she applied for a

Homemade bread soon became a major attraction at the commissary...

small loan at a local bank. "I was able to get the loan on my own credit rating," she says.

A local health food store that she approached agreed to take her bread on consignment, and now, "homemade bread is a feature in their ads." Debbie also does special orders, such as no-salt bread. "Making bread is a very creative and satis-fying way of bringing in some extra income," she says. "My family reaps the benefits of my staying home while enjoying the 'fruits of my labor!' "

Shop for Others Who is better qualified as a judicious shopper than a saving homemaker? When Jean McNertney of Texas goes to market she often buys food or clothing or does the banking and general errands for others as well as her own family. "And I always have my children with me," Jean says of her money-earning efforts.

When shopping for others, it's important to keep the things bought and all sales receipts separate from the family's purchases, Jean stresses. An older child will often push one grocery cart while Jean guides another, with the assistance of a second little helper. "Having the children help encourages their participation and cooperation; so does a small treat!" she says. Jean charges $6 to $7 an hour for shopping chores and delivery to the house. For an extra charge, she also does the laundry for one of her customers. "I pick this up when I deliver the groceries and generally wash it that day, then return it the next day," she says. "At the moment the earnings are small, but a little pocket money can make the day look brighter and the small treats which would never have been squeezed from the monthly budget are welcomed by all."

Sew Up Some Profits If you're on good terms with a sewing machine, consider converting your sewing skills into cash. It's an accommodating field, allowing quite a range of expertise, creativity, and the option to take on either small or more involved projects. Of course, the seamstress who is also the mother of a young one who requires quite a bit of attention is wise to stay with simple projects or those without an urgent deadline.

Carol Barshack, Illinois, has arranged to do the mending for two working friends. Says Carol, "I do my family's mending as it is, so what's a little more?" Since so much of what she does "depends on the job," she doesn't have a set price for her work. The longer a repair takes, the greater the charge.

Earning at Home

Jessica Butler plays nearby while her mom sews the baby carriers she sells.

Jean Detrich of Kansas says that "flexibility is the biggest factor," in her choice of sewing as a way to supplement the family's income. "Whether I sew only a few hours a week or several hours a day is up to me," she says. Those seeking Jean's services often select their own patterns and material and have her make up the garments for them. She figures her charges according to the amount of work involved. She will make a basic A-line, sleeveless dress for about $12, a simple blouse or elastic-waistband slacks for about $5. She then charges from 50¢—$4.00 extra for each additional detail such as zippers, collars, buttonholes, sleeves, etc. She also charges extra for working with complicated patterns or difficult fabrics. She adds 50% to the price if it is a rush job, and charges $3.00 if the customer fails to keep a fitting appointment.

Another seamstress, Linda Evans of New York, taught school for five years before her children were born and has since done some substitute teaching. But when she speaks of the sewing and alterations business she has now in her home, Linda says,

"The money per hour is better than teaching!" And Linda, too, appreciates the fact that with sewing, "I can do it any time I like." Based on her own experience, she advises anyone who is thinking about sewing as a way to earn extra money to do alterations, if possible, rather than "sew from scratch." "Making clothes is very time-consuming," she says, "and not as profitable per hour as alterations." She finds that for the most part, alterations consist of "simple hems on pants, skirts, and sleeves."

Payment for Dottie Gill, Alabama, is in the form of free material, patterns, and notions. Dottie contracted with a local variety store to sew outfits for display in their material section. The store furnishes all needed supplies and "at the end of the display season, the garments are mine," Dottie writes. Of course, she is always working a season ahead. In summer, she's putting together fall and winter garments. But since these come down about the middle of December, there is still plenty of time to wear them that season. She regularly makes outfits that become stylish additions to her sons' wardrobes. "I simply estimate what size they will wear six months from now," she says.

Becky McDaniel of Oklahoma has been sewing since high school days, but recently has turned it "into a real money-maker." Becky makes baby quilts, diaper bags, carriers, and dolls which she sells through a little shop in the area. Developing an area in which one is adept is often the way to attract customers. Teresa Strom, Illinois, has gained a reputation for making pretty bridal veils. The work is not as time-consuming as is dressmaking, yet is the perfect outlet for a creative touch, which brides-to-be appreciate. Teresa can charge well below bridal salon prices, yet still make a worthwhile return on her work.

Use Your Phone   "With the economy as it is today, many business and professional people are having difficulty with overdue bills. Collecting them is something that can often be done by telephone in your own home," says a voice of experience, Debby Sizer of North Carolina. "I make phone calls for a local radio station either when the baby is asleep, playing quietly, or when my husband is at home to watch her," she explains of the half hour to three hours a week that she gives to collecting outstanding bills for the radio station.

As for the return on her efforts, "I receive from ten to twenty percent of the amount collected. My weekly earnings vary; I've received anywhere from $50 to over $300."

In regard to the skills that are most needed in phone collecting, Debby lists them as "a good telephone voice, the ability to be persistent and firm if necessary, and the ability to get along with and understand the public." To this she adds that having a nice manner and being considerate are always appreciated. On occasion, she has gone in person to collect a bill, at which time she takes her two children with her. Debby is convinced that there is a demand for such a service. "A couple of people that I've collected from said that they wished that I would collect for their businesses also."

The Paper Route   Christine Heck may well hold the title of being the youngest person who, come sleet or snow or burning sun, faithfully travels a newspaper route in Michigan—for that matter, she could be the youngest "newspaper carrier" in the world. Christine was three days old when she accompanied her mother on the three hour, sixty-mile trip by car along country roads delivering papers. "When economizing isn't enough and you do need extra cash coming in, it is something you can manage while keeping baby with you," writes Patricia Heck, Christine's mother. Patricia notes that the arrangement worked "because baby slept much of the time and I could stop to nurse her whenever necessary."

Christine's dad was one of the workers caught in an eleven-month layoff in the auto industry, and so the Hecks "were glad to get the newspaper route." When he was recalled to work, Pat took over the paper route. His job security remains uncertain and the news route, which nets approximately $400 to $500 a month, is a financial lifeline.

Pat, who has four other children, adds that the older chil-

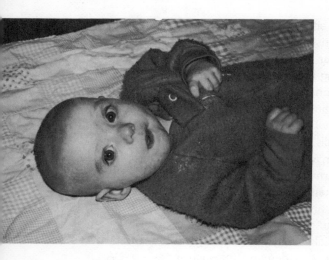

"Youngest newspaper carrier in the world" may well be Christine Heck.

dren help her in the approximately twenty-one hour work-week. The oldest, fifteen-year-old Ken, earned his driving permit, and with his mother sitting next to him in the car, could take a turn at the wheel. And one of the older girls "has always been with me to help since Christine was born." Observes Pat, "My older girls are now eleven, eight, and four and since we've been driving we have enjoyed a lot of togetherness and talking time in those many hours." She adds that "books, picnic lunches, and small toys, along with a messy car, are basic to the job."

The Direct Sales Scene Direct sales is a big business, and more than likely you know someone who sells or who has sold cosmetics or household cleaning products or sold products through home parties. Two mothers we heard from, Joyce Reis of Ohio and Ruth Ann Hager of Missouri, wrote in detail about their home business as distributors for a company which offers household cleaning products, personal care products, and vitamin and nutritional supplements.

Most of the companies who market their products through direct sales use a pyramid system to encourage growth. The distributor benefits by sponsoring others to become distributors, and those so sponsored can then sponsor others. Fundamental to the plan is that the one doing the sponsoring receives a percentage of the sales of all in the pyramid or chain.

The Reises concentrated on sponsoring new distributors, and Joyce explains the mathematics of it. "Salary comes in the form of bonus checks based on the total volume of sales. For example, in our first month, I sold about $400 worth of products to five couples who had joined, and I received a check of about $27." After several months of ordering from a supervisor who lived some distance from them, Joyce borrowed $1000 on an insurance policy and invested it in her own inventory stock. Says Joyce, "Within five months, we had sponsored about thirty-five couples and some of them had sponsored couples and so on until we had about 150 families in the total group. My income ranged between $200 and $400 a month." In that five-month period, she reinvested much of this income back in the business, building up an inventory "worth about $5000."

Ruth Ann reports, "There are fourteen people or couples in my 'chain,' some ordering once a year, others ordering monthly. My average check for a month is $40. That's not large, but my expenses are small."

Volume is the key to earnings. When sales in their "chain" were consistently $3000 a month, the Reises qualified to be supervisors, which in turn entitled them to bigger, more varied bonuses. "We were supervisors for about nine months and then fell below the minimum," Joyce writes. "The business requires a steady and consistent effort of six to ten hours per week." She says that they continue to supply the families in their group or chain who were using the products. "We average about $300 sales volume a month," she says, most of which is filled from the inventory that they had already purchased.

For Ruth Ann, her experience in direct sales of vitamin supplements has been a stepping stone. Her involvement led her to investigate the use of vitamins and other nutritional supplements in health maintenance. An "avid reader," she was in library work for eight years. "I have started a Nutritional Resource and Reference Library," she says. The person seeking information on the use of a particular vitamin-nutritional supplement can ask Ruth Ann to research the matter, and she'll search for printed material from reputable authors. "I usually try to find two or three sources which cover both the pros and cons of the matter," she says. Decision-making is left to the one raising the question, and she encourages people to discuss their new-found information with their doctors.

In describing her office, Ruth Ann writes, "My desk and bookcase are in a finished room in the basement. The children's play area is a few feet away. There's a 'kid's desk,' a table with a yard-sale typewriter, cash register, paper, and pencils. The kids are happy for quite a while because they can also ride their tricycles in the unfinished part of the basement."

Not all selling situations engender such positive feelings. Another mother, Linda Ritter of New Jersey, has a different story to tell based on her experience in demonstrating products at home parties. "When you become a demonstrator," she writes, "most companies require you to hold approximately six initial parties within a short period of time, such as two weeks. Although these companies *say* you only work when you want to, you still get pressure in many cases from your manager because the more you earn, the more the manager earns and so on up the line. Also, these companies have monthly rallies which you will be 'encouraged' to attend."

She worked as a demonstrator for a year, booking parties one or two nights a week and earned about $2000. In recalling that period, she says "It was emotionally and physically draining." As a salesperson at a party in a home, Linda was in the company of other women who, "would discuss ideas, say on child care, that were far from my own way of thinking," she relates. She had to keep her thoughts on such matters to herself, of course. "My role was that of demonstrator, an outsider. My input wouldn't have been appropriate or welcome," she notes. Far more, Linda prefers the role of mother-at-home. "Being home has liberated me," she says.

A Clean Sweep Wield dust cloth, vacuum cleaner, scouring pad, and mop, bring a fresh clean look to a place, and earn $35 to $40 a day doing it. The job can be congenial to a mother with a youngster or two. Be sure to bring snacks and an assortment of interesting toys to occupy your child. A baby in a backpack usually enjoys the activity and new surroundings.

Several mothers-at-home have a regular job cleaning a nearby church. "I do janitorial work once a week for our church," writes Mary Kastendieck of Colorado. "My sister-in-law and I split the work and the pay. We set our own hours and, of course, take the kids along. They napped in the church nursery as babies or I kept them happy in the baby carrier. Now, my children are older and they play or help. I usually spend one day a week cleaning for about six hours." Mary makes $40 a week this way, an amount that "looks mighty good at the end of the month in helping to meet the house payment."

Rusty Peterson applied for and was given the job of custodian and groundskeeper for their church in Oklahoma. The janitorial work inside is year-round, she says, and the grounds-keeping "involves all the months that the lawn needs to be mowed—from March through November." Rusty's children were aged seven and almost three when she started in her new job and "they are always welcome at the church," she says. "They help by emptying wastebaskets, straightening books, sharpening pencils, while I do the heavier cleaning—vacuuming, mopping, cleaning bathrooms, and such. They always finish before I do and then play in the preschool classroom." She can complete the inside work in one to three hours and earns about $14 for these duties. Groundskeeping consists of mowing, at least three hours a week—$15; edging, which her husband does, two to three hours—$12.50; and extra pay for any additional work. Rusty says this could be trimming bushes, pulling weeds, trying to keep the grass out of the parking lot, "and anything else that I see needs to be done or the trustees request that I do. I make out a bill and I am paid monthly."

A Joint Venture   When jobs are scarce for the man of the house, the answer to making a livelihood may lie in husband and wife creating a job and working at it together. This was the situation for the Taylors of British Columbia, Canada—Rhonda, her husband, and their three boys, aged eight months to five years. "Basically, we garden," writes Rhonda Taylor of their family business. "We cut lawns, dig flower beds, plant shrubs, trees, and the like. We do not landscape. The customer chooses the plants, and we do the planting."

With the approach of the summer season, the Taylors placed an ad announcing their service in the local paper. "We were inundated with calls," Rhonda reports. Gradually, they're building up a permanent clientele, and now have two steady customers and one who has work done every so often. "All are older people," she says. "The two long-term customers are like extra grandparents to our children. They are friends as much as customers. Taking time out for a little visiting makes our yard card service unique. I listen a lot." Rhonda observes, and "people come to rely on you." The Taylors stress the value of establishing a routine. "Stop by one day each week even if there isn't any work that needs to be done. Just making an appearance is appreciated."

In describing how they manage their business, Rhonda says, "On workdays, my husband and I evaluate what needs to be done, and he loads the truck and heads off to the site. I come along later after having done any errands. Often, the customer wants some items picked up from a garden shop or hardware store. I also bring our lunch, snacks for the boys, the baby's stroller, and the backpack and toys."

As part of the working team, Rhonda "pushes the lawnmower, rakes and digs." She says, "When the baby was tiny, I strapped him in his front carrier, taking care to cover his head and ears to protect him against the sun and noisy equipment.

I do as much as I can and I am paid at a reduced rate because I feel I'm often pulled away to care for the boys. For four hours at the job, I am usually paid for two." Rhonda worked through her pregnancy, weeding and planting. "In fact, being on all fours was extremely comfortable," she says.

As for equipment, anyone interested in doing this type of work probably already has the essentials—shovels, rakes, a mower, and other miscellaneous garden tools. Often, the customers have tools which can be used. When bringing your own, you'd want to be sure to mark them clearly so as to avoid any mix-ups. The Taylors invested about $3,000 in their company, most of which went toward a four-door pickup truck, a riding mower, and another heavy duty lawn mower.

Customers pay extra for reliability...

Setting the terms is something that the Taylors work out right at the beginning when talking to a new customer. "Our rates are low," Rhonda says, "$8 an hour for labor with no charge for mileage or travel time." Other such firms in their area bill at $15 an hour plus travel time. "Even so," she says, "it can come as a surprise to people to see a bill for over $100 for a day's work." The Taylors took care, too, to see an accountant and "have our books set up properly." Their gross earnings vary from $1,000 a month in the summer to $100 a month in winter.

To other would-be yard care entrepreneurs Rhonda says, "The main criteria before starting a business like this is to consider if you really like gardening. Can you stand to spend a day shoveling manure? Or pushing a lawn mower or turning sod? If you don't like doing it at home, don't try to do it for someone else. Customers pay extra for reliability and quality work—after all, a teenage boy is a lot cheaper." As a family, Rhonda says that "generally, we enjoy ourselves. The boys have room to run, and within reason, to make noise." She emphasizes, "Be prepared to leave early if the kids need to. We usually take two vehicles so my husband can stay and finish if I have to leave." An added bonus, she says, is that "The work keeps us all fit and healthy."

The Craft Makers

Craft-making is the grandfather—or more appropriately, the grandmother—of the home business if ever there was one. That venerable institution we call "home" had scarcely been established when a woman first picked up some nearby materials and fashioned them into an attractive and useful piece, one which, upon her neighbor's next visit, turned out to be just what the neighbor was looking for. The neighbor and then the neighbor's friend commissioned the making of similar items and a home crafter was born. Her progeny have been going strong ever since.

Of the mothers who wrote to us, a large number make craft items regularly for their own use and to give to others as gifts. They may occasionally sell their handiwork, but they do not think of this as a home business. It's just something they enjoy doing along with numerous other money-saving and moneymaking efforts. Maureen Cristall of British Columbia is typical of many others when she writes that she makes a number of crafts—"cloth dolls, woven wall hangings, appliqued hangings which I use for gifts. I enjoy sewing." she says, "and need an outlet for my creativity."

Some others have expanded craft-making into a home job, though it isn't necessarily just the mother's business. Other family members are often involved in making or marketing the craft goods. Sandi Campanell of New Jersey talks about this family aspect of craft-making. "My husband, Denny, helps me find the cheapest supply of the materials I need," Sandi writes.

Maureen Cristall sews at home with "help" from Erin and Jamin.

"This enables me to keep my prices down. Also, he figures out the cost per item." This last, as any business person knows, is important to know in order to cover one's costs. Sandi also gets help in assembling her creations, which may be potpourris, Christmas wreaths, stained glass pieces, or some other craft item, from her six-and-a-half-year-old daughter. Her husband has taken her crafts to various outlets such as a community food market and a dollhouse store. She advises anyone trying to market a new craft to approach a number of different stores. "Try those that you go to a lot," she suggests. "To get started, just look around you and see if there is a need. Then decide on a craft you can do that is fun and rewarding to make."

Another crafter, Judi Myers of Wyoming, urges others to try different approaches and not give up. "I have done such a variety of crafts I could never recall them all. I kept trying till I found one that sold." She explains, "In my case, it's salt dough figurines. I make them specific to the area for sale in tourist shops. Cowboys and moose are the best sellers." Judi, too, gets help in craft-making from her family. "My children have always helped me," she says, "first by mushing their fingers in the dough and now that they're older, by creating figurines themselves."

In the search for outlets, Judi and a friend looked beyond their local stores to those in a larger town some distance away. "We went from store to store till we found one or two that would buy them" Their efforts paid off. "I make a thousand dollars a year," Judi says of her craft business. As for her friend, "out of the ordinary" best describes her medium of expression. Or perhaps the more fitting term would be "off the beaten path." And, furthermore, only in the wide open spaces of the West is it likely to be found. Writes Judi, "My friend gathers animal droppings, varnishes them, and makes funny creatures out of them. They sell like crazy!"

Think Small Writes Holli Rovitti, New York: "I crochet, although not that well, and have found that I can sell teeny crocheted doilies, placemats, coasters, and those little whatchamacallits that go on the backs and arms of chairs." Holli's creations are part of the world of doll house miniatures. "The financial outlay to start this business is truly minuscule," points out Holli. "One ball of the thinnest crocheting thread, either white or ivory, and a #14 crochet hook."

In selecting her designs, she says she experimented with different patterns until she found ones that are "easy to put down, half-completed, in favor of the more important things in life." The latter often involves her young children, so Holli likes the fact that it only takes about ten minutes to crochet an item.

With finished pieces slipping through her fingers so quickly. Holli's inventory increases rapidly. "Volume counts," she says, "because I can distribute my work among several stores." For maximizing the return on making miniatures, Holli offers the following suggestions:

1. Don't be afraid to change, combine, or simplify patterns. Holli found the inspiration for her patterns from

an inexpensive doily book and a booklet on miniature
needlework.
2. Strive for a good effect and low prices. You want prospective customers to say "Oh!" when looking at your
creations—"How cute! How clever!"—and sigh "Ah!"
at the price.
3. For *all* work on miniatures, have good, strong lighting.
Holli says there is also a demand for miniature pot
holders, bedspreads, afghans, tableclothes, and rugs.
You would use a bigger crochet hook and heavier thread
on some of these items. Miniatures in general are good
sellers.

When the question of staying home versus going out to
work comes up, Holli is quick to say that she is home with her
children "because I want to be their mother, and to me, a
mother is not the person who biologically gives birth to a child,
but the one whose personality is indelibly stamped on that child
through continual exposure. Having been adopted myself,"
she explains, "I probably appreciate this distinction more than
most."

The Artist in You   Don't hide your artistic talent under a bushel
basket or, as Connie Phillips of Ohio did, in the closet. With a
little exposure, it could be a source of income for you. Connie
says that she had studied art in school and "occasionally would
sketch or paint," but, she says, "I always kept it all hidden
away in the closet." Her husband, David, is a firm believer
that people do best what they enjoy doing, and so when Connie was looking for a way to earn money, he encouraged her
to display and sell her art work.

She recalls that for a time she borrowed a table and she
shared booths at area craft shows. "We were all nursing mothers," she explains, "so we divided the sitting time at the booth
and split the booth fee." Connie now has her own tables (a
plywood top with screw-in legs is simple and inexpensive) and
display boards that her husband made from pegboard. The

Connie Phillips checks over her supply of buttons with daughter Jeanine.

start-up money came from their "music fund," money that David had earned giving music lessons. Last year, Connie participated in eight one-day shows and earned over $500. She's hoping "with the knowledge I've gained," to double that amount next year.

Along with the more costly paintings and sketches, Connie makes sure she has several low-priced items, things which sell for a dollar or less. The sale of these assures her the recovery of her booth fee. Some of the dollar favorites are copies of several poems that Connie lettered in calligraphy and had reproduced by a printer. Her cost was about six cents each. Bookmarks made of pressed autumn leaves and dried flowers sell for seventy-five cents each. "My fastest moving item is a wooden nickel which I make into a magnetic button," Connie says. "I got the wooden nickels free because they had advertising printed on one side and the business had closed," she explains. Connie paints over that side and adds a catchy saying. She then glues a small amount of square magnetic tape on the other side. They sell fast at three for a dollar. To help her keep track of the buttons that need to be replaced, she has developed an efficient inventory system.

Earning at Home

Meryl Butler Perry at an outdoor art festival when Christy was small.

Meryl Butler Perry, Louisiana, a free-lance artist and art teacher, has combined work and home life since the birth of her daughter, Christy, five years ago. She resumed teaching art classes on a reduced schedule with Christy in a baby carrier. "I would nurse her on the right side before class so that during class she could nurse on the left side while I demonstrated with my right hand," Meryl explains. The most valuable situations for me, Meryl notes, "occur when I create a moneymaking activity directly related to my current interactions with my daughter." Such an approach, she finds, "creatively fulfills many needs simultaneously." When Christy was an infant, Meryl worked on a "Creative Perception" course for parents to use with their infants. The games and other activities promote perceptual growth as well as enhance the parent-child relationship. Recently, in conjunction with Christy, Meryl created another course, "Art-Related Learning Experiences for Young Children." She says that this course, too, is designed to help parents use art as "a basis for interaction with their children."

Meryl sees many advantages in "being one's own boss." There's much greater freedom concerning hours worked and bringing baby along. "And don't be afraid to slow down or quit if things don't work out," she advises. "Having a 'trial period' is a good idea. If things go well—fine! But it's not a 'failure' if they don't." Meryl suggests, too, that whenever possible, "have the customers come to you. This does away with the time and cost of commuting and allows your children to be with you, in a familiar environment." In fact, whenever possible, "include the family in your moneymaking activity," Meryl recommends.

Another talented and resourceful mother established an at-home business based on a gift. "Before I was married, a friend gave me a book on calligraphy," writes Laura Avery of Idaho. With the book as a guide, Laura taught herself "the fine art of chancery cursive, the calligraphy style most often seen in books and on posters." Shortly before her first child was born, she quit her teaching job to be a full-time mother, and her calligraphy skills were used mainly "to address the birth announcements and holiday greeting cards." Laura joined the local La Leche League Group and volunteered to do a poster in calligraphy announcing the meetings. Copies of the poster were displayed around the county. "To my surprise," she says, "that poster led to my first calligraphy job. A friend saw one and asked me to do the brochure for a local fair."

Soon, small jobs were coming Laura's way once or twice a month. "The jobs have been ideal for me," she says. "Necessary supplies are few—one or two calligraphy pens, ink, parchment paper, a ruler, and a kitchen table." Laura does the rough copy while Jesse, her now two-year-old son, is up, but usually waits to make the actual copy till he's asleep or when his father is playing with him. "It's the kind of work I can stop and start as Jesse needs me," Laura explains. As for financial return, Laura says the work pays well. "I charge by the job and take into consideration the client's financial situation. I generally charge $15 to $25 for a page of calligraphy and have been told by clients that they felt they were getting a bargain."

Matthew Kluvo plays with soft-sculpture pumpkins made by his mother, Laura.

Let the Mails Help You   A second generation League mother, Laura Stanton Kluvo of Florida spends her days caring for her young son at home and running her own mail-order business. Her company, appropriately named "In Stitches," offers patterns, instructions, and kits for making crafts. The soft-sculptures, ornaments, and other designs are all Laura originals. "In Stitches" is incorporated and all of Laura's patterns are copyrighted. A mail-order business does not require a large outlay of money to start, but as Laura says, "You must come up with a product that is unique, appealing, and easy to mail!" She advertises her designs in needlework and craft magazines. Laura explains that this gives her a lot of flexibility. "You can make the business as large or small as you like simply by varying the number or size of your advertisements." Creativity and persistence are a winning combination, Laura has found. Some of her work was accepted by *Better Homes and Gardens* to be included in a special craft edition of the magazine.

Shawn Ramsey enjoys the Christmas Craft Fair with her daughter Anastasia.

Fair Thee Well

What mother-at home would think of putting on a fair, a fair that's truly a bustling marketplace with buyers and sellers, entertainment, and plenty of good things to eat? Shawn Ramsey, a California mother of two, thought about it and did it. She now considers "promoting craft fairs" as her home business.

"Promoting comes naturally to me," says Shawn. "Before I became a mother, I worked for six years in the advertising field." Even so, organizing a fair from start to finish—arranging for a site, contacting craftspeople, and attracting buyers—was a new experience for her. Shawn credits "a lot of encouragement from my husband" as seeing her through the project. He kept saying, "You can do it!" and "I did it," she says. For her efforts (she spent "maybe two hours a day" starting two months before the event) she reports that she earned over a thousand dollars.

The idea for the fair came to her "when it hit me in the

fall that there would be no Christmas Craft Fair in our town," a community of about 10,000 people. She did some preliminary research, checking into the cost of a business license, whether a fair had been staged before in that town, whether the auditorium was free on a weekend in December, and "I realized I could get started with only twenty-five dollars for a license," Shawn says.

Start-up money was also needed to place ads in craft art periodicals inviting crafters to come and display their wares. They could reserve a booth for fifty dollars. To avoid losing money on the venture, Shawn worked out a break-even point. If the ads didn't generate enough of a response to cover basic expenses, "I could change my mind, back out, and return everyone's money," she explains. Some of her expenses were: Autditorium—$400 a day, plus custodian's wages; business license—$25; insurance—$50. Forty-six six-foot tables to be used for displays came with the hall. Shawn rented out the kitchen space, thereby increasing her income. Hot apple cider, salads, and pasties, small meat pies made famous in England, were served. Popcorn and baked goods were also sold. Altogether, there were fifty booths at the Christmas Craft Fair. Decorating the auditorium was simple, since a sorority had held a dance there the night before, and Shawn was able to make use of their decorations, including a thirty-foot Christmas tree. To add to the festive spirit of the event, she massed balloons in the foyer. Inside the auditorium, cassette music was broadcast over a loud speaker, and there were wandering carolers, an accordian player, a guitarist, and a flutist. Church groups sang, and a belly dancer performed. At the booths, some of the craftspeople demonstrated their skills—pottery making, glass blowing, making stained glass. A special feature was a Craft Room for Kids catering to youngsters three years old and up.

In the weeks before the fair, Shawn had 2000 tickets printed offering free admission to the fair. These were distributed through the Downtown Merchants Association. The merchants liked the idea of being able to give free tickets to customers, and Shawn was able to attract a large number of people to the fair. A large banner across a main thoroughfare in the town also announced the coming event. On the days of the fair, a high school girl whom Shawn had hired took tickets at the door. (Admission without a ticket was one dollar.) Shawn had decided that she wanted to be free to be with her children, and "they loved it," she says. "They were with my husband and me at the fair all weekend." (Her husband further helped by spending the night at the fair site as a security measure.)

Shawn's family was on her mind when she first thought about the fair. The idea appealed to her, she says, because, "It would be my own business. No one could tell me I couldn't have my almost one-year-old and three-year-old with me." On looking back on her accomplishment, besides the extra income that she made, Shawn found she had also gained added recognition in the community. "I've been asked for advice on other community events," she says.

Have a Sale

The home sale, whether out of the garage, basement, or yard, just could be "all things to all people." It's a source of good buys for the bargain hunter, surprises for those looking for diversion, a good deed for the recycler, and extra cash for the seller. Anyway you look at it, the personal sale fits comfortably with modern-day pioneering. Although it is not usually an on-going source of income, a sale now and again can represent a tidy deposit to your bank account.

Begin, of course, by assembling your merchandise. Rochelle Carothers of Nevada suggests that you look for "duplicates of anything—gifts, unused cookware, clothing which you no longer wear." Rochelle points out that it takes time and practice to spot things that can be moved on and "decide to part with them." She suggests, too, that you remind your husband and other family members to look for possessions that would be worth more on a sale table than left where they are. If relatives have things that they'd like to clear out, offer to include them in your sale and split the profit. Don't overlook items that you may have previously tossed out—half-filled bottles of nail polish or cologne (little girls love to make such purchases), jewelry, including broken pieces, paints, scraps of wallpaper. How about a "green table?" Well-rooted cuttings of house plants or starters for a spring garden lend a fresh touch and usually sell well.

Price your stock realistically. Remember, people expect to find bargains. You may want to visit a few sales in areas near you to get a feel for pricing things. Ask questions: Does clothing move well? Children's items? How extensively was the sale advertised? Also, notice how items are displayed. What looks attractive, and what comes across as "junky"? If you have a collection of odds and ends, group them together in a "Super Bargain" section and price appropriately low. Feature your better ware separately. If you can get a supply of newsprint, use it to cover your display tables. The uniform, clean, white surface will make everything look more attractive. Of course, the pieces that are hauled down from an attic or closet shelf should first be dusted or washed so as to look their shiny best.

What are the possibilities of holding a joint sale with neighbors or relatives? The greater variety of offerings makes a multi-family sale more appealing to would-be buyers, and the larger labor force makes for lighter work and more fun for the sale givers. Susanne Miller of New Jersey joined her mother and sister in putting on a yard sale at her sister Chrissy's house, which was a short distance up the road from a weekly church flea market. To the surprise of the three of them, they netted $200 for their day's work. Nor had they sold out their accumulated finds. "We still had over half the items left," Susanne writes. And so they decided to hold another sale the following Tuesday—and the one after that, and the next one, and the next. "Tuesday began to take on new meaning," she says. "It meant flea market day at Chrissy's house. Every Tuesday from the end of spring to the end of fall, we had a yard sale, unless the weather was bad."

In answer to the obvious question, "Where did all the sale items come from?" Susanne's initial response was "I honestly don't know!" She explains that "actually, we had so much in the beginning, we had a good start. Then, as our friends found out about the sale, they would ask if we wanted things that they were planning to throw away anyway. If it was saleable, we'd take it. Usually, we gave the person a part of the profit if their items sold."

Tuesday proved to be profitable for the trio. "The least that we made in a day was about $100," Susanne says. "Also, it was fun for our family to get together, and we met a lot of nice people. We had our 'steady' customers, and each week we saw plenty of new faces."

A Year-round Market? Why Not! Market Day is a weekly event in many parts of England, according to Jane Hay Hald who lives in West Sussex. It is also an opportunity for countless cooks, gardeners, and crafters to offer their prize wares for sale and earn a welcome bit of change. "It is the type of thing that could easily be set up by a group of women anywhere," Jane emphasizes. She regularly participates in the market near her. "I sell eight loaves of banana bread and eight small chocolate cakes a week in addition to my eggs, and I usually have a profit of $100 a month," she writes.

This highly successful system of marketing, known as Women's Institutes—WI Markets, was organized in England following World War I. Its aim, according to the WI Market Handbook, remains the same today as when founded: "To make it worthwhile financially to keep gardens in cultivation, to prevent waste by encouraging good growing and harvesting and by helping an increasing number of people to develop their skills and market their produce, and to do this by working together cooperatively." WI publications offer instructions and hints on how to make or market a tempting variety of things from bread, chutneys, crafts, eggs, flower arrangements, meat pies, fresh dressed poultry, and wood fuel.

The success of the market concept is evident from a story Jane tells. "A bill was introduced in Parliament to prohibit WI Markets selling jam because it isn't prepared in sterile factories. The Markets are famous for their jam, and so a big argument arose. Parliament lost. After all, what was is it against 100,000 women, the biggest labor force in the country!"

Additional information on the organization of the English WI Markets can be obtained by writing to the National Federation of Women's Institutes, 39 Eccleston Street, London, England SW1W 9NT.

Earn by Tutoring

Are you proficient in a particular subject? Do you have a knack for imparting this knowledge to others? Give some thought to tutoring students in your home. You'll be earning extra money and at the same time keeping your skills sharpened.

Katrina Meek of Illinois was always a good math student and began helping others in the subject while she was still in high school. She earned some college credits in mathematics but decided to forgo higher education "to have babies—much more fun!" she says. In twelve years of tutoring, Katrina found that "a college degree is not necessary. Solid knowledge of the subject is." She has worked with grade school, high school, and college students in math, most of whom hear about her tutoring service by word of mouth or are referred to her by a teacher. If you're interested in tutoring, Katrina suggests, "Let teachers in the local schools know that you're available."

The age and temperament of your own child or children will have a bearing on whether or not to schedule pupils and how many to take. Katrina preferred to tutor when her own children were young. "I could hold a baby, fix peanut butter sandwiches, or kiss a hurt," and still give the math students who would come for a lesson after school the necessary help and attention. But once her children were in school themselves, "they really needed my time after school for a while," she says. For Katrina and her husband, "there has never been any question of my leaving our children. That was always a given fact, and we worked everything else out from that viewpoint."

Jane Hay Hald, who is now residing in West Sussex, England, was living in Norway when tutoring figured as a means of support for her and her child. She writes that she was divorced at the time. "It meant that I had to go to work when my daughter Liv was nearly four," she explains. "I was fortunate that I was in a country where learning English was popular. I gradually acquired a reputation and was often asked to do individual tutoring. Liv was old enough to understand that this was a time when I really shouldn't be disturbed, but it was no crisis if she did need me."

Jane utilized a number of skills in earning a living—working as an English teacher/tutor, a school librarian, and a translator. "For me, the more I could do at home the better," she notes, which was one reason why translating and tutoring were so desirable. Jane points out that, "It was a tremendous advantage not to have all my eggs in one basket. With a foot in the door in three separate jobs, even if the job situation became difficult, I could still expand in the other two areas."

Another free-lance translator, Lisa Robitaille of Ontario, Canada points out that it is necessary to concentrate fully on the work when doing a translation, and so she is careful to arrange her work schedule around her family's needs. "I limit my working to naptime or evenings," she says, "when my husband is home and able to keep the kids occupied for a few hours. There are a lot less headaches that way. It's simply not worth trying to put the kids off—everybody ends up riled, and next to nothing is accomplished." Also, she spreads the work out. "For the present, I'm happy to do one translation every six weeks or so, spending four days to a week on each job.

This schedule is not overtaxing, and when I do have a translation to do, I find it a nice break. I feel professional for a few days, and our savings account gets a little boost." Translators such as Lisa earn "between ten and thirty dollars an hour, depending on the difficulty of the text."

From Teacher to Zoom Zoom the Clown! If you're a former teacher who is wondering how, as a mother-at-home, you can put your training to profitable use, Peggy Koegler of Minnesota has good news. "My background is elementary teaching and social work was the ideal preparation for my present occupation—that of being Zoom Zoom the Clown," she writes. "Put aside the idea that you can't do something," Peggy advises. "Give vent to your imagination, to any inner calling, and go with it!"

In Peggy's case, she always had "a passing fancy with the theater and especially the clowns at circuses and parades." Nothing came of her interest, however, until a fellow League Leader told her of a class in clowning that was being offered at the local community education center. It was a tip that set her on her way to her new career.

The course covered the many different aspects of clowning, Peggy says, showing that there is much more to the art than "just putting on a funny suit." "I began to develop the idea of clowning as an interesting little business," she explains. Peggy specializes in planning children's parties and in her role as Zoom Zoom, she entertains the young party-goers. "I provide the favors and basically plan and prepare the party for the parents or the organization giving the party," she says. Quite often, her own children can come with her and enjoy the fun.

Her expenses are basically low—the favors and whatever she needs for props in the skits she puts on for the children. Other costs are her clown attire and make-up. Her time must also be figured in her charge, both the time spent in preparing and shopping for the party and then in getting ready on the day. "It takes approximately an hour for the make-up alone," she notes.

"The whole thing has been a fascinating experience for our family," Peggy says. To date, an attractive little business card bearing a sketch of a clown holding a balloon is her main form of advertising. She passes these out to friends and at library story hours, children's stores, and the like. Perhaps sometime in the future she'll put an ad in the local paper. "Right now," she says, "I do not want to be overwhelmed. I just want to grow into my new role."

Guarding the Crosswalks When the Worzer family went through a particularly hard financial time Linda found another way to supplement the family income and still keep her young children with her. She became a school crossing guard.

Mothers are frequently seen serving as school crossing guards, and many times with their own little ones in tow. "I learned about the local police department's school crossing guard program through a friend," Linda writes. "There is a great amount of freedom in what I do. I can go home between shifts, and I can bring my children along with me!" Linda works four hours a day on school days and earns $325 a month. When on the job, she usually has the youngest in the backpack and holds her five-year-old's hand while walking the school children across the street. "We keep apple juice and water in the car, along with snacks and coloring books for rainy days and times when we're just plain bored." But most of the time, Linda says, her two little helpers "enjoy watching the 'big kids' on their way to school."

Music, Music, Music

The mother-at-home with a background in music may have a number of options open to her for earning extra money. Musically talented moms tell of giving private lessons in their homes and directing church choirs, often with a baby in a backpack peeking over a shoulder. Flexibility is a necessity, they say. So is being alert to any conflicts between the job and the family's

Musically talented mothers-at-home find they can give private piano lessons with a little one at their side or in their arms.

needs. (This last, of course, holds true for any extra activities.) Pam Mills is a case in point, both in combining mothering and a home business in music and in stepping away from such involvement for a time.

"I had been teaching private piano and flute lessons for several years and planned to continue doing so," this Minnesota mother writes. She arranged to have pupils come in the evening when her husband could be with their two-and-a-half-year-old and newborn infant. But things did not go as planned. "Our new son was an extremely fussy, dependent baby who wanted only me," she explains. Pam says that she realized "my teaching would take time away from my very sensitive baby," and so, since she still wanted to contribute to the family's finances, "I applied for a day-care license," she says.

Pam was a day-care mother for several years, but her story does not end there. "Our very dependent infant is now an independent three-year-old who no longer needs my constant reassurance and attention," she says, "and our newest son at seven months is easygoing and loves everything and everyone. I have given up day-care to go back to teaching privately at home. Music has always been a special love of mine, I am a certified teacher, and I do love it. But my family will *always* come first," she adds. One much appreciated advantage to teaching over day-care work is the earnings per hour. Pam can earn $12 to $15 an hour giving music lessons and thus makes as much in seven hours as she did in fifty to sixty hours of day care.

A musician who has set aside her instrument to be a full-time mother, Marsha Rullman of Arizona, can readily relate to new mothers-to-be who are facing the decision of whether or not to work outside the home after the birth of their babies. "I can sympathize," she writes. "I have a degree in music and particularly enjoy giving lessons and playing in an orchestra."

Marsha decided against the commitment that would be necessary to pursue a career in music. As attractive as it would have been to continue in serious music and to bring in extra money, "I do not do these things because I know without a doubt they would compromise my relationship with my children," she says. Marsha has no doubt that, "Bonds broken or stretched are harder to repair than daily maintenance of what is established by a good childbirth experience and nursing."

Glenda Wattenbarger of Georgia recalls the time she spent as a choir director in a small rural church as "most enjoyable." "Musically," she says, "it was not the most challenging church choir I've directed, but the choir members' acceptance of my children meant so much to me. I truly enjoyed teaching music to them since I didn't have to leave my little ones to do it." More recently, Glenda has been teaching music once a week to her son's third-grade class. "It isn't a paid job, but it's good for me and my son," she states. And, of course, the younger Wattenbarger children are welcome along with mother in the classroom.

With a degree in Music Education, Linda Worzer is able to get piano students readily, and she gave lessons in her home when her first two children were small. "I was careful to schedule lessons with breaks in between," this Texas mother says, "and usually only one student in the afternoon, with one or two in the evening when my husband, Richard, was at home." Linda would nurse a baby as needed during the lesson, but she made a point of first clearing the practice with the student's parents. "I talked with the mothers of all my students and explained that I would probably be nursing the baby at one time or another during a lesson," Linda says. "Most of the mothers were not the least bit concerned about it, though I did lose one or two students whose mothers thought it 'unseemly' to breastfeed in front of a young child." Teaching while at the same time mothering seemed natural for Linda in her situation and she says she never thought of herself as a working mother. "For the most part, we all enjoyed the lessons," she says.

With the birth of her third child, Linda discontinued giving lessons. Shortly thereafter, she was offered the position of choir director at their church. "I was delighted at the prospect of directing a choir again," she says, "but I was unsure how it would work out. I agreed to take the job on a temporary basis. Two years later, I'm still directing the choir." The job pays $125 a month and allows Linda and the choir members to bring their younger children with them. "We have no nursery as such," she explains. "The older children are supervised by teenage volunteers, but have free access to their parents at all times. Younger babies are usually in their parent's arms."

At-home Office Work

Do you type well? Do you have some accounting or other record-keeping experience? Such skills transfer easily to an at-home setting.

Writes Christine Hilston of Ohio: "For about the first year after my son Erik was born, the small company for which I worked before his birth brought me work to do at home for an hourly rate. They also brought an electric typewriter from the office for me to use. I typed reports and about once a

Editor Kathy Wolter checks galley proofs at home while son Adam draws monsters.

month, the company's owner came over to dictate correspondence to me, often while I held Erik on my lap."

Since she was a secretary before she became a mother, Alice Oldag of California also arranged to do office work at home. "When my daughter Ashley was nine months old," Alice writes, "I approached my former employer with a plan where I would do work at home on an hourly basis. I picked up the work, which gave me the chance to take Ashley to visit my friends at the same time. I did the work, about five hours a week, during Ashley's naptimes. My employer was delighted with the arrangement. He had no benefits to pay, and it eased the workload of the secretaries in the office."

Four years ago, when her youngest child was four years old, Peggy Moran started her home typing service. "Lately I have had to turn work away," she says. Peggy, who lives in New York, tells her story:

I work anywhere from four to six hours a day, five days a week, and have quite often worked on weekends. My main job is transcribing tapes for a man who provides me with the transcribing machine and paper and brings and picks up the work for me. I transcribe tapes of speeches, seminars, conferences, interviews, and the like. In addition, I do work for schools in the area, typing copy for their yearbooks, literary magazines, and such. I also typed for a professor for a couple of years and occasionally I do work for the assistant principal of my children's school.

Prior to starting work at home, I was editor of the League's Area Leaders' Letter and secured an old electric typewriter with which to do all my typing. That job helped me sharpen my skills. Last year, however, I bought a brand-new typewriter. Although I now have a contract on my typewriter, I incur few other expenses. I average about six dollars an hour and feel I'm working almost as many hours as a full-time office worker, not counting their coffee breaks and lunch hours. Of course, I'm spared the travel time to and from work and I can spread my work out over the whole day and evening. I've learned to budget my time and do several things at once.

On the subject of time, Peggy adds, "Speaking of time, I have my own definition of quality time for a child. Quality time is the exact moment your child needs you, not an hour at the end of the day that you set aside for your child. My little one was home with me all day when I started my typing business. But when she needed me, I could turn off the typewriter and answer her question, give her a hug, and then satisfied, she would return to what she was doing and I could go back to my work. And if you think only little ones need you, wait until they're teenagers and come home literally bursting with things they need to talk about after school."

Donna MacFarlane of New Mexico works for a unique business, one in which the employees come together only once a week, their children with them, and then disperse to their homes where they continue their jobs. "I do distribution, promotion, and some advertising work for *Mothering Magazine*," this mother of three says. "All of the staff members go to work one day a week and their children go, too. We drop off and pick up our work, which we do at home between child care and household duties. I have found this arrangement to be very satisfactory.

It provides a much-needed income along with personal stimulation and challenge. My children have mom all day plus the benefits of playing with the children of other staff members on our workday. I do not need to take large chunks of my paycheck out for child-care, transportation, or clothing for work. All in all, it is a very rewarding arrangement."

In the state of Washington, the long-term volunteer work Judy Hulse and her husband have done for the Childbirth Education Association of Seattle developed into an at-home business for them. Judy explains:

When CEA of Seattle revised and enlarged their basic manual in 1979, we promoted the idea of distributing it nationally to other groups and hospitals. In the end, we offered to do the distribution part of the job.

To start, we worked up an interesting brochure. CEA of Seattle paid the cost of printing the brochure, purchasing mailing lists, and the postage. We bulk mailed a large number of brochures. At first we had lots of orders for single preview copies. Now there is a substantial list of organizations that are regular "customers" and order as they need more books. UPS delivery trucks stop at our house every day.

There's a lot of flexibility to this job. If I'm working and the kids need me, I can come back to it later. It takes a bit of organization and bookkeeping, but nothing fancy. Also a little muscle, since we ship boxes of fifty books which weigh about forty pounds apiece. We get a commission on each sale. This has brought us an average of $270 a month over the past year. I don't think I'd be getting too much more take-home pay from a part-time office job after paying babysitter costs and having to update my wardrobe.

Still More Ways to Earn

Take Baby Along When a private residential school near her home needed a part-time night nurse for a few weeks, Kathleen Hoffman, RN, agreed to take the position on condition that she could bring her one-year-old with her. The school accepted her terms, and the arrangement worked so well, Kath-

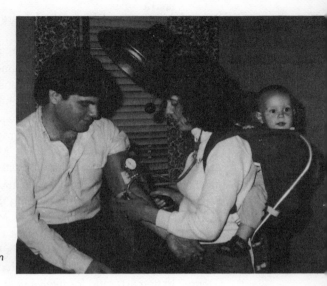

Kathleen Hoffman takes thirteen-month-old Stephen along with her to work.

leen is now on duty between 8 PM and 7 AM every other weekend with her second child keeping her company. She says there may be a few patients who need attention in the evening, but for the most part, she and her little one get a comfortable night's sleep in the nurse's quarters. "I would have to get up for any night emergencies," she says, "but so far there haven't been any." The nurse with the baby is now a common sight at the academy; in fact, Kathleen says the students are very interested in the baby.

Managing Is Her Business   Californian Marilyn Hall, mother of nineteen-month-old Michael, is also a manager of student housing on a college campus. "I take Michael with me," she says regarding her managerial work, which includes checking tenants in and out, arranging for repairs, painting, cleaning, and in general keeping things running. Rents, contracts, and discipline in the ninety-two apartments are not her responsibility, but she is on call five evenings a week and weekends in the event of a maintenance problem. And when a call comes in about a stopped up sink or no hot water in an apartment, it is often mom and Michael who are on their way, tools in hand, to set matters right.

Marilyn is adept at making repairs and keeping an eye on her small son at the same time. "Michael has always had some access to real tools," Marilyn explains. While she works, he will often busy himself with one of her tools. What happens when mother needs the tool? He relinquishes it, his mother reports, adding "when I offer another tool in trade." There are times, it is true, when the budding Mr. Fix-it gets frustrated with the job or, more accurately, with his limited skills. "He takes to hammering on things," Marilyn admits, but quick diversionary tactics succeed in keeping things on an even keel.

"I do not make much money," Marilyn says of her job, but the Halls do get their apartment rent-free. This is an important consideration, since Marilyn's husband is finishing his training as a Registered Nurse. Marilyn herself has a Master's Degree in fine arts, and for twelve years before Michael's birth, had a career as a theater technician-instructor. As for the future, the Halls dream of moving to a rural area, sheep-raising country preferably, where they can be "a working family."

Extra Room? Extra Income!   Do you have a bedroom you're not using as such? Does baby really need a room of his or her own? Could you use some help making the mortgage payment each month? Why not consider taking a boarder or two?

"The opportunity came our way to have a temporary boarder," writes Mary Jean Belrose of Ontario, Canada. "Two weeks after she moved in, she asked if a friend could stay a few days to look for a job. As it turned out," this mother of two little boys explains, "the friend landed a job and still needed a place to stay." And so, two bedrooms at the Belrose house became comfortable rooms for paying guests.

Mary Jean's home business of providing room and meals for two boarders brings in $100 a week. With the additional income, "the financial strain has been lifted," she says. "Before getting the extra income, I often felt guilty about spending money, sometimes even for very necessary things."

Having the young women stay with them involves some added expenses, of course, including the cost of additional food. However, Mary Jean found an unexpected advantage to having two extras at mealtime. "Because I had more people interested in eating what I made, I planned a better meal." Food preparation aside, she notes that "it does take a little extra time and work to change bedding, do the laundry, and clean the bathrooms more frequently." This need to stay on top of things in the house could be difficult for a mother with a new baby, Mary Jean cautions. "But all of these details can be negotiated," she points out. "For a lesser amount, the boarders could change their own bedding and launder it themselves, or just rent the room and have access to kitchen facilities with no meals included."

Write On   Writing isn't only for a select few best-selling authors. There is money to be made, in lesser but welcome amounts, for the occasional author. "I took a short writing course to help me in my work on a publication for LLL Leaders," writes Mary Hurt of Illinois. "Much to my surprise, I've since found it fairly easy to sell a number of non-fiction articles to different magazines."

Writes Mikell Billoki of Ontario, Canada, "I've found that free-lance writing is easily accomplished at home. I've written numerous articles for the local papers on events that I am attending anyway, and I've also written a column on living with little kids—everything from nutrition to arts and crafts."

Computing Profits   "My husband has worked with computers for years, and to better understand what he was doing, I took a college class in programming a few years ago," says Katrina Meek of Illinois. "We now teach occasional classes in basic programming at $12 to $20 a person. We have also begun doing programming for other computer owners—schools, dentists, small businesses. A set of programs, which can be written during the afternoons while the kids are in school, may sell for $200 to $500. Also, it's really enjoyable work."

A Neat Arrangement Vicki Yeley of Texas makes flower arrangements in her basement. A door with a glass pane closes off her workshop area, making it possible for her to watch her children at play while also allowing them to see her.

Never Too Young With three children eager to take summer art classes and the cost per child amounting to over $40, Mary Bell of Virginia and her eleven-year-old son, who was a veteran of several past years' classes, decided to offer their own neighborhood art/craft classes. "My son set up all the supplies and 'taught' the crafts," she writes. "I supervised the whole thing." Five neighborhood children attended. The fee was $5 for five classes plus $3 for art supplies. "My older son learned a lot from the experience, and the other mothers told me that their children loved the classes. We did many things that are difficult to do in a larger class—batiking, tie-dyed T-shirts, sand candles, spin art, stamp art, bread dough sculptures." Mary concludes, "It all worked out very well, and my son earned some extra money, too."

Reference Books to Help Women Choosing to Work at Home

McVicar, Marjorie and Craig, Julia F. *Minding My Own Business.* (New York: Richard Marek Publishers), 1981.

Cardozo, Arlene Rossen. *Woman at Home.* Garden City, New Jersey: Doubleday, 1976.

Hewes, Jeremy Joan. *Worksteads, Living and Working in the Same Place.* Garden City, New Jersey: Doubleday, 1981.

Behr, Marian and Lazar, Wendy. *Women Working Home.* Norward, New Jersey: WWH Press, 1981.

The Days
to Come

There is a time to forge ahead—reaching your goal depends on it—but there is also a time to pause and reflect. Every now and again, step back from your ongoing efforts to save, straighten your back, and lift your eyes. Look ahead to the days to come.

Forget for the moment the ever-present financial concerns, the fact that when it comes to spending money you tell yourself "no" many more times than "yes." Look beyond this time in your life when your children's demands on your energy and patience seem endless. Consider the unfolding of the Plan— *your* Plan. Recall again why it is so very important for you to make this investment of self for the sake of your family, how fitting it is to look upon mothering as a career in its own right, and think a bit about the years ahead.

When your children are small and are at home for the most part, you can make their world a secure place to be. This knowledge is compensation in itself, yet only a small part of the reward coming to a mother-at-home. There are new worlds to discover about yourself, as you will find over and again as time goes by. Most meaningful of all, perhaps, is the relationship that develops between you and your child. A mother and baby establish their own mutual admiration society. When small arms reach out to you and clasp you tightly in an exuberant tribute to your being there, you know you would not trade places with anyone else, anywhere in the world.

But babies don't keep, and along with the wonder of seeing your children grow and become less dependent on you comes the realization that they will soon be venturing forth, going places and making decisions on their own. Their peers will become increasingly more important in their lives. And the kinds and number of challenges that must be met can give even the most intrepid parent reason to pause. With this comes the hope (it is half hope, half prayer) that parents live with— *"That these beautiful young adults who are so dear to us and so eager to test life be spared its harshest lessons."*

There are no guarantees, not in the sense that you can look forward to a smooth, trouble-free future. The years that you give of unbroken mothering are of irreplaceable value, but they are not a vaccine that automatically protects against social ills. The sunny child of six may become the surly sixteen-year-old, much to the consternation of loving parents. Good kids sometimes make mistakes, and good parents find themselves shedding tears because of them.

But the promise holds. You and your child will always be better off because you made the most of the early years. You were there, building the firmest, broadest foundation for the superstructure to come. The groundwork is laid for meeting the new challenges. The basic system for maintaining the lifeline between parents and child is in place.

And what are some of your parenting resources? For one, you know your child better than any outsider can hope to. A toddler and teenager are years apart, but your child's basic characteristics remain the same. Look for them to show through the growing-up changes. Outside professionals—doctors, teachers, counselors—can contribute to the family's well-being in numerous ways, but only on a limited basis. Parents are the sustaining figures and the true experts in family matters. Never underestimate your worth!

You have become well acquainted with the meaning of

The Days to Come

unconditional love. It is what children of all ages need, from the colicky infant to the cranky eleven-year-old. This is not to say that as a parent you can be blind to your children's faults. (How much easier it would be at times to close one's eyes to them.) On the contrary, you need to be very much involved. Parenting is not a part-time job. For all that we speak of meeting the needs of the baby, the same holds true for the older child. There is the need for guidance (which may be questioned before it is accepted) and whatever the age, the need to fit your action to the development of the child. You comfort the infant, counsel the older child, and through it all, make sure always that this child (who may be taller than you), knows he or she is secure in your heart and your love.

How you do this is no mystery. You have only to hark back to the early years with your first child and draw on the understanding you gained then in communicating love to a little creature who was alien in many ways to your adult way of thinking. Express love through your caring touch (rubbing the back is soothing to big and little children), through your interest in what interests your child, with words of praise for all accomplishments however small, with words of endearment: "How special you are to your father and me!" And do these things over and over, exactly as you do with your babies.

Some people may caution you otherwise, telling you that by giving of yourself in this way you're "sacrificing your life for your children's sake" and worse yet, shortchanging your marriage. Turn a deaf ear to them. It's misleading advice since it creates a conflict where there really isn't one, between the roles of spouse and parent. Children don't shortchange their parents' marriage; only the married partners can do that. It is not a matter of choosing in favor of spouse or children, but of accommodating both and building a family.

It is hard to imagine a greater accomplishment than building a family together. Home and family are the bedrock of society. As children are nurtured, the virtues which are essential to the well-being of society as a whole—respect for others, caring for one another, gentleness, the courage to differ at times, and the readiness to resolve differences—are also nurtured. For all members of the family, home is an oasis in an often impersonal world. In times of stress, we return home to regain our strength and rejuvenate our spirits.

There is no more precious legacy that you can leave your children than giving them the chance to grow up in a loving, secure home. Along with a good start in life, you are passing on to them the blueprints for building a family. Building a house can be learned well through instruction; building a family is best learned by having experienced it in all its richness.

Unfortunately, what is good for the family is often at odds with the goals of other sectors of society, and the home will remain a frontier in many ways. There will be a continuing need for pioneering parents who dare to make their own way. The next generation, I am sure, will be most grateful to you for your expertise in the matter. When passing on saving tips and recalling again the reason behind what you did—a commitment to mothering—be sure to convey a spirit of hope. Parenting is meant to be a successful endeavor. The Creator would not have it otherwise. This is the message that has been entrusted to the heart.

*P*ersonal *V*iews of *N*ew *P*ioneers

Nothing can convey the message of this book more accurately than the stories sent to us by mothers who are following the reasons of their hearts and staying home with their children. We have used some of the quotes and excerpts from these letters throughout the book, but here they are included in each family's story.

LAURA RANK, WISCONSIN
Just the Basics

I'm the mother of five children: Amy Sue, nine, Patrick, seven, Benjamin, almost five, Douglas, three, and Erin, one. My husband, LeRoy, is a shipping clerk, earning roughly $15,000 a year. From the time we were married we knew once the children started to come we would be a one-income family. Prior to Amy's birth, I taught school for two years. Even then our main budget and way of life were primarily based on my husband's income. My income just bought our appliances. So the switch was very smooth and easy—no letdown in our lifestyle.

Now eleven years and five kids later we are still comfortably living on that one income. We believe living with just the basics makes a more well-rounded person appreciating life that much more. Of course we *DREAM* of better things, but who doesn't? I just couldn't leave my kids day after day! It is hard enough for me to reenact each child's firsts to his dad, let alone to have a sitter do it for me. Being with your child as he grows enables a mom to know that child's every mood, every whim, and every proud moment, right down the line. That kiss, that hug, that praise, even that occasional criticism, all make your child that much better an adult in the future.

Here are some of the economic secrets that have enabled us to live within our modest means. By no means are we debt-free, but we've never gone hungry or without clothes. Of course, it is hard at times, but what isn't in life that is worthwhile?

From April to October my husband bikes to work seven miles each way. Saves fuel! We also went back to being a one-car family. Once in awhile it is tricky, but with ingenuity it works. I try to keep my shopping to just one day. My husband does errands during his lunch hour. In summer shopping is a daytime venture, maybe even with a picnic lunch. In winter I usually leave immediately when my husband arrives home and take only one child with me. I've found this has the added benefit of getting to know each one as an individual.

I sew for our entire family, husband included. I watch for sales on the bargain material. My daughter's new knickers cost only 75¢ plus a zipper which was laying around the house. That is only one example of many. I watch for pattern sales, but in some cities they can be checked out at libraries. Many times I remodel other people's clothes for my children. Hand-me-downs are nice, too!

Food bills are cut by my husband's garden. We freeze and can most vegetables. We also have our own apple trees, cherry trees, raspberry, and strawberry patches.

Most of our home repairs we do ourselves. We even invested in a few manuals showing us how. It's great to skip the labor charges and only pay for parts! Our biggest investment was a wood burner which greatly cut down heating costs.

Once in awhile we get a little added "pin money." My husband sells his berries and asparagus. It's surprising how many people like to buy organically raised food. I too add a little by doing outside sewing and drapes. My biggest asset is my ability not to get nervous sewing around the kids. The toddler has special toys (spools, old pin cases, ruler, etc.) to play with near me. Also my acceptance of maybe sewing only fifteen minutes at a sitting really helps!

I still substitute teach a day here and there at our parochial school. Some of the times my little one is right there with me. For example, this week I'm teaching the preschoolers at our Vacation Bible School. Why preschool? That way my three- and four-year-olds are my students. My toddler is on my lap while I teach. We've had lots of practice at LLL meetings!

What do we do for inexpensive fun? Well, why not a County Fair, an Art Fair, museum, church activities, and just plain family picnics? The cost is virtually nothing. Just recently we've started hunting our families' ancestors. Visiting cemeteries may not be the most fun for children, but the country roads to get there are quite picturesque and enjoyable when incorporated with stops at parks and waysides.

This gives you a small insight into how our family of seven makes ends meet. But in closing I'd like to add one thing which is probably the most important factor. Our family truly believes the Lord will provide for all our earthly needs. I added this because without this I wouldn't be giving an honest picture of our lifestyle. We strongly believe that those first years of life should be shaped by mother and father even if it means a little sacrifice on their part in regard to earthly possessions. Our kids need us there to help them grow and mature.

SUE HUML, ILLINOIS
Memories of Mother-at-Home

I was born in 1946 in England. Right after the war money was very tight and for a number of years food was on ration. Our home had no heat other than open fireplaces, no hot running water, no bathroom, just an outside toilet. We had no car, washing machine, dryer, or refrigerator—no TV, no carpets on the floor, no toaster or food mixer. I think you can get the picture. Being a young child, the financial state we were in didn't affect me. All I knew was, I was at home with my mother and sister, and dad worked hard to bring in his small salary.

Every day was a struggle for my mother. I recall her selling her wedding ring to a man at the door to buy extra food for us. Every day was a challenge to survive and mum spent her time preparing frugal nutritious meals and, even though we only had two sets of clothes (best and play), we were always clean, well cared for, and, most of all, loved.

It's natural for parents to want the best for their children, but does the best always mean having more material goods?

I now have two beautiful children and a loving husband. I so wish my dear parents were still alive so I might tell them how much they did for me and how much I learned from them. As a young child I *never* felt disadvantaged; in fact I was very happy. My mother taught me a lifelong lesson. I learned the value of people over things, and that for every hardship something good comes of it. As a grown woman/mother the lesson of frugality has never been forgotten. I still shop for the very best bargains, be it garage sales, clothing outlets, buying in bulk, etc. I feel the greatest admiration for my parents, gratitude for the lessons learned *day by day*, and for all the sacrifices they made for us children. I feel I'm a better person for all we endured together and I'm already passing on many of the lessons of life and important values I learned from those experiences.

If today's baby/child could verbalize and have the choice between having mom home and doing without some of the luxuries (which we often view as necessities), I have no doubt at all which he would choose.

I now really appreciate the extras in my life but at the same time realize the importance of family togetherness. In other words, it's nice to have the luxuries of life and material possessions but if it were a choice between that and being separated from our children for hours every day, I would willingly follow in my mother's footsteps.

LILIAN M. KOK-BRINKHUIS, THE NETHERLANDS
Read Between the Lines

As a brand new Leader from the Netherlands I will try to tell you something about the Dutch way of life, and the money-saving projects I try to accomplish. First of all, it is important to know that in Holland the majority of the mothers are at home, and the income of the husband is usually meant to support the whole family. It is very rare if ordinary people have second cars, for instance, not to speak of having a dishwasher or dryer. They are only within the reach of the affluent. So, being a mother and housewife who has to watch the pennies very carefully is not a big exception, which really helps.

Our house is rather big for Dutch standards—for average people—but very small by American standards. We have a garage, a living room, and kitchen; upstairs there is a bathroom and three small bedrooms. In the loft we could make another room if we had the money. Downstairs, where we heat the rooms in winter, we had double windowpanes installed, which saves a lot on cost of fuel. We try to think of turning lights off when we do not really need them, and I use my dryer (very luxurious to have one) only in winter and when it's raining. I try to make many of our clothes myself; the boys have never yet had a store-bought winter coat! In a town nearby they sell all kinds of material cheaply at the weekly market and I go there from time to time (by bus or on the bike—almost the normal Dutch means of transport). Then when we need something, I can make it myself. Also, as a means of income for the local LLL Group, I make baby carriers which I sell privately and put the profits in the Group Treasury.

As for cutting down on the cost of food, I shop nearly every other day, which also is very uncommon in the United States, I believe. But as Holland is so small, the shops are always nearby. I do not have a freezer, so I buy only small quantities in advance. In order to have fresh vegetables and meat every day, we go out and buy enough for one, or maybe two days. This way we only buy what we really need, and when we change plans there is no food wasting in the fridge. It helps to go shopping every day, because we can go there by foot, feed the ducks as we pass the pond, the boys are able to play at some small playground on the way; we do the shopping, and on the way back, if there's time, maybe even drop in at a friend's. Also, in the summer the swimming pool is within cycling distance, and that's something else we can afford. A trip to the park, with a children's farm, where they can feed the goats, sheep, and easels is a favourite, too.

In the evenings I am working on translating Tine Thevenin's book *The Family Bed*. It is a pity that it is a one-time job, but it is very convenient. I can do it in my own time, and the only thing needed is knowledge of English and Dutch, a good dictionary, and a typewriter. I spend about fifteen hours a week doing it, and only work on it after the children are in bed.

I think it is a very sad thing that in the Netherlands the attitude is building up that moms who do not work outside their homes are doing "nothing." One politician was even so blunt as to say that housekeeping could not possibly occupy any mother. After all, making three or four beds was not a full time task, was it? It did make me feel good when the newspapers made a rather big thing out of it! I could not even think of leaving my children in the care of some sitter who does not love them as I do. If we really need the money very, very badly, I think I would try to clean offices, when their father could be with them. The thought of leaving my children never crossed my mind before I had them, and certainly never will, now that I have them. Sure, caring for them is not always easy or even very pleasant, but I would not want to miss the good times for anything in the world! I would be just too envious of anyone who saw my baby smile before I did, or saw my big boy ride his bike before I did. I'm just too possessive, maybe. I do not know the right words in English, but I know you will read between the lines and catch my meaning.

MAURINE JOENS, ARKANSAS
Priorities

There is not enough money in this world to pay me to leave my children! Time with my children is much more precious than any compensation I could receive for taking a job outside of the home. Any energy and love that I expend I choose to spend on my family, rather than on a job that can be done by someone else.

Staying at home with my family has meant making many sacrifices (in spending money that is). Our goal has not been for my husband, Ken, to get two jobs, but to reduce his workload to one part-time job. We have worked for many years on that goal and have accomplished it as we have found that there are so many beautiful things in this world that money can't buy.

We have five children—Christopher, fourteen; Christine, eleven; Victoria, eight; Maria, three; and Anna, one. Our income now is about $350 per month—we lived for about a year and a half on no more than $150 per month. Our priorities are in the line of "needs" instead of "wants."

The first goals we had involved getting out of debt and then staying out of debt. We also made some investments (like a flour mill, wood stoves, milk cow, etc.) that would allow us to keep from spending money.

I would suggest not buying *anything* on impulse. Wait several days, weeks, months—usually when time passes the urge to buy whatever it was that seemed so important usually passes, too. My husband and I also have an agreement that neither of us spends any money without the approval of the other one. This eliminates much spending.

I would suggest getting out from under house and car payments. Save, search, ask for Divine Guidance, whatever it takes—lower one's standard of living—find a bargain!

There are some things a person can't afford, but then there

are some things a person can't afford to do without! Priorities need to be established.

I feel that my family's health is of *prime* importance, and that a balanced diet is extremely important. I will not "cut any corners" that will lessen the nutritional intake of my family.

Food in its natural state purchased as close as possible to its source of production cuts out a lot of "middle man" costs. For example: Locate a dairy and purchase a week's supply of milk at a time. Most dairies have times allotted for selling to the public. Buy wheat (and grind your flour yourself) from a feed store (be sure to ask whether it is clean for human consumption) or, better yet, from the farmer who raises it. Buy fruit by the box or bushel from fruit stands, or, better yet, from the orchards where it is grown. Anything bought in larger quantities is usually cheaper. Look for bargains in large quantities (non-perishables, that is) and "stock-up." That allows one to eat at "last year's prices." Following are some money-saving ideas I've employed:

Never eat out. Take lunches instead. We've taken lunches for five or six days away from home.

I traded a year's worth of piano lessons for myself for house-cleaning for the piano teacher. I put a lot of time into it and as a result I received about three years' worth of lessons. Now I teach my children their lessons.

I learned to cut men's hair.

I don't buy tissues. I make "rags" out of old sheets or flannel and use them like handkerchiefs and wash them.

We don't buy crushed ice. We freeze water in gallon cans, turn the cans on their sides, and hammer (with a hammer) all around the outside of the cans as we turn the cans, and out comes beautiful crushed ice which can be kept in the freezer.

I don't buy paper towels. I keep newspaper handy. A piece of newspaper dampened under the faucet has about as much picking-up power as does a paper towel. I also keep a container of rags handy—some that can do nasty jobs and then be disposed of.

I make my own soap; I make the uncooked kind and it takes very little time—the recipe is on the lye can. We raise our own lard for soap, but animal fat can usually be obtained free from slaughter houses and also old grease can usually be obtained from restaurants.

Check railroad salvage stores for good bargains.

Take close-up pictures with a cheap camera and have them enlarged instead of having photographs made.

Also buy dried corn and make your own corn meal and corn grits cereal. Dried corn, cooked like beans, is delicious.

Make your own cold cereals, if you desire them for convenience.

Cook basic foods without a lot of expensive "frills."

Raise your own herbs and dry them. Good nutritious drinks can be made from things you raise. Winter onions and chives can get you through many months without buying onions.

Raise as much food as is possible. Keep a salad garden. Eat what you have when it is in season. Raise your own seeds. Plants going to seed make pretty flowers.

Make your own gifts and greeting cards.

Make your own entertainment—play games, read and sing together, go hiking, work together, visit with friends, make something together.

MYRA SHRIBMAN, ISRAEL

Reflections on Mothering

The Baby Blues

I had husband, and home, and baby newborn,
Why was I crying as though my heart torn?
Why was I sobbing? Hot tears on my chest,
As she lustily nursed and grew strong from my breast.

And then late one night when our baby lay sleeping,
I told you, my love, why I had been weeping.
How lonesome I felt when you left in the morning,
How this trapped sort of feeling had come without warning.

And then I felt guilty—I shouldn't complain
When my baby was healthy and I had no pain,
Except in my heart—this bottomless sorrow
Stretching forth on and into tomorrow.

You lay with me all through the night and next day,
When the sun kissed the flowers awake, a bright ray
Of hope filled my being, my body, my soul,
And I rose from my bed and saw clear my goal.

I lifted my child and touched her soft face,
I knew that no job could ever replace
My presence here with a baby whose need
Was greater, more urgent, more pressing indeed.

And when I saw clearly my role as a mother,
To nurture, to teach, to care; then all other
Jobs seemed to lose their appeal
And I stepped into motherhood, this time for real.

And now as I nurse her and rock her and sing,
What joy I have found in this mothering thing.
And I wonder whatever makes new mothers cry,
And I wonder if that woman crying was I.

Time

Being at home gives me time to share
Time to surrender and time to care;
Time to listen and learn and wonder
What makes the sun shine; what makes thunder.

Time to take note when all is not well
And to sit with a child who has something to tell;
Time to help soothe the ache of despair
When a child is consumed with worry and fear.

Being at home gives me time to explore
A silkworm's cocoon with a moth at the door;
Time to admire the intricate plan
For a flying machine that will carry a man.

Time to share with my daughter an intimate glance
At our womanly feelings, our hopes, and our chance
To spread gentleness, kindness, love, and compassion,
Even if these are no longer in fashion.

We all have our need for self-recognition
We all have within us some secret ambition;
You reach up towards me, you cling to my breast
And I know I have chosen the job I love best;
I've plenty of time to think, write, and read
But best of all time to respond to your need.

JULINA HOKANSON, WYOMING

Living Royally

Although my secret desire from the time I was small was to marry Prince Charming and raise twelve beautiful princes and princesses, I never openly dared to admit that I'd be an ordinary housewife.

At times during my schooling I was thrilled at the urge to continue a career while raising a family and knew that a really bright woman would not stunt her intellectual and creative abilities just because she chose to marry and have children.

Finally at the age of twenty-four the moment arrived and we joined our love in quiet, serene beauty. Now we are almost middle-aged (I didn't think I would ever admit it) and we speak of decades the way we used to speak of weeks and days, or even moments. We are fulfilling our dreams and raising those princes and princesses. It looks like we may not be able to make it an even dozen. But the eight we have borne are truly royal (though one did not remain with us). We have the usual ups and downs to say nothing of scraped knees, hospitalizations, tears, fears, and hopes, and so *very, very* much uniqueness.

But much of that belongs to another paper as this one is on making ends meet on a schoolteacher's salary.

How do we get by? Where do we economize? Well, we do mostly what everyone around here does, we just do it! When presented with a new challenge, a new baby, another hardship, an extra child or two (a foreign student we are supporting for a few years), we never consider the problems, *we just do it.*

On Saving: We make everything from scratch that we eat, starting with grinding our own flour and whole wheat for porridge (a word adopted from our years of living in Australia). In sixteen years we have not bought more than a few dollars worth of bread. We buy fruit by the bushel and can our winter's supply (about 500 quarts) with the whole family helping. I built a food dehydrator for about $50 which holds about a half-bushel of fruit and by winter we try to have ten gallon jugs filled with a variety of dried fruits and vegetables. The dried fruits are purely for treats. We dry whatever happens to be cheap that year. One year Italian prunes had scarred skins and were not selling, so when the price dropped we loaded up. One year I offered a grocer $1 a box for cherries that were about to mold and he wouldn't take it. Two days later he called me and offered them for free. My dear, patient husband helped me sort through them and we saved over half. We aren't paupers but we do look for every good bargain.

We plant a garden and because of our cold weather and short growing season here in Wyoming we go heavy on carrots, beets, peas, onions, herbs, and cabbage. We store the carrots in a root cellar, bottle the beets, dry the onions and herbs, and turn the cabbage into the most delicious sauerkraut. The first year we could hardly eat it and now the children say "Oh, good! Sauerkraut." Daddy is the sauerkraut expert and has it down to a fine art, cut by hand and done in a crock.

We travel to Idaho and buy 800 or so pounds of potatoes from a farmer friend; they keep in our root cellar. Many people here grow all of their own potatoes. Potatoes are an everyday staple, like homemade bread and milk.

We buy raw milk at about half the store price from a local farmer and use the cream for butter, fun desserts, or home-made ice cream.

We don't use coupons much as we usually don't buy the products that offer them. We buy everything in bulk from canned goods to laundry detergent and try to keep a year's supply of staples, wheat, salt, honey, and powdered milk as emergency storage. (Not that we anticipate a disaster but anyone can be hit with unemployment, flood, earthquake, a strike, or some economic surprise.) The honey is also a real bargain when bought from a local beekeeper at about half the retail price. It is also purchased in bulk (150 pounds a year for our family) practically straight from the bees.

Sewing: I feel smug and creative, when I copy a $40-$80 dress for $10-$15 and my "designer" jeans which are smart and easy to make cost just a few dollars. Shirts are a cinch and cloth can be purchased very reasonably by watching sales, outlets, and end of season closeouts. Until last year I made all the coats for the family including fiberfill hooded parkas, little girls' fluffy fur, dad's and mom's wool dress coats. Sewing can be a tremendous saving as I stock up at a ski-wear factory at end of the season close-outs on waterproof fabric, fiber-fill, and furry linings. The only problem with sewing is that the seam-by-seam, between-family-needs method is *very slow.* I'm always a season and a half behind and what is made for child one is usually worn by number two or three and occasionally not until five or six.

Fun? Our dad loves books and we try to keep an hour in the evening as reading time for the whole family. The girls make up plays and the boys put on magic shows. We sing, although not often enough, and almost everyone plays piano and one other instrument. Hopefully the day will come when we play together. So far the children are content to play football or basketball at the school playground or on church teams. Track is becoming a thing in our life and for the teens a church or school dance will do. If we want to watch a movie we choose something on T.V.

Our bikes are big in our life if and when the snow ever leaves. In the summer we swim in the canal and in the winter we can "tube" (ride inner tubes down the mountains of snow). Mostly we make our own fun as we cannot afford skis or snow-mobiles. Our children just purchased a trampoline with the money they saved from mowing lawns. I think this is a tre-mendous credit to an eleven-year-old and a twelve-year-old. Now all of us are getting a regular workout.

What do the King and Queen do? We meet twice a month with other couples from my husband's school faculty for a dinner where everyone donates a dish, and we have cultivated a friendship with my dear La Leche League co-Leader and her husband who is a composer. We listen to his works, bathe in the beauty of sound and creativity, then discuss some intellectual or controversial and always stimulating point. We attend a seminar once a year related to Paul's teaching and gain some intellectual and spiritual stimulation.

When cabin fever hits, which it often does when winters are nine months long, I call a friend, ride the bike, go for a walk, or sometimes just feel really sorry for myself. Reading helps as does just digging in and working a little harder. Playing the piano is also a source of joy.

Any extra income? In the early years I did some substitute teaching and taught a night class to university students but it became harder and harder to fit it all in. For fifteen years I taught private piano students and then quite by accident I stumbled on to the most exciting new aspect to my musical profession.

We could not afford for me to go to the Chicago LLL Conference in 1981 which was bitterly disappointing. The Chicago area had been my home for some years and I so much wanted to return there. Then a music teachers' workshop to be held the same week as the conference attracted my eye. I'd long been interested in the Suzuki Method of teaching and now a teachers' institute was being held in my home town. I paid the fee and with my infant in tow attended a marvelous week that changed my life.

Perhaps one of the reasons Suzuki music won my heart is because it is family-oriented. The mother attends the child's lesson and then is the teacher throughout the week. Another part of the philosophy that is so in harmony with the rest of my mothering concepts (largely formed by LLL) is that learning cannot begin too early. The infant listens to good music all of his life and then just as he begins to speak his mother tongue because it is around him like the air he breathes, he also begins to play the music he has been hearing from birth to about three years. It is so exciting to see tiny three-year-olds imitate their brothers and sisters. Another exciting aspect of this method is the belief that all children can develop ability, that each develops at his own special rate and comparisons should never be made.

I am delighted to find a way to use my talents in a more creative, loving way and to be involved in a teaching method that involves all my philosophies of family first and the great influence of the mother and the home on the very young child.

We live in a community of low income so I do not make as much as I would in a big city (but I guess our living expenses are also lower). I devote about ten hours a week in actual teaching and earn $80.

We are a long way from Prince Charming on a dashing white charger, and even if my engagement ring was delicately nestled in the golden throat of a white orchid, the nitty gritty of raising that dozen or so is very real, very hard, very challenging, very priceless, very fulfilling, and entirely consuming. I've had a full and enriching life but none of it compares with my curly headed moppet hunting for "baby" (her term for nursing) as I frantically put on a bit of make-up before church. (Yes, she climbed up onto the bathroom cabinet, unbuttoned my blouse, tugged and pulled and found her drink with a giggle and began her delightful snack while I finished off some hurried tricks to enliven the aging face). Nothing compares with the towhead who can't even talk but has learned to recognize the word Mommy in our newest game (reading). Nothing compares with a five-year-old nestling into your bed every night with "I love you Mommy" and a great big kiss. Nothing compares with a fourteen-year-old climbing into bed in the middle to the night just because "I was worried." Nothing compares to a ten-year-old who giggles all the time but would stand on his head all day if you asked him to. Nothing compares to sitting at the hospital bedside with a stubborn twelve-year-old wondering if he will live or die, be handicapped for life or recover completely, and knowing that same stubborness that drives you crazy will pull him through in perfect shape. Nothing compares to knowing that someday you will look back on it all and still be glad that it was family first, no matter what.

JULIE DEMLOW, MICHIGAN

Not Deprived or Defeated

When I was about a year old my mother had to return to work. I was the youngest of three children. My sister is eighteen years older than I and my brother ten years older. I'm sure it was a necessity for mom to work. She and my father always worked hard although they had very little formal education.

While I was a preschooler, I always stayed with a much loved grandmother or an aunt. However, I still remember feeling somewhat shuffled around. After I was in school, or perhaps before that, my mother took a job as a cook in a university dorm. She went to work at five in the morning and was home by three in the afternoon. My memories are of coming home to an empty house although my mother says this actually happened infrequently. I was always terrified someone would "get me." I remember taking the dog and sitting on the floor where no one could see me from the windows. How terrible to be so young and frightened! For many years I blamed my mother severely for this. Now, some twenty-three or more years later, I have taken a more tolerant view. Sometimes it is necessary for mothers to work. I just pray that my children will never have to be "latch key" children.

My husband is a teacher with twelve years of experience. He makes enough for us to get by on and not much more. It is a struggle and a sacrifice for me to be with our children, now two and five. I tried substitute teaching when my oldest, Chris, was about a year old. He had a very regular infrequent nursing schedule and it was very easy for me to nurse and work. But it was very difficult finding a last minute sitter. When my second child, Holly, was born I quit subbing. After I paid for a sitter and gas I found that I made very little money and the hassle just wasn't worth it. I know I will probably have to return to work when they are both in school but my husband and I will fight it as long as possible.

Most months my checkbook balance goes down to $2.50 but we manage. We don't have any credit cards; if we can't pay for something we don't buy it. Therefore, we don't have any unexpected bills to catch us unaware. My husband and I seldom go out alone. We either take the kids or we stay home. We usually go to an afternoon movie ($1 each) or go shopping. We do lots of family things—picnics, walks, flying kites, sledding, or drives. Garage sales and secondhand shops are entertainment and a way to buy things for my family that we couldn't otherwise afford. I buy most of my kids' clothes secondhand although you probably couldn't tell.

Last year I saved our sales tax receipts because I had read that you could usually take a larger deduction than what the government allows. What I found, though, is that we actually spent *less* than what the government said a family of four in our state would spend. That I guess is the key to my being able to stay home.

We live about thirty miles from any large town, in a small village, so we do miss the opportunities that cities offer such as free concerts, parks, museums, classes, etc. However, we find other things to do. A cup of tea with a friend, pot-luck lunches and dinners, or a chat on the phone are precious times and make up for not being in a city.

Some other ways I save: We joined a food co-op. I make most foods from scratch; I sew a lot including all of my husband's shirts; we make gifts and cards; a handy husband is certainly a blessing be it for the car, house, or furniture. I save money from refunds or change and put it in a can for eating out or special treats—it's surprising how fast it adds up. We don't expect to have what our parents worked twenty-five years for or what our neighbors have (mostly on credit).

There are lots of things I would like to have or be able to afford—private school for Chris when he starts, new furniture, a car we don't have to nurse along. But we do get along without these things.

Most of all, I want to say how much I enjoy being with my

kids, what a joy they are most days. I'm frightened to think how close we came to never having any. We were married about seven years before Chris was born. Perhaps this is part of the reason I'm content now. We did what we wanted when we wanted for a good many years and I know we will have this freedom again.

I don't feel deprived or defeated. Saving money is a challenge I enjoy. And just think, today I found $2 I didn't know I had. Aren't I lucky?

DONNA BRYANT, MINNESOTA
A Change of Plans

When I became pregnant with my first-born son, I was the marketing manager for a five-million dollar company. I loved my job and my associates. Since I spent most of my life at work or thinking about work, my job was an integral part of my existence. Even though I would be having a baby, I could not imagine giving up my work. Most of my professional colleagues who had children were still working full-time, and most had returned to work within a few months after delivery.

However, the day my son was born, my conviction to return to work quickly was replaced by an equally fervent conviction never to leave my baby's side. I was awed by his helplessness and his beauty, and could not imagine placing my life's greatest treasure in someone else's care.

During the early weeks at home with my precious bundle of wonder, my only tears were shed at the thought of separating from the babe who nursed sweetly at my breast.

I talked with my husband, friends, and family about my new feelings and change of heart. Most were quite cautious. After all, just a few weeks earlier I had vowed to return to work, and I did have an excellent, prestigious, enviable position. My dearest friends and husband cautioned that this new feeling of utter devotion might be the result of a hormonal imbalance that would pass in just a few months. Feeling quite unbalanced myself at this point in my life, I decided to listen to the advice I was getting from several quarters. The general consensus appeared to be that I would be wisest to return to work "just to see how it would work out." Still feeling vaguely uncomfortable with this decision, I made an appointment with my employer to discuss the terms of my return to work. Because I was breastfeeding and interested in continuing to do so, I hoped to negotiate my return on a part-time basis for as long as possible.

Much to my surprise, I was offered the opportunity to continue my work on a permanent part-time basis. My initial agreement was that I would work twenty-five hours per week, five hours per day. After having worked a minimum of eight hours each day for years, this proposed schedule looked ideal. I would be home each day by 1:30 PM and would miss only one, or at the most two, nursing sessions.

The first day back on the job was agony. I called the sitter three times in five hours. Watching the clock as I had never done before, I rushed out of the office precisely at 1:00. When I arrived at the sitter's home, I found my baby sitting comfortably in the sitter's lap, looking as though he hadn't missed me at all.

This pattern kept up for at least a week, but then changes began to occur. While he was content when I picked him up from the sitter's, as soon as we got home he would begin screaming as though he had colic, something he had never had before. He would be inconsolable, sometimes for hours. Nursing him would often help, but it was usually only a temporary peace. I was frantic and kept telling myself to quit my job.

Already, though, I was committed to an agreed-upon course of action, and felt that I had to prove I could do it. My company needed me desperately; that was gratifying. My baby needed me desperately, too, but his needs were not as well articulated, nor was his praise of my efforts as obvious.

There were many happy moments, at home and at the office, during the time I worked part-time. The joy of coming home to nurse and care for my baby was, I thought, enhanced by our separation. I felt very lucky to have the best of both worlds. I also felt very tired. My son expected my total attention when I was home, my office demanded more than I could give on a reduced schedule, and my husband expected that my lightened work load meant I had more time to cook and clean. His helpfulness around the house dropped dramatically when I decided to work less than full time.

For quite a while, I was very busy trying to fulfill everyone's expectations of me, including my own. I never sat down to figure out what was happening to my life, my marriage, or my child. Gradually, I became more and more fatigued in mind, body, and spirit as career, marriage, and mothering all demanded more than I could give.

After one year, on my son's first birthday, my milk supply dwindled to the point where he refused to nurse and preferred his more reliable bottle. I was crushed, but also too pressed for time to do anything but accept this unhappy development.

In the fall, my husband and I decided to try to have another child. I made it plain to my husband that I would not return to work after the second child was born. In December, I informed my company that June 1st would be my last day of work, as my second child was due in August.

As my last day of work approached, I grew more apprehensive about my decision. What if I were making a mistake? Would I ever be able to regain the status I enjoyed at this company? Would I be bored (or boring) at home? At times I wished to change my decision, but these momentary qualms always gave way to a deep conviction that this decision was a long overdue one for me.

By the second week at home, I was busy enough to hardly think about the office. I was preparing for the new baby's arrival, cooking, and cleaning, but most of all, mothering. It did not take long for me to understand why I had wanted to be home with my son in the first place. I was discovering a delightful and complex little person that I hardly knew.

The greatest benefit I have reaped from staying home is one that I would not exchange for any job or any amount of money. Watching my son grow, helping him when I can, guiding him when I must, and being there when he needs me, is the most rewarding work I have ever known. Like any job, it has its ups and downs, good days and bad. But I know that this is one job I won't be able to apply for later.

NIKKI GALBRAITH, ZAMBIA

True Liberation

Being at home has meant to me true liberation. I am the expert; I set the pace; I feel that I am needed. If one of my children has a bad night we can all sleep in the next day. I work the hours that suit our family, not what someone else dictates. I have never felt conflict between family and work (e.g., a sick child and mother worrying more about her job than the child). I must admit I haven't felt the need to "go out to work." I NEED my children and would be brokenhearted if I were apart from them.

My mother worked and I was also sent to boarding school. I hated it; I felt so lost and abandoned. There was nobody who was "on my side," nobody to tell my troubles to. I am trying to do for my children what I craved those lonely years and hope their childhood will be happier. If there is one thing that has reinforced my beliefs, it's LLL.

It's such an emotional subject—working and motherhood. You can't be a successful business executive, doctor, or any other professional if you are only there part-time, so how can a woman feel satisfied in her role if she's only partly involved? Jobs are always there, the cost of living will always go up, but children won't always be children and if we put possessions before our children that's all we will be left with.

RHONDA TAYLOR, BRITISH COLUMBIA

Nothing Could Be So Rewarding

I'm writing to tell you of some of the special measures our family uses to keep me at home. First a little about our family. We consist of mom, dad, and three little boys: Charles, five; Edward, three; and Steven, eight months. I stopped working when I was seven months pregnant with Charles and have stayed home despite long periods of unemployment or underemployment for my husband. For many months four years ago, I only had $30 a month for groceries. Needless to say, I was grateful Charles didn't need milk from the store! Somehow we always scrounged enough to meet the mortgage and we were always nutritiously fed. Granted it wasn't always our favorite foods. We depended on occasional dinners with my parents to enjoy roast beef or steak. We were also forced to borrow $500 from them at one point, but we managed to pay that off in three months. Did I ever question staying at home? Yes! I often wondered if I could get a job, but we always decided against it. Even buying an ice cream cone wrecked the budget, but we learned a lot about each other and ourselves. There were very rough times. My husband did odd jobs; an electrician's helper one day, cutting brush the next, repairing a cottage the next. We now have the strength of knowing that we can make it no matter what happens. If things get unmanageable at his present job, he can leave and we'll do just fine. It also gave him an extra measure of self confidence. *He* supported *his* family and no one can question his ability as a provider. We used to sit up nights wondering how we could make ends meet. My definition of heaven was to have enough money so that we didn't have to worry about *every* *penny*. Well, we made it.

My husband has a steady job now, but we've kept the odd jobs, only now we have a registered yard care company. (See page 276 for details of this family business.)

There are certainly extremely frustrating days but there are many satisfying ones. I collapse exhausted every night but with a smile, and wake two or three times a night to cuddle a little one into bed with us. My schedule is my own, the pressures I feel are of my own making, and I am learning more about myself then I ever thought I'd know. I'd never want to be anywhere else. Nothing could be so rewarding.